VIRGINIA WOOLF: MUSIC, SOUND, LANGUAGE

ELICIA CLEMENTS

Virginia Woolf: Music, Sound, Language

UNIVERSITY OF TORONTO PRESS
Toronto Buffalo London

ISBN 978-1-4875-0426-7

Library and Archives Canada Cataloguing in Publication

Clements, Elicia, 1970–, author
Virginia Woolf : music, sound, language / Elicia
Clements.

Includes bibliographical references and index.
ISBN 978-1-4875-0426-7 (hardcover)

1. Woolf, Virginia, 1882–1941 – Knowledge – Music.
2. Woolf, Virginia, 1882–1941– Criticism and interpretation.
3. Woolf, Virginia, 1882–1941 – Aesthetics. 4. Music and
   literature – History – 20th century. 5. Music in literature.
6. Sound in literature. I. Title.

PR6045.O72Z5633 2019   823'.912   C2018-906430-7

This research was supported by the Social Sciences and Humanities Research
Council of Canada.

 Social Sciences and Humanities   Conseil de recherches en   Canada
Research Council of Canada   sciences humaines du Canada

University of Toronto Press acknowledges the financial assistance to its
publishing program of the Canada Council for the Arts and the Ontario Arts
Council, an agency of the Government of Ontario.

Canada Council   Conseil des Arts   ONTARIO ARTS COUNCIL
for the Arts   du Canada   CONSEIL DES ARTS DE L'ONTARIO
                                            an Ontario government agency
                                            un organisme du gouvernement de l'Ontario

 Funded by the   Financé par le
Government   gouvernement   Canada
of Canada   du Canada

For Roz, Terry, and Shaleena

Contents

Acknowledgments

This book would not have been possible without the financial support of the Social Sciences and Humanities Research Council of Canada. I am grateful for their sustained funding. Additionally, the Office of Research Services at York University, and specifically Janet Friskney, have been very helpful in securing grants for this project.

I am appreciative of the welcoming and accommodating staff at several institutions that have allowed me access to their archives: The Berg Collection, New York Public Library; the Special Collections of the Sussex University Library for several visits to consult the Monks House Papers and the Leonard Woolf Archive; the British Library Sound Archives; and the Special Collections Archives of the Hogarth Press at the University of Reading. I am grateful to Kirby Smith, Senior Library Assistant, and Thomas Birkhead, Library Assistant, Penguin Random House Archive, UK; Sarah Baxter, Contracts Advisor and Literary Estates, The Society of Authors; and David Plant, the Random House Project Officer at the Hogarth Press Archives for permission to view several files at the Archives of the Hogarth Press. Scott Libraries at York University, especially the RACER Interlibrary Loan staff, have expeditiously helped me with countless hard-to-find materials over the years.

I have also learned more than I can say from several significant and generous mentors, friends, and colleagues, first and foremost Lesley J. Higgins, whose guidance, inspiration, and erudition has fed this project from its inception. I am fortunate to have had the long-standing support and encouragement of Marie-Christine Leps, Leslie Sanders, Gail Vanstone, Lisa Ossowski, Tanya Sweeney, Alison Halsall, Cheryl Cowdy, Candida Rifkind, and Natalie Neill. A special thank you concerning this publication goes to Natalie for her expert indexing of the book, and to Kevin Karst for building my perfect writer's desk. I have had the good fortune to work with helpful research assistants; Kristen Ames and Stephen Van Andel did much proverbial legwork and acquired vital resources for me. My thanks also to Judith Williams for her knowledgeable copy editing and to Barb Porter for her kind, astute, and professional oversight, as well as to Richard Ratzlaff, Mark Thompson, and the anonymous readers at University of Toronto Press. Additionally, I have benefited greatly by the chance to present much of this work at conferences, including several papers at meetings of the Annual International Virginia Woolf Society, the Modernist Studies Association, and Performance Studies international.

Long before the completion of this book, my love of music and literature was shared with and fostered by instrumental people in my life. My mother, Roz, my father, Terry, and my sister, Shaleena – all of whom, in many ways, went on this journey of ideas with me – have unfailingly buoyed my life and my academic pursuits. I dedicate this book to them, and in the memory of my late father.

At the time of writing, only four of the Cambridge Editions of Virginia Woolf's novels were available: *Mrs. Dalloway, The Waves, The Years,* and *Between the Acts.* I have used these editions and supplemented the rest of Woolf's oeuvre with the Oxford Classics editions. While this book was in production, the Cambridge Editions of *Night and Day* and *Orlando* came out. At this late stage in the publication process I was unable to use them in the current manuscript.

Permissions Credits

The following permissions are gratefully acknowledged:

The unpublished transcription of the letter from Elizabeth Trevelyan to Virginia Woolf dated 1 September 1940 is reproduced courtesy of The Keep, Brighton, UK, and Philip Trevelyan.

The unpublished transcription of letters from Basil de Sélincourt to Virginia Woolf, one dated 26 October [1926] and one undated, are from The Random House Group Archive and reproduced courtesy of The Random House Group Ltd., the Library of The University of Reading, Special Collections, and Mary Lowe.

The unpublished letter from Leonard Woolf to Eric White dated 30 November 1927 is from The Random House Group Archive and Library of the University of Reading, Special Collections, and reproduced courtesy of The Random House Group Ltd., The University of Sussex, and The Society of Authors.

A revised version of my essay "Transforming Musical Sounds into Words: Narrative Method in Virginia Woolf's *The Waves,*" *Narrative* 13.2 (May 2005): 160–81, is reproduced here by permission of The Ohio State University Press.

Abbreviations

Citations from Virginia Woolf's novels, letters, diary, and essays are abbreviated in the book as follows:

AR *A Room of One's Own*
BA *Between the Acts*
CR *The Common Reader*
D   *The Diary of Virginia Woolf*
DM *The Death of the Moth and Other Essays*
E   *The Essays of Virginia Woolf*
JR *Jacob's Room*
L   *The Letters of Virginia Woolf*
MB *Moments of Being*
MD *Mrs. Dalloway*
ND *Night and Day*
OR *Orlando*
RF *Roger Fry*
TG *Three Guineas*
TL *To the Lighthouse*
TW *The Waves*
TY *The Years*
VO *The Voyage Out*

VIRGINIA WOOLF: MUSIC, SOUND, LANGUAGE

Introduction

Then I was always conscious of a beautiful rhythm in the book – perhaps in the sense that Roger used the word? – but also more closely in the musical sense, and in a way which I have felt before in your books. Drawing the analogy too closely is misleading, but the feeling is as of listening to a large scale symphonic movement with a quiet introduction, hinting at later themes – then the gradual statement of those themes & their development & interweaving, and recapitulation & development in other keys – it is all there, and then the quieter Coda with remembrance of earlier themes. This may all sound non-sensical to you, and it probably only means that your biography, like all real works of art, convinces one by its own sense of form.

Elizabeth Trevelyan, née van der Hoeven, to Virginia Woolf,
1 September 1940; unpublished

It was delightful of you to write to me about my life of Roger. You have found out exactly what I was trying to do when you compare it to a piece of music. Its [*sic*] odd, for I'm not regularly musical, but I always think of my books as music before I write them. And especially with the life of Roger, – there was such a mass of detail that the only way I could hold it together was by abstracting it into themes. I did try to state them in the first chapter, and then to bring in developments and variations, and then to make them all heard together and end by bringing back the first theme in the last chapter. Just as you say, I am extraordinarily pleased that you felt this. No one else has I think.

Virginia Woolf to Elizabeth Trevelyan, *L6*: 425–6

In 1940 Elizabeth Trevelyan, née van der Hoeven, a friend of Virginia Woolf's who was also a musician, made these insightful and quite

detailed comments about the reverberant nature of Woolf's biography
of Roger Fry. Woolf's inviting reply, that "I always think of my books
as music before I write them" (*L6*: 426), is the impetus for this book.[1]
Penned a year before her death in 1941, Woolf's response indicates that
music – its properties and its forms – is crucial to her creative methods
and accomplishments, as does Trevelyan's keen and articulate rendering of the structure of Woolf's work. Trevelyan's observations most
likely refer to sonata-allegro form, commonly used in symphonic (and
other pieces) from the mid-eighteenth century onward in the Western
tradition of art music. It consists of three main sections, exposition,
development, and recapitulation, but is also sometimes followed by
a brief coda (Trevelyan mentions the latter three). But Woolf's return
answer is less structured, proposing, I would suggest, a pattern of organization akin to theme and variation, defined less strictly in music discourse as a technique where material is altered during repetition – a less
"fixed" form to which Woolf will allude several times in her diaries, as
I shall mention below. One derives the impression, given the substance
of the conversation, that Woolf's inquiry at the end of the letter about
the "difference to your music" (*L6*: 426) that Trevelyan's failing eyesight
might have on her playing is a genuine curiosity about how a musician
practises her craft as well as empathetic concern for her friend.

In addition to these provocative analogies, other questions arise
when one considers this exchange about Woolf's biography of Fry.
What does it mean, for example, to preconceive of books *as* music? Or,
as Woolf tells the composer Dame Ethel Smyth (1858–1944)[2] in 1931,
that she composes "to a rhythm and not to a plot" (*L4*: 204)? Or, in 1940
to Smyth again, that she wants to "investigate the influence of music
on literature" (*L6*: 450)? How do the novels elaborate such concepts
and methods, especially given that her remarks are notoriously vague
but also exceptionally evocative? Why does Woolf understand the
sonorous art as a potential point of access into her own medium of language? To which particular musical timbres, rhythms, and forms does
Woolf gravitate? And, ultimately, what is produced from such intermedial and interdisciplinary crossovers? My study of Woolf's novels and
the art form of music examines such queries to argue that Woolf found
new methods for her own mode of fictional writing by exploring such
resonances.

But Trevelyan's letter also details another facet of this project: the
importance of the receiver of sounds for Woolf. In her letter, Trevelyan
acts as what I shall call an apperceptive listener, after Mikhail Bakhtin's

understanding of the function: someone who receives another's speech (in this case, writing) and incorporates it into her own experience in the act of perceiving: "The speaker breaks through the alien conceptual horizon of the listener, constructs his own utterance on alien territory, against his, the listener's, apperceptive background" (Bakhtin 282). In turn, Woolf's response to Trevelyan demonstrates her own excitement that someone has "felt," and one could add, given the aurality noted in the letters, heard, what is submerged in many of her texts, a rhythmic and/or musical pattern that holds the mass of details together. Throughout her oeuvre Woolf will repeatedly return to the idea of music as a metaphor for design, and in *The Waves*, I argue in chapter 6, even looks to a specific piece of music to help her galvanize that novel's method and structure. But the reception of sound, and its art form of music, is also paramount for Woolf. She details such a capacity in many of her characters from the beginning of her oeuvre to the end, as I demonstrate in Part 2. In addition, my goal is to perform a similar apperceptive function by attempting to "hear" her novels.[3]

Transatlantic modernism (for my purposes, circa 1900 to 1945) witnessed a surge of intermedial exchanges; the musico-literary combination was particularly prolific. In many cases fomented by Walter Pater's dictum that *"all art constantly aspires toward the condition of music"* (106), American, British, and Irish writers explored the interstice of language and sonority: from Langston Hughes's innovations in poetry with the employment of jazz and blues rhythms to E.M. Forster's thematizations of Ludwig van Beethoven's Fifth Symphony in *Howards End* (1910); from Gertrude Stein and Virgil Thomson's operatic collaborations *Four Saints in Three Acts* (1927–8) and *The Mother of Us All* (1947) to James Joyce's experiments in language and structural analogy in *Ulysses* (1922). The list could go on much further, as Daniel Albright's *Modernism and Music: An Anthology of Sources* (2004) – a collection of writings about musico-literary ideas by an extensive variety of artists from the period – attests. Tellingly, Werner Wolf's comprehensive and theoretically seminal work for intermedial studies, *The Musicalization of Fiction: A Study in the Theory and History of Intermediality* (1999), investigates three modernists, Joyce, Woolf, and Aldous Huxley, as the "first climax in the history of attempts at musicalization" (125).

Although I do think more work needs to be done, especially in terms of developing the socio-political dimensions of race, class, gender, and sexuality (at least) when it comes to intermedial analysis, modernist criticism over the last fifteen to twenty years demonstrates a promising interest in this particular combination. Brad Bucknell's *Literary Modernism and Musical Aesthetics: Pater, Pound, Joyce and Stein* (2001), Sam Halliday's *Sonic Modernity: Representing Sound in Literature, Culture and the Arts* (2013), and, most recently, David Deutsch's *British Literature and Classical Music: Cultural Contexts 1870–1945* (2015) speak to a desire to understand the significance of music and sound for early twentieth-century literary workers. Although I depart from Deutsch's conclusions about Woolf's "aesthetic elitism" (88) for reasons I discuss below, his cultural study is the only sustained consideration of some of Woolf's work in these projects that examine modernism more widely; commendably, he also explores the class implications embedded in British ideas about "classical" music through a new historicist lens.[4]

But music-related scholarship concerning Woolf in particular has also grown considerably over the last twenty to twenty-five years. Joyce E. Kelley, in her essay for the *Edinburgh Companion to Virginia Woolf and the Arts* (2013), has proficiently detailed the sizeable amount of scholarship on Woolf and music. In addition, two books have appeared since 2013: Emma Sutton's *Virginia Woolf and Classical Music: Politics, Aesthetics, Form* (2013), focusing especially on Woolf's indebtedness to Richard Wagner, and Adriana Varga's edited collection of essays gathered under the title *Virginia Woolf and Music* (2014). Both books contain informative overviews of Woolf's musical background; proof of Woolf's thorough enjoyment, appreciation, and knowledge of music has been ably and amply confirmed as of late. Sutton's historically nuanced Introduction to her book[5] fully enumerates Woolf's (albeit scant) musical training, her record of avid concert going, her essays on music, Hogarth Press publications on the sonorous art, musical friends and relations, as well as her thorough engagement with Wagner's ideas, plots, and sounds, so I shall limit my elaboration of her musical backdrop below to specific contextual instances that relate to my arguments throughout the chapters. Moreover, while Sutton's study ably lays out the historical and political underpinnings of how music and literature interact in Woolf's oeuvre, my project focuses more squarely on the conceptual and aesthetic implications of this intermedial pairing. I agree with Sutton, however, that "attending to the political significance of Woolf's uses of music concerns not only the diegetic representations of music in the fiction but also the politics of form itself" (*Virginia Woolf and Classical Music* 19). Hence, I shall explore Woolf's musicalization of fiction in both thematic and structural terms.

In addition, although my initial impetus for this study was solely the intermedial crossover between music and words, as my ideas have developed I have found that to separate music from sound and focus solely on it as a niche aspect is limiting where Woolf's work is concerned. Because for Woolf "nothing [is] simply one thing" (*TL* 251), what constitutes music in the first place is often at issue in the novels, as much as it is with language and literature. Art and life are, indeed, various but inseparable for Woolf, and this intermingling is manifested in what I believe is one of her most thoroughly investigated artistic crossovers. But further, music is often amorphous and in flux in her rendering, so where sound (ambient, official, natural) begins and formal music (Western traditional, folk, even jazz) ends is seldom strictly determined, especially in the novels from 1922 onward. Sounds, less so for what they signify than for their own sake, enable Woolf to develop her ideas about music and to think specifically about how a different art form with divergent medial properties makes meaning alternatively from literature. Moments of singing in the novels, such as the children's song at the end of *The Years*, for example, demonstrate the instability of linguistic meaning (the "chorus" is not in any recognizable language) while foregrounding the effect of vocalizing on auditors. The result solicits a plurality of possible interpretations from the impromptu "audience" and the reader, particularly because sound, without an identifiable signified, is the foremost signifier. Thus, this book is as much about sound and language as it is about music, hence the list in my title, and the focus in both Parts 1 and 2 on new aspects from sound studies.

Woolf criticism has also explored her employment of the aural domain more generally, with a focus on sound, noise, and technology. I shall return to these critics especially in Parts 1 and 2,[6] but Melba Cuddy-Keane deserves comment here, as her essays have been key to my approach to how to "listen" to Woolf's novels. In addition to her early examination of music and communal relations in "The Politics of Comic Modes in Virginia Woolf's *Between the Acts*" (1990), her two article-length analyses – "Virginia Woolf, Sound Technologies, and the New Aurality" (2000) and "Modernist Soundscapes and the Intelligent Ear: An Approach to Narrative through Auditory Perception" (2005) – of new conceptions of aurality in the early twentieth century are groundbreaking studies of the sonics that inundate much of Woolf's oeuvre. In these latter two discussions, Cuddy-Keane's analysis is geared towards a particular historical interchange among New Music, inventions in

sound technologies, and Woolf's perceptions of aurality. Her delineation of terminology collected and developed from sound studies will
be instrumental in what follows. Cuddy-Keane was the first to apply R.
Murray Schafer's notion of soundscape to Woolf's work, for example,
an equivalent term to landscape that refers to the sounds heard in a
particular environment – my concentration in Part 1, where I examine sound and space together. Auscultation, a parallel to focalization,
which I shall focus on particularly in Part 2, where I explore the act of
listening, denotes the aural perspective through which a narrative is
presented. To indicate the emission of sound as opposed to the aural
placement of the listener, Cuddy-Keane suggests the term diffusion.
And lastly, her distinction that "there is a significant difference between
the linguistic representation of sound and the linguistic conceptualiza-
tion of it (sonicity as opposed to semantics)" ("Virginia Woolf, Sound
Technologies, and the New Aurality" 4), will be developed in Part 2
with the help of Michel Chion's theory of the different modes of listening in film. Thus, while Cuddy-Keane establishes the importance of
soundscapes to Woolf's fiction, my study offers sustained close examination of the activities of sound production and reception.

Despite this burgeoning scholarship on Woolf, the areas I examine
have not been fully mined for all the connections that help us to understand her novelistic innovations in new ways. In this book I argue that
sound, and its most representative art form of music, is integral to
Woolf's understanding of language and literature. More specifically, the
sonorous enables her to explore further issues of meaning in language
and art; it helps her to elaborate a politics of listening; and music itself
provides a potential structural model that facilitates the innovation of
her fictional method in *The Waves*. Thus, in what follows I explore several new areas in musico-literary scholarship: I expand and develop
concepts about the idea of song in literature, investigate the intersection
of sound and space, elucidate the act of listening as an ethical practice,
explore rhythm as a concept and in language, investigate scenes of performance in the novels, and posit a musical structural analogy.

I. Woolf's Musical Ear

Woolf had specific ideas about what the phrase "having an ear"
denotes. Her description of Thomas De Quincey's prose, in which
she mentions the "fineness of his own ear" (*CR2* 134), demonstrates
that she also contemplated how such an "ear" manifests in language.

Indeed, musical training and appreciation, I would suggest, teach one to listen in perceptive and attentive ways; significantly, such practices are also borne out in Woolf's writing. Below, I shall offer a brief account of Woolf's lifelong fascination with music to provide some indication that it is as comprehensive and significant as the connections she made to visual art.[7]

Woolf employed at least the *idea* of music in all of her novels, from her first fictional work, *The Voyage Out* – the protagonist, Rachel Vinrace, is a passionate amateur pianist – to the "scraps, orts and fragments" (*BA* 136) of her final text, *Between the Acts*. Although Woolf's musical acumen was admittedly limited, she was an astute and avid listener to traditional Western art music. Growing up in a late Victorian household, she took music lessons as a child and so was capable of hearing different melodies, tempo changes, or rhythmic alterations. Her sister Vanessa Bell recalls their early music lessons: "music naturally, since we were girls, had to be drummed into us, and the piano mistress succeeded in reducing us to complete boredom" (*Notes on Virginia's Childhood* 147). In addition to piano, they also took singing lessons. On one occasion in August 1908, in the same paragraph in which she explains in a letter to her sister how she is "trying to arrange a method of imagining scenes, and writing them," Woolf describes how she sings from "musical hieroglyphs" sent to her by Clive Bell in the morning's post:

> halfway through breakfast, I sang my song to keep myself in spirits, and saw it, as though in a mirror before me – mocking me. I at once changed my tune, and sang the second song, which no one knows. Tell the Chipmonk [Clive] his malice is thwarted; I sang for half an hour, and all the house crouched on the step to listen. (*L1*: 348–9)

It is doubtful that this means she was adept at reading music, but the episode suggests that neither was it a completely foreign language to her. The playfulness with which she describes the experience is also telling, especially in the context of her first novel, featuring the talented musician Rachel Vinrace, which most critics agree she had begun to compose at this time.

Thus, Woolf's interest in music for aesthetic purposes begins early in her career, well before her first novel was published in 1915. As early as 1905, as many critics have indicated, Woolf wrote a paper for the *National Review* entitled "Street Music" in which she discusses music's special "power over us [...][8] whenever we give ourselves up to its sway that no picture, however fair, or words however stately, can approach" (*E1*: 30). This essay was written within the same timeframe as she was reading Pater's *The Renaissance*, as well as writing a review of *The Oxford History of Music*, published in the *Guardian* of June 1905.[9] In 1909 she also penned a short non-fiction piece titled "The Opera" in which she discusses the multiple reactions of the audience, and what creates an audience's preference for Gluck or Wagner. Such audience-oriented scenes occur in several of the later novels, and play particularly important functions in them. In *The Waves*, Rhoda attends a vocal concert; in *The Years*, Kitty Lasswade watches Wagner's *Siegfried*; and the whole of *Between the Acts* is devoted to exploring the audience's perception of Miss La Trobe's pageant.

Woolf's diary records her own attendance at many musical concerts, including her visit to Bayreuth in 1909 – the same year she heard Ethel Smyth's opera *The Wreckers* at its British premiere at Covent Garden, long before Smyth introduced herself after reading *A Room of One's Own* (1929).[10] In Bayreuth she made a careful study of several of Wagner's operas, which she frequented with Saxon Sydney-Turner and her brother Adrian, first reading the opera (in German), then listening to it, and afterward discussing it. This experience was also realized as an article, "Impressions at Bayreuth." Thus, during her formative years as a writer, Woolf was herself an apperceptive listener where music is concerned; she had spent some time and energy working out what constitutes the sonorous art form in terms of its enunciation, performance, and reception.

From 1915 onward she attended concerts at Queen's Hall, Langham Place – at the time, London's principal concert hall. Also, during the winter seasons of 1918–21, Woolf went on her own to a number of private subscription concerts at Shelley House, Chelsea, and Cromwell House, South Kensington. She faithfully attended the Beethoven festival week in 1921 at Æolian Hall, during which the London String Quartet played, in chronological order, all seventeen of Beethoven's string quartets. Thus, her familiarity with Beethoven, and particularly the quartets, begins at an early stage of her fictional work. As she records in her diary, "But every afternoon for a week I've been up to the Æolian Hall; taken my seat right at the back; put my bag on the floor & listened to Beethoven quartets. Do I dare say listened? Well, but if one gets a lot of pleasure, really divine pleasure, & knows the tunes, & only occasionally thinks of other things – surely I may say listened" (*D2*: 114).

As sound technologies changed and listening at home became more common in the 1920s, the frequency of Woolf's enjoyment of the sonorous art did also. After the Woolfs obtained an Algraphone in 1925, they listened to music in the evenings on a regular basis, in part because Leonard wrote record reviews for the *Nation and Athenaeum* between 1926 and 1929 (*D*3: 42). Victoria Glendinning documents that they also purchased a new gramophone in January 1929 (247). Most likely, they continued their tradition of listening to it in the evenings in front of the fireplace at Monks House, their summer home in the south of England, throughout the 1930s. Leonard kept a loose card catalogue of the record reviews, as well as a *Diary of music listened to, 1939–69*, both of which can be found in the Monks House Papers at the University of Sussex. From the record reviews, the loose and randomly dated card catalogues, and Leonard's music diary, a pattern of receptive, up-to-date (in terms of record publications and performers), and knowledgeable listeners emerges; I shall discuss their listening practices further in chapter 6.

Also at this time in the late 1920s, the Hogarth Press published several pamphlets about music and related topics, as well as two book projects. In the same essay series that begins with Gertrude Stein's *Composition as Explanation* (1926), a signal that the sequence was to continue to circulate groundbreaking yet potentially "unpopular" publications, the Woolfs published two pieces by Robert H. Hull, *Contemporary Music* (1927) and *Delius* (1928); Eric W. White's *Parnassus to Let: An Essay about Rhythm in the Films* (1928) – White also penned the book-length *Stravinsky's Sacrifice to Apollo* (1930) for the press; as well as Basil de Sélincourt's *The Enjoyment of Music* (1928), which speaks to the growing trend at the time towards music appreciation spearheaded by the British Broadcasting Company (1922–6), later Corporation (1926–38).[11] They also published the two-volume study *An Outline of Musical History* (1929), by Ralph Hill and Thomas J. Hewitt.

Intriguingly, Virginia Woolf might have been the driving force behind de Sélincourt's piece, as the following transcription from the Hogarth Press Archives in Reading reveals:

Oct 26 [1927][12]

Dear Mrs Wolfe [*sic*],
Very many thanks for your letter. I'm glad you like the title "The Enjoyment of Music". I'm afraid it may take me rather a long time to get on with it; I am in any case a slow worker, and the reviewing

season is at its worst. Then I have a Choral Society to keep going in my village here, and this costs me at least a day every week. I would rather therefore not suggest a time for the delivery of the essay; it will be my first "free" piece of work.

As to the terms you suggest, I can only say that I hope they will not involve you in loss. Music is not a popular subject, & I am not a popular writer. And I am already paid for the essay, in the fact that you cared to ask me for it –

Sincerely yours,
Basil de Sélincourt

This unpublished letter from de Sélincourt documents that Virginia, rather than Leonard,[13] made the overture to de Sélincourt (who was an essayist, reviewer, and journalist) to write a piece on music for the Hogarth Essays, Second Series. He was also an "on-the-ground" supporter of music, as the letter records. Because he is glad that she likes the title, it is likely that they have had a back-and-forth correspondence at least once previously, so his misspelling of her name is (embarrassingly) absent-minded on his part, even though he is clearly delighted she has asked for the essay.[14] In a subsequent (undated) letter he corrects the mistake, rightly addressing her as Mrs Woolf, laments that he has worked so much on the essay that he is "at present in the condition of hating it more than everything else in the world," and asks for a final deadline date of submission. Lastly, a third handwritten letter from de Sélincourt (undated) is addressed to "Mr Woolf" (properly spelled); it mentions he is very pleased that Leonard likes his essay but is quite formal, noting clauses he would like to amend; it is substantially different in tone from the other letters addressed to Virginia. Significantly, for my purposes, what all four essays in the Second Series have in common, in addition to discussions of the significance of contemporary music and film, is a focus on rhythm, an aspect of Woolf's writing that becomes particularly important in the time leading up to *The Waves* (1930), as I shall discuss in chapter 6. The fact that she most likely played an active part in encouraging this component of the Hogarth Essays is new information for Woolf scholars interested in her musical connections.

As her novels and her letters to Ethel Smyth in the 1930s also document, Woolf was aware of the different registers of instruments. Appositely, Woolf describes to Smyth how her mind wanders during discussions with people: "merely what one thinks when someone else is talking – [*handwritten*]: in fun; by way of playing a tune on the bass. I like trying to play tunes while people are talking – with a view to the whole symphony" (*L5*: 354). This last phrase is beautifully suggestive of the wide-ranging ways by which Woolf integrates music and sound with the concepts of subjectivity and social interaction. In addition, Diane Gillespie suggests that Woolf's self-deprecating comments about her knowledge of the other arts were almost disingenuous at times: "Woolf's attitude toward the other arts combined emotional and intellectual, respectful and playful, even irreverent responses. Maintaining her self-image as ingenuous amateur, she still looked to art forms as diverse as painting, photography, cinema, dance, and music when works in her own medium, and words themselves, failed to inspire, clarify, or communicate what she wanted to say" ("Introduction" 1). A letter to Stephen Spender, for example, confirms her ability to detect musical tuning, something that would suggest, whether she was a musician or not, that she had, perhaps, the aforementioned "musical ear": "Again, living writers are to me like people singing in the next room – too loud, too near; and for some reason I am so exacerbated by their being flat or sharp; as if I were singing my own song, and they put me out" (*L5*: 408). Ultimately, although she was not an amateur musician, she was a dedicated student of the pleasures of organized sound and a lifelong connoisseur of the Western musical tradition. The novels also document familiarity with English folk tunes, jazz, and nursery rhymes.

II. Interdisciplinary Methods

For this study, I define music as organized or arranged sounds that are produced for the purposes of art (even sometimes while dislodging the implications of "order" or questioning what constitutes "music" in the first place). Woolf's intermedial thinking, I shall suggest, emerges not only because of the culturo-historical changes that took place at the start of the twentieth century, but also because she was always concerned with the social relevance of aesthetics. Indeed, throughout this book I shall argue that Woolf understood music as a socio-cultural force, and was far ahead of her time in doing so. Appreciating Woolf in these terms where music is concerned would not be possible without the growth over the last thirty years of the field of critical musicology. Since Susan McClary argued in 1991 that "music does not just passively reflect society; it also serves as a public forum within which various models of gender organization (along with many other aspects of social life) are asserted, adopted, contested, and negotiated" (8), the idea that "notes" are culturo-politically benign has become untenable.[15] Hence, critical musicologists (informed by feminist, gender, queer, Marxist, postcolonial, and cultural studies, as well as critical theory) insist it is necessary to examine music as an art that differs from language through specialized medial means, certainly, but one that is not exempt from the power and knowledge relations that govern the society in which it is produced.[16] A reading of the social dynamics of musical discourse is integral to my project, therefore, as I investigate how cultural differences manifest in Woolf's writing through her effort to think of language, and what constitutes the novel, in musical terms.

Thus, my project also develops further the critical concern that has emerged since the 1980s to understand Woolf's novelistic experiments not only as being formally innovative but also as elaborating sociopolitical critique, counter to Leonard's misleading description of her in his autobiography as the "least political animal that has lived since Aristotle invented the definition" (*Downhill* 27).[17] Through a thorough engagement with her ideas and methods concerning music, I arrive at a wide-ranging consideration of what I would deem her politicized, intermedial aesthetics. This is not only significant for Woolf criticism, feminist studies, and musicology, but also for the field of modernism more generally. As Susan Stanford Friedman has shown in her efforts to internationalize feminism, Woolf is an excellent case study for "developing strategies to interpret the geopolitical axis of difference that threads itself throughout her work, always mediated by other axes of difference like gender, sexuality, and class" (115). Similarly, not only does an examination of Woolf's interartistic thinking advance new avenues of investigation for the current interdisciplinary scholar, but her thirty-five-year exploration of the subject also points the way.

Woolf's novels reveal a considered engagement with intermedial practices, therefore, demonstrating that her feminist politics emerge compellingly when she travels between the two media of music and language. This study investigates her multilayered approach to sonority in the novels: her treatment is figurative, conceptual, and linguistic. Such manifold employment of sound and music would be enough to justify another full-length study, but she also experiments with musical ideas and forms to develop and innovate her novelistic methods, as I shall discuss in Part 3 – "to give the effect of the whole – again like music" (*TW* 214). Nevertheless, these interartistic strategies do not follow a model of progress in the novels. Instead, the musical ideas that are present from start to finish transform alongside her political and aesthetic views. Although her ideas change, they do not culminate in the last novel as a finished product, a complete resolution, or final cadence (to use a musical analogy). As with her prose, Woolf's deployment of sound and music also resists closure. Her thinking purposefully revisits previous ideas to explore new facets of her aesthetic principles.

Woolf's way of combining the two art forms is also significant in terms of larger trends in modernism. If intermedial studies theorist Klemens Gruber is correct, that in the early twentieth century a certain "semiotic fundamentalism" (247) dominated modernist interartistic crossovers, then Woolf's deployment of intermediality runs counter to this trend. In his study of Samuel Beckett, Martin Harries[18] also suggests that there is a "desire for medium specificity" in modernism (14). Indeed, Woolf might even concur: she contends that Roger Fry held similar views in her biography of him, as I shall return to in this book's Coda. But time and again, Woolf's openness to other media in combination with her own does not provide a competitive or binary version of their relations. Music is not found to be privileged over and above other art forms (even though it is highly esteemed at times), or transcendent, I shall argue. Instead, foretelling our current intermedial and digital age, Woolf is not interested in clear-cut oppositions or strict boundaries where musico-literary connections are made, in similar fashion to her political and social views.

Thus, I am not concerned so much with the accuracy of Woolf's employment of musical form when I make those connections in Part 3, but rather with the effect of that intersection. For this reason, because I have only found one *possible* structural link between a specific piece of music by Beethoven and *The Waves*, I have not forced the issue with the other novels; put simply, I do not see such a close tie between the forms of the other fictions and particular pieces of music, although others have certainly made associations.[19] The focus of this book will be to explore what can be gained from studying Woolf's far-reaching and experimental intermediality, not in mapping one medium onto another. The latter closes down a text and often leads to the somewhat redundant assertion that literature does not replicate music sufficiently, or vice versa. Instead, I am interested in the possibilities that arise when these two media meet, clash, conflict, and complement one another. This includes, I believe, in the case of *The Waves*, the overall structure of the novel in addition to its content.

I am not attempting to instantiate a typology, therefore, in chapter 6. Although direct links between specific literary texts and musical compositions can be made, I am mindful of both literary and musicological critiques of formalism.[20] But for my own part, I would suggest that to ignore the formal properties of texts that explicitly attempt to revolutionize literature by breaking open the possibilities of its structures in favour of solely historical and contextual approaches overlooks not just the political potential in formal innovations but also the medium of language. I would also propose that Woolf's methods demonstrate such political potential, particularly when her forms are inseparable from the content of her texts – most explicitly exhibited in *The Waves*. Thus, I attempt to strike a balance between close reading and contextualization because I am concerned with the concrete materials that we deploy in our art forms; indeed, this type of scrutiny is part of my materialist focus.

I use direct musical comparison to demonstrate the depth of Woolf's intermedial thinking, therefore, not to provide a study that unlocks the "key" to her text via musical analysis. The close examination of language and musical sound, I believe, is still essential for intermedial criticism. If it is ignored, one risks leaving the concrete materials that produce art by the wayside. Studies that avoid formal comparisons also have a tendency to turn musico-literary analysis inadvertently into plot comparison (especially when opera or song is under discussion), when the fruitfulness of the connection for me is the fact that music does not contain a plot in the same way that literature does. (Debates abound in musicology on this front also.)[21] Woolf gravitates towards music not simply because of its kinship with language and literature but perhaps even more so because of its distinctiveness from the verbal. I argue that Woolf's attention to these intermedial crossings is about experimenting with both the aesthetic and the ideological limits of art forms, rather than fixing one form onto another.

Correspondingly, throughout this book, I maintain an overriding focus on Woolf's materialist feminism, finding that it thrives in the interstices of music and literature. As I shall demonstrate in each part, the material reality of sound is paramount for Woolf, not its seeming elusive ability to escape the phenomenal world in mystical transcendence, an idea about music that has a long history.[22] Thus, my argument runs counter to Deutsch's, for example, in which he suggests, speaking of *The Waves*, "Woolf's merger of music and prose indeed exhibits an attempt to formulate such transcendental equivalences, to evoke the sound and sense, for instance, that 'like[n]' music to writing" (86). Instead, sound is heard to ricochet in the class-bound, aural architecture of Wigmore Hall in *The Waves*; represented in the attachment of the acousmatic voice to heterogeneous bodies in *Between the Acts*; or shown to demonstrate that performance remains, to use Rebecca Schneider's phrase, in *The Years*. Accordingly, I argue that Woolf's deployment of sound and music, like her feminism, is materialist.

Schneider summarizes (after Karen Barad) what has become a recent critical "turn" in performance studies:

> the new materialism commits not only to acknowledging matter as agential but also to acknowledging matter as *discursive*, though not linguistic, unsettling the precedent prioritizing of "language" as the sole or primary means to think about meaning-making (Barad 2003). This latter, of course, is something the new materialism shares with dance studies and performance studies, which both have been working diligently on these issues across several generations of scholars. ("New Materialisms" 7)

Work in this area has also been done in critical musicology. Nicholas Cook has been a front-runner in regard to music and performance studies, and I shall refer to his theories particularly in Part 3. I have also undertaken the study of music *as* performance in literature in my writings on Pater, as well as on Woolf's *The Years*. For me, this type of interdisciplinary critical study includes the analysis of scenes of performance (a focus of chapter 5), but also how language (often inspired by music or sonic experimentation) becomes performative. Where Woolf is concerned, her writing is particularly charged with performativity when rhythm is at issue in her texts (chapter 6).

Furthermore, the traditional tendency to understand the literary modernist enterprise as largely psychological seems to go hand-in-hand with a rejection of the physical and material world, precisely the domain to which women were (and often are) relegated. Long-established critical interpretations of Woolf's ideas about subjectivity have also tended to reiterate the notion of "pure being," often categorized as a mystical state that transcends both time and space. But as Jane Goldman has argued, Woolf herself, most succinctly in *A Room of One's Own* and *Three Guineas*, "brings to bear an emphatically materialist analysis in her feminist tract[s]" (5). The same is true of her novels. Woolf's insistence on the "real world" – exposed here by examining her focus on the material nature of sound and its art form, music – is a strategic destabilization of the mechanism of the gaze and the consequent limits it enforces on the female body. Put another way, Woolf's particular concentration on music and sound reveals an alternative modernist aesthetic, one that is concerned with the political and social ramifications of the material domain and takes a fundamentally different approach to the largely accepted notion of modernism as interior and visual. Some of her most vivid methods for doing so are to think sonically and across the art forms of literature and music.

The purpose of this project, therefore, is to explore crucial areas in Woolf criticism, intermedial studies, and the modernist period. Contributing to the growing exploration of cultural material across disciplines, a study that investigates Woolf's musico-literary processes is poised to produce fresh perspectives on one of the early twentieth century's major cultural workers. "Hearing" her fiction, then, brings to the fore new insights into her use of language, her understanding of her own methods, her evolving generic experimentation, and her theorization of the relationship between art and life.

III. "Hoity te, hoity te, hoity te ...": Tripartite Woolf

Eleanor's imitation of the 3/4 metre of the waltz in *The Years* (*TY* 274) captures a rhythmic pattern of threes that often permeates Woolf's novels – Louis's repeated "it stamps, and stamps, and stamps" (*TW* 5) in *The Waves*, the gramophone's thrice recurring refrain, "dispersed are we" (*BA* 69–70), in *Between the Acts*, and the tripartite structure of *To the Lighthouse* are just a few examples. Likewise, my structure is made up of three parts, each split into two chapters. Within these sections, the notion of theme and variation to which Woolf often refers in her letters and diary is the primary model. In addition to her reply to Trevelyan, her early designs for *Between the Acts*, for another example, suggest this musical form: "Its [sic] to be first the statement of the theme: then the restatement: & so on: repeating the same story: singling out this & then that: until the central idea is stated" (*D5*: 114). Inspired by the musical nature of Woolf's methods, my goal is to engage thoroughly with the umbrella topic by examining it from three significant perspectives: the intersection of sound and space; practices of listening; and performance, both scenic content in the novels and the performativity of language and structure. In addition, I employ theories in each chapter that cross disciplines. In Part 1 I use concepts from the study of aural architecture but also actor-network theory; I deploy film theory and historical sound studies in Part 2; and I draw largely upon performance studies from both theatre and musicology in Part 3. The project, therefore, is about intermediality and interdisciplinarity, but also attempts to utilize theoretical concepts that explore such issues as well.

Furthermore, the chapters are largely chronological in terms of Woolf's oeuvre, not because I want to instantiate a notion of progress, but because there are developments, new directions, or redirections that illuminate particular patterns in her thinking that arise when the novels are read in succession. Although chronology can inscribe its own linearity, I endeavour to understand the series of her novels contextually, but not as a rationalized, historical evolution with a finale or swan song, so to speak, musically. The texts are certainly tied to personal, social, and historical shifts, of course, such as her changing aesthetic methods, access to publication, her evolving/revolving feminist ideas, the world wars, the international politics of the 1930s, etc. I choose a chronological organization, however, in order to allow for various overlapping, sometimes even conflicting, patterns to emerge within each overarching, larger focus. To cohere the myriad patterns that arise when I concentrate on the earcon (the aural equivalent to an icon) – I find that a cross-section of novels, *The Voyage Out*, *To the Lighthouse*, and *Between the Acts*, sound the earcon in similar places, for example – into a chapter on its own fixes associations in a way that is counter to Woolf's methods, aesthetics, and politics; it also leaves out other aspects that come alive when I explore the trajectory of the novels, as I hope the reader will experience.

My discussion of the singing women in several texts cuts across Woolf's oeuvre, for instance, in fruitful ways, connecting seemingly inconsequential characters: the old women (Woolf's phrase) in *Jacob's Room*, *Mrs. Dalloway*, and *To the Lighthouse* (Mrs McNab) are linked with central ones such as Sara in *The Years* and Miss La Trobe in *Between the Acts*. Woolf's concept of the "outsider" is at issue with each of them: homeless, working-class, poverty-stricken, and lesbian characters vocalize the earcon themselves or enable others to do so. Space and sound together are often grounded in tangible, albeit elusive, bodies. Consequently, readers looking for clear-cut, overall summations of the novels will, I suspect, be disappointed. I do think, however, that by the end of this study, a comprehensive understanding of how sound and music function in the novels is achieved. As noted, my reasoning for this approach is inspired by Woolf's prose, methods, and aesthetic ideas, which rarely, if ever, fix language or structural elements. My book, in dialogue with her fictional output, works by layering.

As one might expect from Woolf's prose, therefore, my examination reveals the exceptional depth of her experiments in language and her wide-ranging employment of sound and music throughout her oeuvre. Taken together, all three parts elucidate several reasons why sound and music are important to her aesthetic: (1) because it is an art form that resists precise meaning; (2) because of its aural nature, which foregrounds the process of listening; (3) because it is active – it must be performed to be heard; and (4) because it is imbricated in the material and social world.

Part 1, "An Emerging Earcon: Woolf's Singers," traces her employment of a particularly musical earcon used in a variety of her novels, both to resist and reconfigure the burden of meaning in language (the old woman's song in *Mrs. Dalloway* is a good example of this "melody"). Indeed, as noted, seemingly inconsequential singing figures emerge in my survey of the texts from the 1910s and 1920s in chapter 1. In chapter 2, these vocalizations are shown to be integrated more thoroughly with significant characters in the novels from the 1930s. Tropic deployment of sound and music demonstrates an uncommon capacity to dislodge assumptions about knowledge acquisition. Moreover, what I am calling, after Mladen Dolar, a postlinguistic vocal declaration emerges in particular spaces in the texts, demonstrating the link between sound and space in intriguing ways. I employ the concept of aural architecture – the properties of a space that can be experienced by listening as defined by Barry Blesser and Linda-Ruth Salter – to reveal that Woolf's effort to articulate an earcon in the public sphere counterbalances then-contemporary trends in music and sonic practices. Indeed, the pattern of a network, in Bruno Latour's sense, a Gilles Deleuzian assemblage, is reflected in the movements of sound. Thus, in Part 1 I also argue that Woolf is interested in investigating the nature of sonicity to query many of the epistemological assumptions and circumstances of her age. Ultimately, her interartistic strategies enable new ways of making meaning as well as alternative models for subjectivity and artistic expression.

To clarify here, because the issue will come up in each part, by public I mean a space that incorporates more facets than a traditional notion of separate sphere ideology, maintained by thinkers such as Jurgen Habermas. Significantly, in Woolf's fiction, public space is not solely in fundamental opposition to a private, domestic sphere, even if these were admittedly pervasive and even useful terms for her that she herself incorporates throughout her writings. As Anna Snaith has argued,

> [Woolf's] questioning of their meanings and connotations [public and private] comes ... in the variety of context in which she places them. She unsettles them, moves them about – makes them work for her, refusing to be labelled by them. Historically, Woolf's use of the terms was influenced, and played through, the ideology of separate spheres. For a woman living at the turn of the century, the division of public and private would have had immense significance even as it began to be challenged. (*Virginia Woolf* 11)

Indeed, in the last twenty years, and as Woolf's novels demonstrate, theorization of Victorian separate sphere ideology has been ably problematized to demonstrate that these are not mutually exclusive domains, binary oppositions that inevitably privilege one space over the other (typically the public over the private).

More helpful is an associational understanding of social spaces. As Seyla Benhabib has maintained after Hannah Arendt,

> the "associational" view of public space suggests that such a space emerges whenever and wherever, in Arendt's words, "men act together in concert." On this model, public space is the space "where freedom can appear." It is not a space in any topographical or institutional sense: a town hall or a city square where people do not "act in concert" is not a public space in this Arendtian sense. But a private dining room in which people gather to hear a *Samizdat* or in which dissidents meet with foreigners become public spaces; just as a field or a forest can also become public space if they are the object and the location of an "action in concert," of a demonstration to stop the construction of a highway or a military airbase, for example. These diverse topographical locations become public spaces in that they become the "sites" of power, of common action coordinated through speech and persuasion. (93)

In Part 1, Woolf's pattern of sound and space demonstrates that "sites" of power do exist that are more various than official, public spaces; simultaneously, she challenges the political importance of seemingly benign and presumably "private" domestic conditions. Natural and built environments in both rural and urban settings in the novels are also shown to commingle when the earcon is voiced, questioning separate sphere ideology from another angle.

Part 2, "Profound Listening and Acousmatics," examines this other important dimension to the processes of the utterance, arguing that Woolf understood the apperception of sound as being integral to ethical communal relations. By employing Chion's three modes of listening – causal, semantic, and reduced (although I shall re-term it "profound") – I examine audition as it appears in Woolf's novels. Her multilayered representation of perceiving sonority reveals more of the political function of augmenting the aural domain, demonstrating that Woolf explores the receptive side of sonority to put forward an alternative social ethics. Woolf is interested in new ways to make meaning, but she is just as concerned with the reception of those practices, as well as the variety of different forms, ideas, and words that inhabit the world, particularly new technologies. With the help of sound theorists Jonathan Sterne and John Picker, I argue that her novels teach the reader new ways to listen. In chapter 3 the telephone and the wireless affect the reception of sound at significant moments in the novels. In chapter 4 texts such as *The Years*, with its air-raid scene heard from the perspective of characters in the basement of a London house, urgently bring home the intertwined circumstances of a lack of listening and the calamity of war. Hence, this part demonstrates how very integral the other side of the utterance is to Woolf's social principles, an outgrowth, I contend, of her musico-literary explorations.

Part 3, "Music *as* Performance in Woolf's Fiction," investigates Woolf's employment of musical scenes to explore Schneider's concept that performing remains instead of disappearing. Woolf, I suggest, although with variations, puts forward a tangible notion of the sonorous art in many of her characters' performances. In addition, in the later novels especially, her performers do not become automatons reiterating the value and longevity of the "great composer's work." Instead, Woolf explores the actual, embodied process of performing as a non-discursive resistance to sanctified history. In *The Years* and *Between the Acts*, the significance of the performative archive grows. In chapter 6, I switch the focus to Woolf's materials in order to explore the effect of performativity on language when sound and music are in the foreground. Rhythm becomes especially important in this chapter as a trigger for Woolf's active installation of language and method. Writing to a rhythm and not to a plot makes Woolf herself the performer of language. The innovations that emerge from this intermedial thinking, which are revealed to be particularly inspired by the music of Beethoven, help create the vital experiments that manifest in her groundbreaking novel *The Waves*.

In the Coda I come full circle, returning to the opening epigraph from a different vantage point to discuss the text to which Trevelyan refers when Woolf responds that she always thinks of her books as music before she writes them. Exploring Woolf's biography of Fry, her take on his artistic theories (particularly those about rhythm) and his life, provides me with some final comments on Woolf as a proto-intermedial writer. Ultimately, throughout the book, I find that Woolf's texts demonstrate an awareness of sonority that celebrates the phenomenal world, rather than attempting to transcend or circumvent it. In this way, her fruitful musico-literary ventures reveal how very mediated the world is.

PART 1

An Emerging Earcon: Woolf's Singers

Chapter One

Finding a Voice

In the middle of the night a loud cry rang through the village. Then there was a sound of something scuffling; and then dead silence. All that could be seen out of the window was the branch of lilac tree hanging motionless and ponderous across the road. It was a hot still night. There was no moon. The cry made everything seem ominous. Who had cried? Why had she cried? It was a woman's voice, made by some extremity of feeling almost sexless, almost expressionless. It was as if human nature had cried out against some iniquity, some inexpressible horror [...].

One lay in the dark listening intently. It had been merely a voice. There was nothing to connect it with. No picture of any sort came to interpret it, to make it intelligible to the mind. But as the dark arose at last all one saw was an obscure human form, almost without shape, raising a gigantic arm in vain against some overwhelming iniquity.

Virginia Woolf, "Three Pictures" (1929), 13–14

The epigraph elaborates a nexus of issues that circulate around a particular sound, albeit in silent words, that Woolf articulates with growing intensity in her novels. The title of the lesser-known essay, "Three Pictures," a short piece that details three scenes, does not suggest anything about aurality (and even implies the visual domain). Yet, a heightened sonic experience is illustrated, depicting an utterance rendered as a poignant cry from "human nature." In this chapter I explore what this "cry" might convey because it is found in most of the novels, including her first major work of fiction, I argue. Indeed, this sound is significant enough, I contend, to be described as what acoustic theorists Barry Blesser and Linda-Ruth Salter term an earcon: "the aural analogue of a visual icon ... a sonic event that contains special symbolic meaning not present in the sound wave" (83).

Particular sonic patterns also emerge in specific places and spaces (I shall define the difference below) in Woolf's texts, often revealing social ramifications, especially in terms of gender. Woolf's musico-literary endeavours disclose the relationship between aurality and spatiality. Blesser and Salter define and elaborate auditory spatial awareness by examining the interconnections between space and sound from pre-history to the present. If they are correct, and an aural architect, "acting as both an artist and a social engineer, is therefore someone who selects specific aural attributes of a space based on what is desirable in a particular cultural framework" (5), then Woolf performs this function when she makes particular choices in her novels that illuminate various experiences of sonority in built and unbuilt environments. This role is not the same as an acoustic architect, "a builder, engineer, or physical scientist who implements the aural attributes previously selected by an aural architect" (ibid.). Instead, "an aural architect can create a space that encourages or discourages social cohesion among its inhabitants" (ibid.). Woolf demonstrates such effects by voicing this earcon in distinct places and spaces in her fictional (and nonfictional) output. A seemingly incidental woman, for example, emits a significant vocal utterance in a village in the jungle in *The Voyage Out*, in the streets of London in *Jacob's Room* and *Mrs. Dalloway*, and in the Ramsays' summer home in the "Time Passes" section of *To the Lighthouse*, demonstrating that Woolf arranges the aural architecture in her narratives sometimes to encourage socio-cultural inclusion, and at others to reveal an experience of exclusion.

The study of sound, music, and space has blossomed in recent years, partly as a result of Blesser and Salter's work, as well as that of Emily Thompson and John Picker, and the growth of Sound Studies more generally.[1] Musicological perspectives that take space into account have also surfaced lately. The collection *Music, Sound, and Space: Transformations of Public and Private Experience* (2013) edited by Georgina Born is a recent case in point.[2] Moreover, Woolf scholars have taken up the task of analysing spatiality in her texts,[3] and the combination of sound and space emerges in Melba Cuddy-Keane's work on aurality, although not in an overt fashion. In addition, her understanding of the relational nature of auscultation also informs my reading below; throughout I shall employ the terminology of sound analysis she puts forward in her essays (see Introduction).

In what follows I shall distinguish place, meaning "environments that have been shaped and molded by human action and habitation," from space, "certain key characteristics of the environments or settings within which characters live and act: location, position, arrangement, distance, direction, orientation, and movement," drawing on definitions provided by Marie-Laure Ryan, Kenneth Foote, and Maoz Azaryahu (6). In addition, "there is a close relationship between place and the concept of sense of place, the latter referring to the affective, emotive bonds and attachments people develop or experience in particular places and environments on a variety of scales, from the microscale of the home (or even room), to the neighborhood, city, state, or nation" (6). Where Woolf's work is concerned, as Anna Snaith and Michael Whitworth have argued, her "writings on space negotiate the complex interrelationship between the bodies that inhabit space and the symbolic meanings that govern and regulate that habitation [so that] space is no longer static, neutral and objectified" (Snaith and Whitworth 5). I shall explore what happens to sound (often musical) in Woolf's reconfiguration of private and public spaces.[4]

Although Part 1 is largely about the interplay of Woolf's literary geography and her employment of sonics, the art form of music is also significant, as it is often enlisted in the voicing of an earcon. Indeed, I shall suggest that a pattern of understated and even elusive singers emerges in the novels from the time of *Jacob's Room* onward. Thus, I explore Woolf's characters (usually seemingly incidental ones) who sing or are related to vocalizing in same way. Recent theories about the voice – after Jacques Derrida and deconstruction, which dislodged the concept of presence from it – can help explain why Woolf gravitates towards the singer to utter this earcon. Mladen Dolar theorizes that the voice is the agent of enunciation in a way that separates it from the signifier/signified binary. He argues that the voice "opens a zone of undecidability ... an intermediacy" (13), describing it as separate from, although related to, language: "If we speak in order to 'make sense,' to signify, to convey something, then the voice is the material support of bringing about meaning, yet it does not contribute to it itself. It is, rather something like the vanishing mediator" (15). Thus, he defines it as *"what does not contribute to making sense"* (ibid.; italics in original). As I shall demonstrate, Woolf's enunciations of an earcon suggest it is "postlinguistic" – meaning "beyond language, the voice which requires a more sophisticated cultural conditioning than the acquisition of language ... most spectacularly illustrated by singing" (Dolar 29); it is, however paradoxically, a resistance to language, which often seems inadequate to capture significant moments in Woolf's texts, according to some of her characters. As Bernard, the writer, expresses in *The Waves*, he is in search of a "soaring, lark-like, pealing song to replace these flagging, foolish transcripts" (*TW* 201).[5]

I do not want to suggest from Dolar's definitions, however, that the postlinguistic voice is transcendent or that it achieves some sort of presence, nor does Dolar, but the idea that the postlinguistic is "beyond" the voice is not quite what I think happens in Woolf's work. Instead, this articulation of the earcon through the voice, which most often surfaces as song or chorus, articulates the material nature of sound. Although there is certainly learned, technical skill involved in the trained singing voice for musical performance (and I am referring here to the Western art tradition with which Woolf was so familiar), such practices and vocalizations are fundamentally rooted in the body. The proficiencies one learns when attempting to reach the level of craftsmanship are numerous and vary depending on the vocal method, but some commonalities might include the expansion and control of the breath, a connection to the diaphragm, and the opening up and placement of sound in cavities of resonance in the head and the body, for just a start. A singer learns to move sound around within and out of her or his body. Whether coached or not, moreover, the sound that issues from the mouth is at the mercy of the larynx that produces it, the distinct voice box that creates each person's specific timbre (or sound quality). Learning music itself, and all that is involved physically and mentally, is yet another layer of aptitude, as well as meaning making, that comprises interpretation through the combination of melody with words. Singing, then, is an intermedial experience that is saturated with negotiations among the body (its abilities, its shortfalls, and its health), the "notes" (breathing and phrasing, for example), and the words (language being the presumed area for clarifying meaning and composer "intent," although it too, of course, is subject to the free play of the signifier, as Roland Barthes would have it). All of this is to say that the postlinguistic, as I understand it, is not necessarily beyond language, but perhaps beside it, behind it, within it, around it, yet nevertheless distinct from it, primarily because it is "*what does not contribute to making sense*" (Dolar 15) – it is all of those other non-articulable things.

The aural domain, then, enables Woolf to imagine new possibilities in terms of the material world. Because she recognizes the physical conditions of aurality, that sonorities can travel where optics cannot, for example, she uses it to transgress seemingly concrete spatial borders in her texts, often disclosing the constructedness of place. Indeed,

I shall argue that a discernible shift from place as container to a spatial network, along the lines of Bruno Latour's actor-network theory (ANT), occurs in the novels of the 1920s. I have two primary reasons for using ANT to understand the connection between Woolf's earcon and place/space. First, it puts the focus on material relations. According to Latour, ANT "is a simple material resistance argument. Strength does not come from concentration, purity and unity, but from dissemination, heterogeneity and the careful plaiting of weak ties ... [a] feeling that resistance, obduracy and sturdiness is more easily achieved through netting, lacing, weaving, twisting, of ties that are weak by themselves, and that each tie, no matter how strong, is itself woven out of still weaker threads" ("On Actor-Network" 3). Second, ANT equalizes the human and the nonhuman through the concept of the actor/actant. Latour explains that an actant is "something that acts or to which activity is granted by others. It implies *no* special motivation of human individual actors, nor of humans in general. An actant can literally be anything provided it is granted to be the source of an action" (ibid. 7). In my study this includes nonhuman entities such as the house and its airs in *To the Lighthouse*, for example, but most important for my purposes, the singing voice as postlinguistic. One more caveat: I do not *apply* Latour's theory below; instead, in keeping with the approach of ANT, I shall attempt to tease out heterogeneous associations and patterns created by sonic movements, rather than searching for or imposing a predetermined map of a network. Nevertheless, in unveiling a connection between sound and space, Woolf voices an assemblage of sonics that has typically gone unheard. Moreover, I argue that the cry grows in its political urgency in the 1930s, which will be the focus of chapter 2.

I. Resonant Beginnings: *The Voyage Out*

Woolf's first novel, *The Voyage Out*, employs the art of music directly through the main character, Rachel Vinrace, who is a pianist. The first part of the novel takes place aboard a ship, the *Euphrosyne*, which functions like a moving domicile, albeit one that is in a somewhat ramshackle state for bourgeois passengers; it is a mercantile ship used for the transportation of goods across the Atlantic Ocean. The second half is located at the ship's destination, Santa Marina, a fictitious South American colonial port town. This latter part follows the exploits of a group of upper-middle-class English tourists at a resort and its surroundings but focuses primarily on the developing marriage plot of Rachel and Terence Hewet. But before a wedding can take place, Rachel falls ill and dies, thwarting the typical expectations of the female bildungsroman.

Perhaps because the protagonist is an instrumentalist, the vocal art form is not very important in this text. Occasionally, Rachel does sing to herself and finds it freeing, "knowing it doesn't matter a damn to anybody" (*VO* 248), but practising and performing on the piano are much more significant, which I shall discuss in detail in Part 3. Yet, one scene, which occurs in the same chapter as the enigmatic and muted engagement proposal between Rachel and Terence, does contain the enunciation of a cry with many of the attributes that will adhere to the earcon in the later novels: it questions presumed direct and simple linguistic communication described as unintelligible, its auditors explicitly do not understand it but it makes them question themselves and the world around them, and it is voiced in the open-air space of a clearing, as opposed to a place indoors with clearer, demarcated boundaries. The scene reveals that Woolf engages aurality to destabilize the conventional binaries of optics: subject/object, colonizer/colonized. It is the villagers' voices, despite the specifics of what they are saying, that trouble the usual dyads, if only for a fleeting moment.

The proposal scene when Rachel and Terence declare their feelings for each other takes place during a river excursion to visit a village in the jungle,[6] suggesting a link between the "new territory" of their relationship and the apparently undeveloped landscape – for "since the time of Elizabeth very few people had seen the river, and nothing had been done to change its appearance from what it was to the eyes of the Elizabethan voyagers" (*VO* 308). Woolf's depiction of the English in this scene is notable for its satire, which reveals the colonialist presumptions of the European travellers. In *Imperial Eyes*, Mary Louise Pratt argues that such presuppositions were rampant in the travel literature of the nineteenth century and that interpreting geography in these convenient terms served to enable the acquisition of territory. With this mindset, English explorers often proceeded to "discover" new regions of supposedly uninhabited space, despite the fact that the local inhabitants were guiding them to such places (which the residents already knew about). The novel demonstrates the interplay between space and place when the English travellers view the vast and purportedly unseen landscape but then retreat to their hotel, a British-identified place, a colonial hotel in Santa Marina. While the "undiscovered" space connotes movement and adventure, tinged with the excitement of fear based on stereotypes about "foreignness" and the unknown, the hotel provides the comfort and safety of a familiar place with the requisite British conventions.

Before reaching the village but just after the "engagement" scene, Mr Flushing, the organizer of the expedition, mentions an explorer named Mackenzie (*VO* 323), who has died because he ventured (like Joseph Conrad's Kurtz) beyond the bounds of any other white man, and fomented the potential "dangers" lurking in the wild in a way that is often detailed in Victorian travel literature. Yet, time and again, those on the sojourn are shown to be oblivious to the material world they are traversing. Instead, they interpret what they see as though they are still reading it in a Richard Burton travelogue, or even one by Mary Kingsley (to whom Woolf refers in *Three Guineas*).[7] As the party approaches a clearing, for example, Mr Flushing comments, "'it almost reminds one of an English park'" (*VO* 325). And the narrator confirms, "As far as they could gaze, this lawn rose and sank with the undulating motion of an old English park" (ibid.). Thus, the travellers understand the visual discourse of the scene as a reflection of their own geography, comforting themselves by establishing a sense of place and the prospect that perhaps the villagers they will encounter, therefore, will be just as "civilized" as they are.

Nowhere is the presumed privilege of the English more poignant than in the visit to the village in the jungle; this is also the first instance in which an ineffable cry is voiced in Woolf's novels. The scene is highly imagistic; it is, therefore, often interpreted by critics in visual terms. Appropriately, they point out that the narrative gaze reflects the colonial tactics deployed by the English. Christine Froula, for example, contends that Woolf's novel is a response to Conrad's similarly anti-colonial text, *Heart of Darkness*, suggesting the Amazon village is akin to Marlow's "Inner Station": "Rachel and Terence flinch under the village women's strong gazes in an ethnographic encounter that makes Rachel feel her world as strange and inexplicable in their eyes as in her own" (56). Similarly, Andrea Lewis argues that the gaze is panoptic and oppressive, part of a largely intrusive moment in which "the private activities of the natives become a public spectacle for the English, a point of ethnographic interest for them. In particular, it is the bodies of women which provide the focus of the tourists' vision … the women are portrayed in a strangely static and silent manner" (117). Natania Rosenfeld suggests the opposite, that Woolf utilizes the moment to subvert the colonial power struggle: "The intense, shaming gaze of the native women is a refusal of objectification and an assertion of autonomy" (35).

Whether or not the power relation of the gaze is deflected or reinscribed, the open-air space affects sound differently than it does sight, and Woolf reflects the variance in her chosen literary geography. The scene is oddly but repeatedly linked by the travellers to the particularly English landscape noted above (however problematically): the communal park, suggesting a manicured, exterior site, very different and indeed strikingly less contained than Rachel's room on the *Euphrosyne* or at the villa in Santa Marina, a "room cut off from the rest of the house, large, private – a room in which she could play, read, think, defy the world, a fortress as well as a sanctuary" (*VO* 136). In *Jacob's Room* and *Mrs. Dalloway*, Woolf will utter the earcon in London parks, exterior places identified in the novels with Englishness and a love of the natural world (embedded in the urban environment of the city at large), as a resistance to the fact that "it is the partition of space that structures it," as Michel de Certeau reveals in *The Practice of Everyday Life* (123). The solitary room, on the other hand, subscribes to a narrative pattern of space as container, which evokes a common ambiguity found in enclosed space: "emotionally fulfilling sense of place versus freedom-depriving prison" (Ryan et al. 18). And the room, of course, will be central to Woolf's theorization of it in gendered terms in her polemic, *A Room of One's Own*. In this early instance of the cry (and several after), therefore, it is voiced in a space that is antithetical to the, albeit delimited, security and freedom that Woolf will associate directly with female liberation. Instead, its enunciation is in a social and public arena fraught with relations of power.

Accordingly, a requisite effect occurs in terms of the aural architecture of the scene. Clearly, the stare of a woman, which "never left their faces," makes the English uncomfortable and uneasy, so much so that they "finally turned away, rather than stand there looking at her any longer." Despite their presence as "tight-coated soldiers," eventually "the village took no notice of them; they had become absorbed into it. The women's hands became busy again with the straw; their eyes dropped" (*VO* 332). But then, the intensity of this "contact zone" – "the space in which peoples geographically and historically separated come into contact with each other and establish ongoing relations, usually involving conditions of coercion, radical inequality, and intractable conflict" (Pratt 6) – shifts from the gaze towards aurality. Sound is employed to characterize the everyday life of the villagers; the utterances are no less meaningful for being indecipherable to the English:

> If they moved, it was to fetch something from the hut, or to catch a straying child, or to cross the space with a jar balanced on their heads; if they spoke, it was to cry some harsh unintelligible cry. Voices rose when a child was beaten, and fell again; voices rose in song, which slid up a little way and down a little way, and settled again upon the same low and melancholy note. (*VO* 332)

Movement and a lack of restriction characterize both the women's bodies and their voices in the scene. The everyday life of the village, its materiality, is active, with children playing and mothers calling after them with a "harsh unintelligible cry," a description that will be echoed repeatedly in the novels and not necessarily a negative quality for Woolf – such as the fierceness noted when the caretaker's children sing their indecipherable chorus at the end of *The Years*. Moreover, the voices in another language are described in terms of their tangible existence (moving sound waves) as an undulating song; somehow these words that come to the auditors as incomprehensible nevertheless cohere into meaningful sonics even as they resist propositional content.

But notably, there is a primitivist undertone to what Woolf seems to be after here with her association of these South American women and an albeit subdued sort of violence. She would have encountered this pervasive and highly problematic modernist trend in the paintings of Paul Gauguin, for example, which were included in Roger Fry's "Manet and the Post-Impressionists" exhibit in 1910. His *L'Esprit Veille*, now referred to as *The Spirit of the Dead Watching* (1892), an instance not only of racist but also of gendered objectification, shared a room with Vincent van Gogh's canvases.[8] Although Woolf will develop her earlier ideas into the Outsiders Society of *Three Guineas* and typically depicts these differences from restrictive, English codes of behaviour as exhilarating, it does not erase the derogatory links among women of colour, homelessness, and working-class conditions (the latter two occur in subsequent novels) that depend on racialized and classist assumptions about a "savage other."

Yet, the effect of the harsh, unintelligible singing voices on Rachel and Terence is to make them consider, however momentarily, their place in the world: to self-reflect. Immediately after the "melancholy note," Terence ponders: "'Well,' [he] sighed at length, 'it makes us seem insignificant, doesn't it?'" (*VO* 332). Prior to this aural moment, they appear content to retreat into militarism. After the sounds breach the English travellers' acoustic horizon – "the maximum distance between a listener and source of sound where the sonic event can still be heard" (Blesser and Salter 22) – Rachel and Terence have, however briefly, this moment of contemplation: maybe they are not as important as they had previously thought? But once Rachel and Terence turn away, walk through the "trees, leaning, without fear of discovery, upon each other's arms" (*VO* 333), and are no longer within range of the village sonics, they return to their affirmative discussion about happiness and love (even though being in love also involves pain, according to the narrator): "they had not gone far before they began to assure each other once more that they were in love, were happy, were content; but why was it so painful being in love, why was there so much pain in happiness?" (ibid.). Nevertheless, the gaze, thoroughly imbued with the colonial dynamic, is disrupted in this scene by the postlinguistic voices of the villagers. Dolar might argue that this is because singing "reverses the hierarchy [with language] – let[ting] the voice take the upper hand" (30).

II. Sonic Networks in *Jacob's Room*

In *Jacob's Room* the links between courtship scenes and imperialism are deployed more overtly, and they are underscored by the death of soldiers in Flanders Fields and every other acre of "the Front." The novel details the life of a young man who both epitomizes the entitlements of the Edwardian society from which he comes and is a victim of them. The narrative thoroughly interrogates the cultural practices that led to the devastation of the world's first global conflict. The life of the aptly named Jacob Flanders[9] is chronicled from childhood to his education at Cambridge, from experiences in London as a young man to travels on the continent and his eventual death in the First World War. The text gives the appearance of being a bildungsroman, yet it deftly dislodges the assumptions of such a progressive narrative. Various techniques – a multitude of perspectives (120 characters in total dot the novel), unexplained gaps in time and space, and an intrusive yet dubious narrator – combine to create the effect of an empty protagonist, one that is already absent, even dead. The reader does not "know" Jacob in the way one typically might in a traditional realist novel either. As Mrs Norris, a fellow traveller on a train, reflects in regard to him, "it is no use trying to sum people up. One must follow hints, not exactly what is said, nor yet entirely what is done" (*JR* 37), a summary of Woolf's method in the novel as a whole. The remark foregrounds the illusion of a solid sense of subjectivity and the requisite effect on genre, something Woolf will theorize in another train scene in "Character in Fiction" (1924) (*E3*: 420–38).

The voicing of the earcon not only grows in intensity in *Jacob's Room*, it also proliferates, elucidating the aural nature of Woolf's comment that the text is a "disconnected rhapsody" (*D2*: 179). The cry, therefore, becomes an all-out lament in this elegiac book. It surfaces variously: in Jacob's name, as the booming of guns, as birdsong, and as a homeless woman's "wild song" (*JR* 89). In each case the sonicity of the earcon, as opposed to its semantics, as Cuddy-Keane has formulated, is foregrounded, while the meanings of the words that articulate it in the novel are questioned and destabilized. In addition, distinct patterns in terms of space and place emerge in this text, ones that suggest that Woolf's understanding of her literary geography changes after the First World War. The significance of the room, not surprisingly given the novel's title, is certainly maintained, but an expanded sense of space more akin to a network also surfaces when one traces the sounds of this earcon. As Ryan et al. explain, "while space as container is delimited by boundaries often imposed on the subject, space as a network is a dynamic system of relations that allows movement, and that is often actively created by the subject" (18). In Woolf's case, the leaps made in the novel's spaces and places make new connections via sound.

Thus, networks of spatial relations (international, natural in urban, private and social/public) are created via Woolf's deployment of sonority to close up and challenge what Latour might suggest is the "'tyranny of distance' or proximity" ("On Actor-Network" 4). The novel as a whole, and especially through its aural bridging, demonstrates that "elements which are close when disconnected may be infinitely remote if their connections are analyzed; conversely, elements which would appear as infinitely distant may be close when their connections are brought back into the picture" (ibid.). This is a result, no doubt, of the overall methodological project of the novel – "Let us record the atoms as they fall upon the mind in the order in which they fall, let us trace the pattern, however disconnected and incoherent in appearance, which each sight or incident scores upon the consciousness" (Woolf, "Modern Fiction," *E4*: 161) – but also the product of Woolf's sustained investigation into the properties of sound and its articulation in the relations of domestic and social space.

Significantly, this text and its protagonist have been interpreted by critics as being infused with the concept of spatiality; the connection that space has to aurality, however, has not been addressed, nor has the more general relationship to music, with the notable exception of Brad Bucknell's essay on silence as being linked to history in the novel. Alex Zwerdling, on the other hand, was one of the first to make the quintessentially important link between the subject matter of the war and Woolf's novelistic innovations and experiments. Similarly, Edward Bishop, whose editorial work on the novel informs his interpretation of the text, argues for the impact of the topographical. Spatial gaps between sections are highly suggestive: "the format is part of the memorializing impulse in *Jacob's Room*: the sections are like individual photographs; the book as a whole is like an album of snapshots" (42). In the following section I explore how both rooms and exterior spaces are infused with an earcon, creating surprising geographical relations in her text.

Intriguingly, Jacob is introduced to the reader with a simple, plaintive cry: his brother, Archer, is searching for him on a beach in Cornwall. Beginning the novel by marking the absence of the central character, the sound of "'Ja – cob! Ja – cob!'" (*JR* 4) is repeated three times in the opening segment, a sonic signifier that marks the fact that he is missing as the novel begins. Extra blank spaces between the paragraphs visually accentuate the first two iterations of this call. But in case the reader has missed the effect of the three utterances, the narrator informs her or him of its sonics directly after the thrice repetition: "'Ja – cob! Ja – cob!' shouted Archer, lagging on after a second. The voice had an extraordinary sadness. Pure from all body, pure from all passion, going out into the world, solitary, unanswered, breaking against rocks – so it sounded" (*JR* 5). These initial enunciations of his name encapsulate, already, his ethereal, drifting, and empty existence; Jacob, of course, will eventually be broken against the boulders of militarism, so to speak, in the war. This proleptic cry becomes a textual earcon in the novel, reiterated to mark the protagonist's absence (his brother is looking for him, but in a sense, he is already dead from the start – the novel demonstrates that what leads to war is the same mentality that produces "masculinity"). But in this first segment, the call is voiced in an expansive space without partitions, "going out into the world" and "unanswered," suggesting the openness of network connections rather than a delimited house or room.

The call of the protagonist's name also haunts the final pages of the book when Richard Bonamy, Jacob's university friend who is in love with him, echoes the exclamation of his name just after he has died. The description of the melancholy voice accompanies this final declaration as well, but it emanates from the city streets this time, wafting into the window of Jacob's room: "Engines throbbed, and carters, jamming the brakes down, pulled their horses sharp up. A harsh and unhappy voice cried something unintelligible. And then suddenly all the leaves seemed to raise themselves. 'Jacob! Jacob!' cried Bonamy, standing by the window. The leaves sank down again" (*JR* 247). The reader is brought full circle not only in terms of the subject matter of the text, but also by its sounds. An elegiac outcry is deployed by Woolf to mourn the social consequences of imperial conflicts, this time in Jacob's room, which, instead of containing Jacob with a sense of security and liberation (as in Rachel's case), marks his absence, as harsh cries from the city streets suffuse its soundscape.

Jacob's Room, largely set in London, also contains significant commingling of urban and natural environments. Examining the earcon illuminates the linkage between the two. The penultimate chapter, for example, depicts contrasting scenes: a happy episode of family life on the Mediterranean coast (an echo of the Cornwall beach at the start of the novel but also the village scene of mothers in the Amazon in her first novel) and the intrusive sound of the guns of war on Grecian soil:

> But the red light was on the columns of the Parthenon, and the Greek women who were knitting their stockings and sometimes crying to a child to come and have the insects picked from its head were as jolly as sand-martins in the heat, quarrelling, scolding, suckling their babies, until the ships in the Piraeus fired their guns.
>
> The sound spread itself flat, and then went tunneling its way with fitful explosions among the channels of the islands.
>
> Darkness drops like a knife over Greece. (*JR* 245)

A community of women and their children are irreparably disrupted by nationalist agendas. This aurally and visually dense panorama is followed, after a notable gap on the page, by Betty Flanders being roused from sleep by the sound of the same guns: "'The guns?' said Betty Flanders, half asleep, getting out of bed and going to the window, which was decorated with a fringe of dark leaves. 'Not at this distance,' she thought. 'It is the sea.' Again, far away, the dull sound, as if nocturnal women were beating great carpets. There was Morty lost, and Seabrook dead; her sons fighting for their country" (*JR* 246). Sounds reverberate in an expanded acoustic network, one that links the English mother of Jacob with a community of mothers in Greece and crosses nationally constructed borders. Using sound to make new relations across space troubles the seemingly sequestered perimeters of the "safe" rooms back on English soil, enough for Betty Flanders to be woken from sleep. The remarkable aural and visual metaphor of "nocturnal women [...] beating great carpets" strikingly conjoins the hollow boom of detonation with the domestic labour of wives and mothers.

Similar female-centred communal moments occur on British soil as well. Fanny Elmer, another of Jacob's love interests, who, notably, thinks he has a "beautiful voice!" (*JR* 160), hears a wordless earcon – this time the song of a thrush (or a work whistle) – as she sits "on a bench in Judges Walk looking at Hampstead Garden Suburb" (*JR* 162). This particular community has a significant social history. Located approximately seven miles from the centre of London, it was founded in 1907 by Dame Henrietta Barnett for an explicit purpose and internationally recognized as an exemplar of early twentieth-century domestic architecture and town planning.[10] Its founding principles were those of community and green space. A joint cooperative endeavour by "a group of like-minded citizens," the suburb initially came into being because of the attempt to build the Hampstead Tube station that would connect the less urbanized town and heath with central London. According to Barnett, the construction of a tube station would produce the "ruin of the sylvan restfulness of that portion of the most beautiful open space near London" (Barnett 312). The idea of the Garden Suburb grew out of the work of the Heath Extension Council, which eventually succeeded in having the land dedicated to the public as an open space. The formation of the suburb was a social experiment with a specific and unique agenda to provide for people of the city from all classes, a beautiful and healthy place in which to live. Although the connotations that surrounded Barnett by Woolf's time suggest the Victorian mindset of her parents that she and other Bloomsburies pointedly rejected, Barnett's philanthropy might also have won from Woolf the same sort of respect she had for her mother, whom she witnessed ministering to the sick outside the family home (she was a practising nurse). Thus, the suburb represents an explicit effort to bring the natural world into urban space and to buffet the encroaching city. Moreover, however problematic in terms of class (it is, after all, beside the wealthy suburb of Hampstead), it maintains significant tensions: it is on the periphery of the urban centre and it commingles the natural and synthetic worlds.

Like the location chosen for the village scene in *The Voyage Out*, this geographical place also seems to have a particular connection to sound. Although the intentions for Hampstead Garden Suburb were forward-looking and altruistic, Woolf suggests that traditional gender scripts are, nonetheless, thriving, codes to which Fanny would seem to subscribe whole-heartedly and uncritically. As dogs bark and motor cars hoot, "young women walk out into the air. All the men are busy in the town. They stand by the edge of the blue pond. The fresh wind scatters the children's voices all about. *My* children, thought Fanny Elmer" (*JR* 162). Links are again made between the open-air space of the natural world, mothers, and playing children. "The women stand round the pond, beating off great prancing shaggy dogs. Gently the baby is rocked in the perambulator" (ibid.), yet they seem to be in a trancelike state: "The eyes of all the nurses, mothers, and wandering women are a little glazed, absorbed. They gently nod instead of answering when the little boys tug at their skirts, begging them to move on" (*JR* 162–3).

The narrator describes a scene of compulsory heterosexuality, as Eve Sedgwick would put it; the women in the scene are methodically playing their parts, despite the new mobility they enjoy in this social, urban space. Subsequently,

> [...] Fanny moved, hearing some cry – a workman's whistle perhaps – high in mid-air. Now, among the trees, it was the thrush[11] trilling out into the warm air a flutter of jubilation, but fear seemed to spur him, Fanny thought; as if he too were anxious with such joy at his heart – as if he were watched as he sang, and pressed by tumult to sing. There! Restless, he flew to the next tree. She heard his song more faintly. Beyond it was the humming of the wheels and the wind rushing. (*JR* 163)

The restless nature of the thrush belies the seeming simplicity of the scene and the philanthropic goals of the suburb; it also emulates Fanny's sentimental "love" and her hopes for marriage with Jacob. Woolf is critical of Fanny, and by association the community suburb, for a lack of reflection. The mothers' situation as the nation's breeders, in which Fanny includes herself, is foregrounded, even as the little boys are ignored as they tug at their skirts. The earcon signifies intense disquiet, something Fanny also seems to be experiencing, although she interprets this as being in love. Woolf again chooses an exterior, collective, yet delimited, built environment in which to sound this ineffable cry. Although in this case, the suburb follows a master plan prepared by Barry Parker and Sir Raymond Unwin, its architects, it echoes the moment in *The Voyage Out* in the village (poignantly thought of as an English park by the travellers, but also an open-air built environment created by its community). Both are also shown to be sites of associational power relations, even though "common action" is not necessarily achieved.

Yet, as noted, the interior space of Jacob's room is also privy to the earcon. In another instance, after Jacob visits the British Museum Reading Room (much to the annoyance of Miss Julia Hedge, "the feminist"), he returns to his apartment to read Plato's *Phaedrus*. The narrator pauses to reflect on the "greatness" of Plato, Hamlet, and Ulysses. Interrelated issues about access to knowledge that Woolf will illuminate in *A Room of One's Own* intrude into Jacob's ironic reverie of self-importance:

> Meanwhile, Plato continues his dialogue; in spite of the rain; in spite of the cab whistles; in spite of the woman in the mews behind Great Ormond Street who has come home drunk and cries all night long, "Let me in! Let me in!"
>
> In the street below Jacob's room voices were raised.
>
> But he read on. For after all Plato continues imperturbably. And Hamlet utters his soliloquy. [...] Plato and Shakespeare continue; and Jacob, who was reading the *Phaedrus*, heard people vociferating round the lamp-post, and the woman battering at the door and crying, "Let me in!" (*JR* 149)

Effectively, the lineage of "great masters" is juxtaposed to the aural refrain of "Let me in!" from voices outside the walls of Jacob's room. Anticipating the Oxbridge library scene in *A Room of One's Own*, the episode's concurrences encapsulate the exclusion of both the working class and women from higher education. Peripheral sound infiltrates the acoustic arena of this private and domestic place, and again it functions as an ironic comment on the character who hears it. Jacob ignores the cry that sounds on the edge of his acoustic horizon; he has been educated to do so "imperturbably," the young male version of the trancelike mothers. The reader, however, might notice its thrice repetition, and engage in a critical dialogue with the narrative from which Woolf's central, but ghostlike, character is almost excluded.

One last scene in the novel evokes the Woolfian earcon. Although several critics have discussed the importance of the old woman who sings in *Mrs. Dalloway*, a strikingly similar character makes her appearance first in *Jacob's Room*.[12] Between Jacob's arrival at St Paul's Cathedral and his meeting with Clara Durrant at the Opera House, an old woman is heard singing in the city streets. She is introduced by the narrator's enumeration of stations in the "underworld" (*JR* 88) of the Tube, an association that will be repeated in *Mrs. Dalloway*. Subsequently,

> Long past sunset an old blind woman sat on a camp-stool with her back to the stone wall of the Union of London and Smith's Bank, clasping a brown mongrel tight in her arms and singing out loud, not for coppers, no, from the depths of her gay wild heart – her sinful, tanned heart – for the child who fetches her is the fruit of sin, and should have been in bed, curtained, asleep, instead of hearing in the lamplight her mother's wild song, where she sits against the Bank, singing not for coppers, with her dog against her breast. (*JR* 89)

Striking social commentary infuses the passage. Pointedly, the old woman has no home. Although she does not sing for coppers, the reader assumes – because of the child's presence as witness to her mother's song – that there probably is no bed into which the child will be comfortably tucked either. This injection of a specifically musical sound into the exterior acoustic arena of the city street makes an (albeit ambiguous) statement through the novelistic technique of juxtaposition. Conjoining issues of the traditional private sphere (gender, motherhood) with those of the official public sphere (national interest, capitalism – ironically, the impoverished woman's back leans against the Bank,[13] noted twice in the paragraph), the scene demonstrates the indissolubility of the two spheres. Moreover, the fact that the homeless woman is singing a "wild" song (evoking the harshness of the unintelligible cry) is also significant because it incriminates the passersby who are on their way to the opera (including Jacob). The narrator notes, "But few, it seems, are admitted to that degree. Of all the carriages that leave the arch of the Opera House, not one turns eastward" (*JR* 89). This *other* opera, then, is voiced (whether listened to or not) on the acoustic margins of Covent Garden – a highly privileged sonic arena and classed space. The earcon is infused into the acoustics of the London street, marking its geography as a place of capitalist exploitation and societal exclusion. In this novel, no one but the narratorial voice (and perhaps the reader) seems to take notice. When this specific version of the earcon sounds again in *Mrs. Dalloway*, it breaches the consciousness of several significant characters in the text, increasing in intensity as it does.

Moreover, Blesser and Salter explain that earcons "acquire symbolic meanings by repeated exposure to a particular event in a corresponding context, which then creates an associating linkage between the sound and its context. Subsequently, such sounds, even without the original context, trigger the thoughts, emotions, and memory associated with that context" (82–3). Exploring the aural architecture of *The Voyage Out* and *Jacob's Room*, therefore, reveals that matters of overt concern in *Three Guineas* – imperialism, class and gender inequity, war – are palpable in the earlier novels through Woolf's longstanding interest in how sound and music make meaning differently from language. A specific nexus of issues emerges in each text at the crossroad of sound and space, demonstrating that Woolf's project to illuminate the relationship between ideology and material reality, so persuasively argued for in *A Room of One's Own*, is underway in *The Voyage Out* and *Jacob's Room*.

III. Urban and Rural Interrelations in *Mrs. Dalloway* and *To the Lighthouse*

As Woolf continues to reconfigure novelistic prose in the 1920s, the ineffable earcon is uttered by characters who have similar traits to those who have uttered it previously. These selective moments in each text further illuminate shifts in aural architecture and point the way to this utterance's expansion in the 1930s. Yet, there are few "unintelligible" sonic signifiers in *Mrs. Dalloway*, a novel that traces the movements and thoughts in a "day in the life" of the titular protagonist and her double, Septimus Warren Smith, a shell-shocked war veteran. In fact, the text is markedly inundated with the coded aurality of London. Since the novel is concerned to disclose the consequences of discipline and order – Dr William Bradshaw's sense and enforcement of "proportion" (*MD* 87), for example – it is apposite that it is saturated with London's official sounds, just as it is with its urban, authoritative, and publicly sanctioned architectural structures. Indeed, as Cuddy-Keane argues, "Woolf uses the striking of Big Ben to redraw London with a significantly expanded geographical range. For the single sound source of Big Ben brings into temporal harmony a multiplicity of listeners positioned in a variety of locations" ("Modernist Soundscapes" 387). Big Ben's leaden reverberations, the pistol shot from the motor car, the "strange high singing of some aeroplane" (*MD* 4), or the young soldiers marching up Whitehall into whose rhythmic step Peter Walsh reflexively falls all typify the text's sonics.

Yet, one ambiguous, "quivering sound" (that recalls and develops the old woman's "wild" song in *Jacob's Room*) does "interrup[t]" (*MD* 72) Peter's ruminations as he meanders into the acoustic horizon of Lucrezia (Rezia) Warren Smith. Moreover, this is another instance in which an earcon is uttered in an exterior, public place that is a natural, yet highly ordered and somewhat contained, setting: Regent's Park. During the Industrial Revolution in Victorian England, "the combined assault on all the senses by a profusion of crowds, animals, machines, and a vast array of moving objects became a source of civil discomfort" (Blesser and Salter 106). As silence became a precious commodity, control over sound became a class issue. Blesser and Salter suggest that "the loud, coarse music of seedy organ-grinders provoked the wrath of the upper classes. As if their private property was being confiscated, the ruling class responded socially, politically, and emotionally" (ibid.). Indeed, John Picker has demonstrated that such disdain and fear were underscored by xenophobia (49). In contrast, then, to the pattern of sequestering pure sound in private space in the early twentieth century, Woolf repeatedly obscures and distorts sonic "purity" in interior places and employs it in exterior environments that are large, even unwieldy for acoustical physics, disrupting the assumptions of separate spheres. This earcon is often intrusive in an effort to get the attention of human perceivers, but most times (and as in the earlier novels), these moments demonstrate an inability on the part of the ruling classes to hear the significance of the sound and what it might represent. The female vagrant whose vocalise,[14] "ee um fah um so" (*MD* 72), echoes in *Mrs. Dalloway*'s central pages is a good example of Woolf's questioning of the presumed distinction between traditional private and public space, for the soloist, according to the passages that follow the indistinct sounds that issue from her lips, just might be singing an art song.

The segment in question begins and ends with a rendition of a melody that is wordless, in terms of linguistic meaning. As the passage records,

> A sound interrupted him [Peter Walsh]; a frail quivering sound, a voice bubbling up without direction, vigour, beginning or end, running weakly and shrilly and with an absence of all human meaning into

> ee um fah um so
> foo swee too eem oo –

the voice of no age or sex, the voice of an ancient spring spouting from the earth; which issued, just opposite Regent's Park Tube Station, from a tall quivering shape, like a funnel, like a rusty pump, like a wind-beaten tree for ever barren of leaves which lets the wind run up and down its branches singing

> ee um fah um so
> foo swee too eem oo,

and rocks and creaks and moans in the eternal breeze. (*MD* 72–3)

Obviously, the words of the song are deliberately obscured at the start of the segment, as incomprehensible as the children's song at the end of *The Years*. The language of it is initially indecipherable, except perhaps as a series of vowel sounds such as one would find in a singer's vocal warm-up. Yet, the vocalise is set apart from the paragraphs of the text, suggesting it claims the same status as the earlier, indented quotation of Shakespeare: "Fear no more the heat o' the sun" (*MD* 8). It is as though Woolf is attempting to capture, in language, a non-verbal song, bringing "the voice energetically to the forefront, on purpose, at the expense of meaning" (Dolar 30), as singing often does. When the words of the song are alluded to, they are fragmentary (a few catches of phrases, such as "'look in my eyes with thy sweet eyes intently'" *MD* 74); the rest of the words in the song are paraphrased; and the title of the piece is pointedly not given. Thus, the content of the song is purposefully suggestive but simultaneously elusive – a "flourishing of the voice at the expense of the text" (Dolar 30) – notably, a focus on the voice for its own sake that one could find in a musical performance such as an opera or an art song recital.

Nora Eisenberg has argued for the importance of a figure very similar to this singing woman; for her she is "Anon," the androgynous vocalist from Woolf's last essay.[15] Eisenberg validates the significance of this personage by suggesting that Woolf "imagines an old world in which a communal life flourished free from conventional language, which she thought a male dominion, ruling and often ruining her world" (253). Others have also noted the import of this character in *Mrs. Dalloway*, although few link her musical significance. Angela

Frattarola understands the moment as an instance of "found sound" overheard by Rezia and Peter. Although "Rezia and Peter momentarily participate in the London chorus by listening to the sample, they still fail to make complete sense of the old woman's song and ultimately remain separate, not harmonized, and consumed with their personal tasks" ("Listening" 151). Frattarola suggests that "complete sense" is the objective here and necessary for social connection. I am proposing otherwise, that the old woman's ineffable song is part of a larger pattern for Woolf that asks its auditors to reflect precisely by resisting fixed signification.[16]

Despite its inscrutable quality, however, the song and its singer are described as being almost indestructible and given a historical expansiveness:

> Through all ages – when the pavement was grass, when it was swamp, through the age of tusk and mammoth, through the age of silent sunrise – the battered woman – for she wore a skirt – with her right hand exposed, her left clutching at her side, stood singing of love – love which has lasted a million years, she sang, love which prevails, and millions of years ago her lover, who had been dead these centuries, had walked, she crooned, with her in May. (*MD* 73)

The reference to the lover who has died and a walk in May is what has led J. Hillis Miller to conclude that the old woman's song is a reference to Richard Strauss's *lied* "Allerseelen" ("All Souls"), a popular (although technically difficult) piece written in 1885 when Strauss was only twenty-one. According to Miller, "the episode scarcely seems to justify the space it occupies unless the reader recognizes that Woolf has woven into the old woman's song, partly by paraphrase and variation, partly by direct quotation in an English translation, the words of a song by Richard Strauss, 'Allerseelen,' with words by Hermann von Gilm" (189–90). Equally fashionable in the 1910s and 1920s, if not even more popular in an amateur musical setting because of its technical and harmonic simplicity, is Eduard Lassen's setting of the same text. I think it is more likely, as Stuart Clarke has argued, that the song setting Woolf might have had in mind is this Belgian-Danish composer's.[17] Comparing the variations in English translations, Clarke supports the identification of this other version with a comment Woolf makes in a letter that refers to Leonard singing about "purple heather" at Vanessa Bell's. As Woolf notes in her correspondence: "Everybody was there […]. And we had a bottle of audit, and got very merry. We sang old catches [...] oh and Clinker had the mange, and lay by my side, while Leonard sang Lay by my side a bunch of purple heather" (*L4*: 276).

Moreover, not only is Strauss's setting for a full-voiced soprano (the dramatic soprano Jessye Norman is an example of the appropriate voice type) but the piece is also very difficult for both the accompanist and the singer, complete with late Romantic Straussean harmonies and unexpected melodic material; it is not "tuneful" in the way Woolf describes Leonard singing it, and would likely be heard (and learned) in the original German, as is customary practice for singing Strauss's *lieder*. Comparatively, the Lassen version of Gilm's "Allerseelen," for which the composer was chiefly known, is very simple for both the pianist and the singer. It is also more traditionally melodic and strictly strophic, with some variation for a slightly climactic ending. Strauss's song is a departure from the strophic settings of traditional *lieder*. His "Allerseelen," which resists exact repetition of the melody, especially in the last verse, would not be what Leonard Woolf would somewhat disparagingly call "light music" in his record reviews; Lassen's setting, on the other hand, could be regarded as melodious, although it was also prevalent at recital venues, according to reviews in *The Times* that span 1890 to 1941. Both versions of "Allerseelen" were routinely sung in concert halls, but Lassen's is referred to slightly more than Strauss's (nine as opposed to six) in these appraisals. Its popular circulation lends credence to Clarke's argument.

Regardless of which composer's setting Woolf had in her auditory mind, the passage reveals that she also musicalizes her prose effectively by risking nonsensical language in an attempt to emulate the sonorous art form during this musical scene in the novel. In addition, the anaphora (repetition of "through" and "when") in the passage quoted above foregrounds the repeated length of segmented phrases in the song (alternating four- to eight-syllable prepositional phrases in succession, separated either by dashes or commas). Indeed, the five paragraphs that describe the old woman's song are full of these four- to eight-syllable (sometimes doubled) phrases that rhythmically emulate the source text (four-line stanzas that hover around ten, ten, ten, and eight – "as once in May, as once in May" is the last line). The five-syllable kernels of "ee um fah um so / foo swee too eem oo – " (*MD* 72) are together, notably, ten syllables long. Thus, Woolf patterns her phrases (with some variation) in the same syllabic metre as the song alluded to and imitated but not named. When the scene shifts to Rezia's thoughts about Mr Bradshaw and her hopes for her future with Septimus in a new subsequent paragraph, the rhythm of the language gradually changes to contain larger clauses and more variation in terms of phrasal length: "So they crossed, Mr. and Mrs. Septimus Warren Smith, and was there, after all, anything to draw attention to them, anything to make a passer-by suspect here is a young man who carries in him the greatest message in the world, and is, moreover, the happiest man in the world, and the most miserable? Perhaps they walked more slowly than other people" (*MD* 75).

Commingling what seems to be impossible in terms of temporality – the past and the present – the old woman and her vocalise are at once as old as time and jarringly modern, standing, as she is, outside a Tube station. Although she confounds gender inscriptions, "the voice of no age or sex, the voice of an ancient spring spouting from the earth" (*MD* 72), the narrative specifies that she wears a skirt and uses female pronouns to refer to her. Old but ageless, no sex but female, and excluded from the capitalist marketplace, her subject position fundamentally questions attributes typically interpreted in binary terms. Yet she and her song are also described as issuing an "invincible thread of sound" (*MD* 74). Resilient yet variable, the figure and her sonority enact the attributes of the earcons from the earlier novels, now evinced more specifically in the form of the singing voice.

The thread of her sounds also builds a network of auscultators through the consciousness of Peter Walsh and Rezia Warren Smith. In the published version of the novel, the song interposes into Peter's reverie about his meeting with Clarissa, just after he thinks "Clarissa was as cold as an icicle" (*MD* 72). But in Notebook One of the manuscript, the song follows from a different place in Peter's thoughts, right after a paragraph (which ends up being used earlier in the book in the final version) about Clarissa's ability to gather together societal connections:

> Infinite numbers of old women conglomerated round her of course. ~~She had a She had a foot in a great many worlds. And she still knew some of the~~ And odd, unexpected people turned up, an artist sometimes; <sometimes a writers; though she made no ~~pretence of~~ <attempt at> a salon. ~~The whole thing depended on her.~~ Behind it was all that network of ~~calling, kindnesses, keeping up with~~ <of visiting> being kind to people […] (Woolf, *Virginia Woolf "The Hours"* 94)

It is salient, for my purposes, that Woolf foregrounds Clarissa's social network, even calling it such, in the early draft, directly preceding the entrance of the old woman and her song; it suggests rhizomatic (Latour often describes a network as analogous to Gilles Deleuze and Felix Guattari's term), or at least eclectic, relations in social terms (old women and odd, unexpected people) and connects this with the central character of the book, more so than with Peter, who is still the filtering consciousness. In the manuscript, the section concerning the "battered woman [...] singing of love" begins abruptly after the phrases "Or take this view of Clarissa. It was Sallys" (Woolf, *Virginia Woolf "The Hours"* 96, 94). Woolf's choice, in the end, to have Peter interrupted by the sound suggests that she takes a different approach in the final version, one that utilizes the earcon to point up the stark socio-economic contrast between Peter (a colonial administrator) and Rezia (a milliner). It also recalls the earlier function of this cry, which asks its listeners to reflect. While, like other upper-middle-class characters in the novel, Peter does not do so, Rezia does contemplate both the old woman's circumstances and her own.

A "foreigner" who is almost completely isolated in London and disenfranchised by her dependency on her husband (and his growing mental instability), Rezia also foregrounds the issue of social exclusion in gendered terms throughout the novel. At the end of the battered woman's scene, Rezia's thoughts make the connection for the reader between the singer and the possibility of another life: "Oh, poor old wretch! She said, waiting to cross. Suppose it was a wet night? Suppose one's father, or somebody who had known one in better days had happened to pass, and saw one standing there in the gutter? And where did she sleep at night?" (*MD* 74).[18] In contrast, Peter's response is neglectful: although he "couldn't help giving the poor creature a coin," he promptly leaves the uncomfortable scene "as he stepped in his taxi" (ibid.). In Notebook One of the manuscript, the "ee um fa um so" passage occurs only once: in the middle of this section that focuses on Rezia. In addition, she is described as particularly receptive to song, perhaps, as Woolf suggests, because of her Italian background – opera being a staple of that culture in ways it was not for the English: "She had an extraordinary, a southern, susceptibility to sound" (Woolf, *Virginia Woolf "The Hours"* 100). A sentence that does not make it into the final version, it nevertheless lends support to why Rezia is so receptive to the old woman's plight, and also her vocalise.

Heterogeneous responses span the built yet green space of the lower end of the Broad Walk of Regent's Park (which is surrounded by the Avenue Gardens), as the "old bubbling burbling song, soaking through the knotted roots of infinite ages, and skeletons and treasure, streamed away in rivulets over the pavement and all along the Marylebone Road, and down towards Euston, fertilising, leaving a damp stain" (*MD* 73). Coupled with the metaphors of "knotted roots," the movement of the sound helps Woolf conceive a rhizomatic relation among things: both east and west (Marylebone and Euston) and north and south into and below the park where "the pavement was crowded with bustling middle-class people" (*MD* 74), but also the meandering walking paths of Rezia and Septimus, as well as Peter. The vertical axis of space is also incorporated: "Cheerfully, almost gaily, the invincible thread of sound wound up into the air like the smoke from a cottage chimney, winding up clean beech trees and issuing in a puff of blue smoke among the topmost leaves" (ibid.). Such patterns, enabled by imagined sonics, suggest there is no inside or outside in terms of aurality; as Latour argues, "a network is all boundary without inside or outside" ("On Actor-Network" 6). Moreover, the sonicity of the voice itself is as much of a connector as the old woman who sings it, an equally important actant described as separate from the singer. Like the rhizomatic footpaths of the park itself, the earcon has turned into an integral part of Woolf's social and material network in the novel.

The fact that these sounds are potentially based on the Western tradition of art song but voiced by the nameless and homeless woman in the street also crosses the traditional interpretation of separate private and public spheres. The choice of an art song, in addition to the conceptual material it contains in its poetry, is purposeful on Woolf's part: it implies this woman has had another life, as Rezia ponders, one in which she learned the bourgeois codes of the drawing room in preparation for the marriage market, much as Elsbeth Siddons sings at the Durrants' party in chapter 7 of *Jacob's Room*.[19] At the very least, the upper-middle-class connotations of Lassen's "Allerseelen" overlie the poverty into which this woman has been thrown. Woolf again depicts a crossover of spheres that counterbalances the contemporary trend towards the ownership and control of sound in privatized space.[20] Instead, a "female vagrant" sings a drawing-room song, a practice explicitly associated with privileged domesticity (even in Woolf's own novels) in a decidedly publicly sanctioned place that commingles the natural and urban worlds. In this instance, the earcon marks the lack of social cohesion, indeed disenfranchisement, in the city, particularly for women. But spatially, it makes relations among its receivers with the sound of a singing voice. The connections make a network of links among social classes that would not be associated otherwise: the old woman, Rezia, and Peter do not speak to each other, but sound bridges both the spatial and social divide, however momentarily. The reader, again, experiences this network, even though the characters themselves are less aware of it. This is a similar associational function to the airplane that also connects its viewers and auditors throughout the metropolis, but the singing voice that bubbles and burbles in urban places conjoins, more specifically, the issues of gender and class.

In To the Lighthouse the earcon retreats indoors but still manages to cross the boundaries of the natural and built environments, as well as to foreground similar social concerns. Woolf's next novel, about an upper-middle-class family, the Ramsays, illuminates several commonalities between the city singer and a working-class character, Mrs McNab. Structured in three large sections, the text is set in the Scottish Hebrides. The first part of the narrative, "The Window," centres on Mrs Ramsay and her relationships with her children, husband, and guests (particularly Lily Briscoe, a painter) who stay at the summer home west of Scotland. Mrs McNab, the charwoman, makes her appearance in the "Time Passes" section of the novel (ten years are fused into one allegorical night). This middle portion of the work disrupts the regularity of narrative temporality by bracketing significant events from the family members' lives, while focusing on the deterioration of the empty summer home. The middle "passage," as it has been called, is followed by a third section, "The Lighthouse," that occurs after Mrs Ramsay's death and the end of the First World War, and focuses on the, now older, siblings' journey to the lighthouse alongside their aged father. Lily Briscoe's completion of the painting she began ten years earlier supplies an artistic and "visionary" ending, albeit one that resists closure.

In the first section of the book, "The Window," Mrs Ramsay provides much of the filtering consciousness, and at times she seems particularly receptive to sound. Indeed, she experiences a sort of sonorous reverie in chapter 3. Inside the house, she is cutting out pictures with her son, James, to distract him from his disappointment about not being able to go to the lighthouse. Mr Ramsay has brusquely said no to any excursion for the day, and he is out in the garden. The narrative records that Mrs Ramsay hears a "gruff murmur, irregularly broken by the taking out of pipes and the putting in of pipes which had kept on assuring her, though she could not hear what was said (as she sat in the window), that the men were happily talking" (TL 23). Woolf then turns these noises into a comforting backdrop of daily life tinged with moments of shock. (The quotations in this final section of chapter 1 are necessarily long because Woolf's prose changes in *To the Lighthouse*; it becomes even more fluid than in *Mrs. Dalloway* and often consists of numerous, extended compound sentences):

> this sound which had lasted now half an hour and had taken its place soothingly in the scale of sounds pressing on top of her, such as the tap of balls upon bats, the sharp, sudden bark now and then, "How's that? How's that?" of the children playing cricket, had ceased; so that the monotonous fall of the waves on the beach, which for the most part beat a measured and soothing tattoo to her thoughts and seemed consolingly to repeat over and over again as she sat with the children the words of some old cradle song, murmured by nature, "I am guarding you – I am your support," but at other times suddenly and unexpectedly [...] like a ghostly roll of drums remorselessly beat the measure of life, made one think of the destruction of the island and its engulfment in the sea [...] – this sound which had been obscured and concealed under the other sounds suddenly thundered hollow in her ears and made her look up with an impulse of terror. (*TL* 23–4)

The sonic trance continues for two more paragraphs, "as if she waited for some habitual sound, some regular mechanical sound; and then, hearing something rhythmical, half said, half chanted, beginning in the garden, as her husband beat up and down the terrace, something between a croak and a song, she was soothed once more" (*TL* 24–5). Sound wafts in and out of the window, from as far away as the shore of the beach, to as near as the children in the yard, auscultized and processed as simultaneously comforting and alarming by Mrs Ramsay. Into this daydream

> Suddenly a loud cry, as of a sleep-walker, half roused, something about
>
> Stormed at with shot and shell
>
> sung out with the utmost intensity in her ear, made her turn apprehensively to see if anyone heard him. (*TL* 25)

The set-apart line is from Alfred Lord Tennyson's "Charge of the Light Brigade" and it is bellowed by Mr Ramsay. As Kelly Sultzbach, in her ecocritical study of Woolf, rightly suggests, this exclamation foretells the doom that will befall the family because of the war; the reader will be abruptly informed in brackets of Andrew Ramsay's death in the "Time Passes" section. But, especially given its immersion in Mrs Ramsay's aural musings, it also acts as an instance of the earconic cry of lament so poignantly attached to war in *Jacob's Room* and *Mrs. Dalloway*. It is not a vocalise, nor is it described as meaningless, for Tennyson's Victorian poetry is a marker of Mr Ramsay's retrograde mentality in the novel. Yet, it is unexplained in the passage. The assignment of Mr Ramsay's voice to the words is difficult to discern and the poetry itself not explicated in the least nor attributed to Tennyson. Instead, the reader must infer its significance and is left primarily with the "intensity" of the sound of it for Mrs Ramsay, the sonicity of the words.

In the "Time Passes" section of the novel, Woolf not only elaborates further on the singing figure discussed earlier but also resituates her in a rural and domestic setting, the inverse of the contrived, yet green space, of the public park. There are several shared traits among the homeless and working-class figures who voice the earcon in Woolf's books from the 1920s. In chapter 5, Mrs McNab sings a similarly non-descript tune while she works in the house:

> As she lurched (for she rolled like a ship at sea) and leered (for her eyes fell on nothing directly, but with a sidelong glance that deprecated the scorn and anger of the world – she was witless, she knew it), as she clutched the banisters and hauled herself upstairs and rolled from room to room, she sang. Rubbing the glass of the long looking-glass and leering sideways at her swinging figure a sound issued from her lips – something that had been gay twenty years before on the stage perhaps,[21] had been hummed and danced to, but now, coming from the toothless, bonneted, care-taking woman, was robbed of meaning, was like the voice of witlessness, humour, persistency itself, trodden down but springing up again, so that as she lurched, dusting, wiping, she seemed to say how it was one long sorrow and trouble, how it was getting up and going to bed again, and bringing things out and putting them away again. It was not easy or snug this world she had known for close on seventy years. Bowed down she was with weariness. (*TL* 177–8)

Again, as with the earlier earcons, the words to a song do not matter as much as the "sound issu[ing] from her lips," which uncannily encapsulates an entire life in a day. Likewise, in addition to the ambiguity of the song, which is never specified, it is similarly "robbed of meaning";

Mrs McNab has been "bowed down" for decades, almost ageless, much like the "sinful, tanned heart" of the woman who sings "not for coppers" in *Jacob's Room* and the "battered woman" from *Mrs. Dalloway*. Noting the many paradoxical binaries that are disrupted in the passage, Mary Lou Emery suggests, "no simple inversions or reversals explain their metaphorical connotations. They seem to partake of the female, the inhuman, the natural, and the mechanical simultaneously and indeterminately" (221).

Yet, despite being "trodden down," Mrs McNab and her song are "springing up again" and "bringing things out and putting them away again," begetting life in the Ramsays' old house, "as if indeed there twined about her dirge some incorrigible hope" (*TL* 178), just as the battered woman's "invincible" song recalls a "love that prevails" (*MD* 73).The airs in both cases, as they are "robbed of meaning," also echo the earlier resistance to language that Woolf deploys in *The Voyage Out*. In each instance, words turned into melodies obscure the propositional content of language, but are highly "meaningful" nonetheless because they are postlinguistic. Indeed, if Dolar is correct, as I have previously noted, that "singing takes the distraction of the voice seriously, and turns the tables on the signifier" (30), then it is apposite that Woolf deploys the earcon through the figure of this working-class charwoman who enunciates, not a song with no meaning because she is incapable, but a tune that, once again, enacts the significance of vocalizing.

Gender and economy are also at issue in the latter chapters of the middle section. Mrs McNab and Mrs Bast, who work, gossip, and occasionally drink tea in the bourgeois rooms of the empty house, question a fixed relationship between private and public spheres. Women who endure the physical toil of domestic labour are the only human inhabitants during the "Time Passes" section. Although the agency of their voices is debatable, the pattern of a former or other life, one that suggests performances in public forums, again functions to cross social borders that illuminate a set of economic strictures on the "daughters of educated men" (*TG* 155) that are different from those of the labouring classes. I do not mean to suggest, however, that these representations completely escape the problematic link between the working classes and violence. Although I do think Woolf makes this association in order to venerate the resilience of these women, this does not void it of questionable overtones – as in *The Voyage Out*, it reiterates primitivist stereotypes that dehumanize subjects, representing them as "other."[22] Nevertheless, the pressure placed by Mrs Ramsay on Lily Briscoe to enter the marriage market serves as a noteworthy contrast to the performance space occupied by Mrs McNab in her youth. Her music-hall experience, as Emery suggests, occurs in a sphere "different from that occupied by Mr. Ramsay and might offer Lily Briscoe as she progresses in her painting career an alternative to the bourgeois masculine realm that in part one is implicitly the only world, other than Mrs. Ramsay's domestic one, to which she might aspire" (227).

Indeed, in many ways, the passage makes it clear that it is on Mrs McNab (and others like her) that the ruling classes obliviously depend to bridge the gap between life and death, appositely in this connecting section of the novel. As I have shown, the earcon often enters Woolf's texts precisely at such junctures, moments when the privileged classes are painfully unaware of the damage they cause by thoughtlessly perpetuating patriarchal practices; it is no coincidence, of course, that the deaths of Prue Ramsay in childbirth and Andrew Ramsay in the First World War are baldly mentioned in brackets during the next chapter (6) of "Time Passes." Indeed, Andrew's demise is introduced by a sound of anguish familiar to readers of *Jacob's Room*:

> But slumber and sleep though it might there came later in the summer ominous sounds like the measured blows of hammers dulled on felt, which, with their repeated shocks still further loosened the shawl and cracked the tea-cups. Now and again some glass tinkled in the cupboard as if a giant voice had shrieked so loud in its agony that tumblers stood inside a cupboard vibrated too. Then again silence fell [...] there seemed to drop into this silence this indifference, this integrity, the thud of something falling. (*TL* 181)

In the next bracketed paragraph, "A shell exploded" (ibid.). A scream of torment marks the passing of time in this abandoned domestic space and enunciates the cost of war: death.

Lastly, the airs that breathe through the house also enact the rhizomatic movement of Latour's network, as Mrs McNab meanders about the domicile: "through the rusty hinges and swollen sea-moistened woodwork certain airs, detached from the body of the wind (the house was ramshackle after all) crept round corners and ventured indoors" (*TL* 172). They are nonhuman, capable of bending around architectural thresholds and filling up rooms, much like soundwaves. They evoke the nomadic amblings of the old woman's "thread of sound" (*MD* 70) that coils up the beech trees of Regent's Park. In a collective and audible sigh, for example, they give the natural world voice: "At length, desisting, all ceased together, gathered together, all sighed together; all together gave off an aimless gust of lamentation to which some door in the kitchen replied; swung wide; admitted nothing; and slammed to" (*TL* 173). Aurality is so prevalent in the "Time Passes" section that it has led Cuddy-Keane to suggest that "sound is represented as auscultated by an ear within the empty house," demonstrating at key moments "the relational nature of auscultation" ("Virginia Woolf, Sound Technologies, and the New Aurality" 85). Similarly, Sultzbach notes the nonhuman, multivalent function of the airs in the text: "Woolf insists on fingering 'airs' … in 'Time Passes' as well as their ability to 'expand,' lift and carry, or 'check,' disturb and disintegrate" (124). Sultzbach also connects these wisps to Mrs McNab and her song because both express the paradox of cohesion and fragmentation. She reads the final unassigned section that describes a "half-heard melody" as potentially issuing out of Mrs McNab's mouth, although "who or what is producing the song becomes unclear" (135).

In Woolf's *tour de force* middle section of the novel, therefore, the house itself and the natural world within and without it also intone a strain as the remaining Ramsays and Lily plan their return:

> And now as if the cleaning and the scrubbing and the scything and the mowing had drowned it there rose that half-heard melody, that intermittent music which the ear half catches but lets fall; a bark, a bleat; irregular, intermittent, yet somehow related; the hum of an insect, the tremor of cut grass, dissevered yet somehow belonging; the jar of a dor beetle, the squeak of a wheel, loud, low, but mysteriously always on the verge of harmonizing but they are never quite heard, never fully harmonized, and at last, in the evening, one after another the sounds die out, and the harmony falters, and silence falls. (*TL* 192)

Again couched as a song, the relational capacity of travelling sound becomes an actant in the passage, revealing, as it does, a rhizomatic network, "never fully harmonized." Latour suggests that similar patterns are found in the "trail of associations between heterogeneous elements" (*Reassembling* 5) with his reconfigured concept of the "social." Indeed, Woolf's aurally infused, rural soundscape captures, as noted earlier, Latour's "feeling that resistance, obduracy and sturdiness is more easily achieved through netting, lacing, weaving, twisting, of ties" ("On Actor-Network" 3).

Fittingly, then, in this novel that is set in a summer home in the Hebrides rather than in London, the natural world also articulates the earcon. Indeed, in the next and last chapter of "Time Passes," one final voice is heard:

> Through the open window the voice of the beauty of the world came murmuring, too softly to hear exactly what it said – but what mattered if the meaning were plain? – entreating the sleepers (the house was full again; Mrs Beckwith was staying there, also Mr Carmichael), if they would not actually come down to the beach itself at least to lift the blind and look out. They would see then night flowing down in purple [...] if they still said no, that it was vapour this splendour of his, and the dew had more power than he, and they preferred sleeping; gently then without complaint, or argument, the voice would sing its song. (*TL* 193)

Another instance of the cry wandering into a window, simultaneously inside and outside spatially, night and all of its sounds perform this aural-laden rhapsody. The inhabitants have gone to bed, they have "faltered," unwilling to partake in the animation that surrounds them. Yet, like Rezia, Lily might just hear it. Although the "sigh of all the seas breaking in measure round the isles soothed them" (*TL* 194), Lily wakes up the next morning in a bit of a fright. The final flash of "Time Passes" is tinged with fear: "Lily Briscoe stirring in her sleep clutched at her blankets as a faller clutches at the turf on the edge of a cliff. Her eyes opened wide. Here she was again, she thought, sitting bolt upright in bed. Awake" (ibid.). It is in the third section of the book, of course, that Lily has her artistic vision, perhaps made possible because of this earconic stirring.

In *The Voyage Out*, although the gaze of the women in the village is reversed rather than restructured, it still seems incapable of truly changing the colonial power structure. If anything disrupts the exploitation, it might be the mechanism of sound, an "unintelligible" earcon that the ruling-class English listeners are, nevertheless, incapable of understanding. Similarly, the irony of the homeless woman's predicament as she stands with her back against the bank in *Jacob's Room* is lost on the passersby in the street, although perhaps not on the narrator or reader. The sorrow invoked by the "invincible thread of sound" (*MD* 74) in *Mrs. Dalloway* is not lost, however, on Rezia, although it certainly is on Peter. Finally, Mrs McNab's interlocutor, Mrs Bast, does seem to understand the apparent "witlessness" of her friend and her song, but perhaps the contemporary middle-class reader, Woolf implies now, does not.

Repeatedly, Woolf utilizes the earcon to mark a lack of social consciousness, but it gives symbolic resonance to these incidental characters through sound and its association to place and space. Uncovering the significance of song throughout Woolf's oeuvre, then, can change one's understanding of these, albeit minor, figures, and give them a stronger "voice" when analysed together. What the comparisons also demonstrate is that in both urban- and rural-identified novels, the earcon calls others to account. In addition, something almost beyond human nature, as suggested in my epigraph, is often integral to the articulation of this melody, capable of crossing the borders of seemingly separate socio-cultural spheres and showing them to be constructed, not just by human hands, but also by codes of behaviour. Furthermore, these "old women" discussed thus far are marginal, on the periphery in terms of community and space and in the novels themselves. This is part of their function as challenges to the status quo. In chapter 2, a shift occurs: Rhoda, one of six characters in *The Waves*, overtly ponders the meaning of a "cry" after attending a musical performance, and Woolf integrates singing characters into *The Years* and *Between the Acts*, giving the voicing of the earcon to fully developed characters who straddle class boundaries.

Chapter Two

The Earcon Reproduces

As we listen to the voices we seem to hear an infant crying in the night, the black night that now covers Europe, and with no language but a cry, Ay, ay, ay, ay … But it is not a new cry, it is a very old cry. Let us shut off the wireless and listen to the past.

Woolf, Three Guineas (1938), 362

And then comes the low of the cows in the field; and another cow to the left answers; and all the cows seem to be moving tranquilly across the field and the owl flutes off its watery bubble. But the sun is deep below the earth. The trees are growing heavier, blacker; no order is perceptible; there is no sequence in these cries, these movements; they come from no bodies; they are cries to the left and to the right. Nothing can be seen. We can only see ourselves as outlines, cadaverous, sculpturesque. And it is more difficult for the voice to carry through this dark. The dark has stripped the fledge from the arrow – the vibrations that rise red shiver as it passes through us.

Woolf, "The Moment: Summer's Night" (1940), 7–8

How Woolf's portrayal of the night changes from *To the Lighthouse* (published in 1927 and discussed at the end of chapter 1) to *Three Guineas* (1938). The latter is an essay as opposed to a novel, but Woolf details yet another instance of the earcon in her polemic, suggesting a darker and more insistent version of its enunciation. In that book-length text she describes a possible infant's cry as a response to the menacing black night that covers then-contemporary Europe (an allusion to Adolf Hitler's growing power in the 1930s). In "The Moment: Summer's Night," the nonhuman and the environment utter this exclamation, as though human beings are so far from hearing it in 1940 (the second year of the Second World War) that Woolf cannot envision them expressing it. If "injecting noise of whatever kind into an acoustic arena is nothing more than the exercise of sonic power" (Blesser and Salter 31), I argue that Woolf deploys earcons in her later novels to voice now manifold, harsh but indomitable, ineffable yet evocative cries, beckoning readers to question their own imbrication in patriarchal methods and institutions.

I. "And what is a cry?": *The Waves*

The Waves contains similarly patterned sonorities to the earlier books, but also elaborates other crucial aspects of the earcon – developments that will emerge from musical sound once again. Considered Woolf's most formally experimental novel, *The Waves* traces the inner mind-scape of six "characters" and their interactions with each other, plus the outer life of a seventh personage, Percival. I put "characters" in quotation marks because Woolf reformulates how subjectivity can be represented in this narrative. Her portrayal of the minds of six personalities does not recount plot-centred events; indeed, very little plot content is communicated. Instead, the text explores the responses of these minds to diverse experiences and memories. Paradoxically, Woolf even indicates in her diary that she wants the novel to be character-less. Interspersed among the chapters that explore episodes from different stages in their lives, largely in an ongoing present tense (with the exception of Bernard's final soliloquy, which is in the past), are lyrical, italicized interludes that describe the waves and the progress of the sun through a single day (also in the past tense). Music and sound become more explicit as the novel overtly addresses issues concerning the art form of writing and the constitution of human subjectivity under the aegis of Bernard, who interrogates the system of language – his own artistic medium – as well as art in general. In this exploration of linguistic uncertainty, meaning becomes more indeterminate. Music, in this novel, is used both to critique language and to suggest alternatives to it.

Hence, Rhoda, one of the six "characters," hears the unintelligible cry during a recital at what is most likely Wigmore Hall, just north of Oxford Street in London, where she has been walking westward.[1] Vividly, she describes a female vocalist at the performance:

"Then, swollen but contained in slippery satin, the sea-green woman comes to our rescue. She sucks in her lips, assumes an air of intensity,

> inflates herself and hurls herself precisely at the right moment as if she
> saw an apple and her voice was the arrow into the note, 'Ah!'
>   "An axe has split a tree to the core; the core is warm; sound quivers
> within the bark. 'Ah!' cried a woman to her lover, leaning from her
> window in Venice. 'Ah, ah!' she cried, and again she cries 'Ah!' She has
> provided us with a cry. But only a cry. And what is a cry? (*TW* 128)

The "Ah" of the vocalist, then, can be understood as another instance of
the *"blank melody"* (*TW* 4) heard throughout the novels. Rhoda's singer
enacts the implied existence that women from the other novels might
have experienced before their disenfranchisement or life of domestic
labour. This singer's aria is described in comparable terms: as a woman
calling to her lover, as a quiver of sound, and as intensely expressed –
the singer hurls herself at a note. All suggest the "invincible" nature
of the earlier verbally resistant songs and focus on the voice for its
own sake rather than the linguistic content of it. The scene brings the
voice, almost notoriously, to the forefront, revealing that, often, "singing is bad communication; it prevents a clear understanding of the
text" (Dolar 30). Thus, Woolf focuses specifically on the postlinguistic
aspects of the singer's craft, the sonicity of the vocal utterance. In addition, and as with the old songstresses, the reader does not know what
music is being performed.[2]

The event described above is also saturated with class implications,
revealing the constructedness of place in the process. As Rhoda enters,
she notes, "'here is a hall where one pays money and goes in, where one
hears music among somnolent people who have come here after lunch
on a hot afternoon. We have eaten beef and pudding enough to live for
a week without tasting food'" (*TW* 127–8). Rhoda's preamble critiques
the material conditions that enable some to attend such concerts while
many others cannot (especially given Woolf's earlier representation of
food to contrast the wealth of the male colleges at Oxbridge with the
poverty of the female institutions in *A Room of One's Own*). The passage
illuminates a sated audience that thoughtlessly depends on the working classes for their luxury: "'Therefore we cluster like maggots on the
back of something that will carry us on'" (*TW* 128). The gluttonous side
of class privilege is conspicuous: the listeners "'lie gorged with food,
torpid in the heat'" (ibid.).

The actual concert place is also important, for it is a building that
bridges previously separate spheres: it is a public venue that employs

the acoustics of the shift to privatized sound at the start of the twentieth century. Unlike the other novels, the earcon in *The Waves* is performed in an architectural structure that was built precisely for the purpose of musical performance, instantiating a connection between this "cry" and the sonorous art form. Simultaneously enclosed but also public, a recital hall carries with it insinuations of social hierarchy. Correspondingly, its acoustics subscribe to a model of purity and efficiency, sonics prized by the ruling classes. Wigmore Hall, in particular, was specifically planned to be both grandly impressive and intimate enough for a song recital or chamber music performance. Known to this day for its excellent acoustics, it is often used for recording purposes. From its inception, therefore, its aural architecture would constitute a "new acoustic era ... summarized as spatial designs that emphasized foreground sounds in a background of silence. Soundscapes were to be stripped of living sounds and spatial acoustics, thereby weakening the aural connection of spaces to the social fabric" (Blesser and Salter 108). Thus, voicing the earcon in this space is another instance of its critical function. While the ruling-class audience listens to the performance – as they did in the village in *The Voyage Out* – no one, except Rhoda, seems to understand, or even begin to contemplate, the import of this sound.

Nonetheless, the concert-hall scene further demonstrates that the earcon is more urgently expressed in the novels of the 1930s. Indeed, narrative devices are used in this episode not only to describe this sonority but also to enact such processes in language. The vocalic utterance "'Ah!'" is enunciated five times in the passage, suggesting that the inarticulate sound should be heard on the reader's level, in what Garrett Stewart calls "inner audition" (3), as well as in the narrative. Indeed, the sound seems to pierce the text through persistent repetition (a strategy used with each of these singing figures), insisting that the reader hear the vocal cry being performed in language. But in *The Waves* the issue of the earcon's linguistic uncertainty yet invincibility is also foregrounded by a significant "character." Rhoda's rumination on the meaning of "a cry" is the first instance in the novels that distinguishes it as a sound of remark. In addition, Percival has died in this episode in *The Waves*; Rhoda, like the others, ruminates on his passing. As with Bernard in the last soliloquy, as I shall discuss below, part of the earcon's significance in this novel is an attempt to find some way to articulate the pain of experiencing death (either of loved ones or resistance to one's own).

It is also of consequence that Rhoda is the "character" who listens to the enigmatic earcon. Notably, she has purchased her own ticket and attends the concert by herself: a female listener unaccompanied by a male in the public sphere listens to another woman singing a solo on stage (although perhaps the vocalist is musically accompanied by either a man or a woman on the piano). This is not remarkable in and of itself by 1931, but as in earlier renditions, the articulation of the earcon fore-grounds a female community (albeit of two, although there could be other women in the audience), one that could be read in contrast to the hierarchy of the class-identified codes discussed above. A network of many listeners hear the cry in the concert, enacted as it is in the public sphere. Yet, Woolf's rendition again alludes to other earconic moments by having Rhoda be the perceiving consciousness of the female singer's vocalization in the novel. Like Lucrezia Warren Smith or Betty Flan-ders, another woman hears the utterance of the earcon and interprets it for the reader, however ambivalently.

The Waves enacts another sounding of the earcon in the mind of a male "character" as well: the writer, Bernard. Indeed, unlike Peter Walsh, who simply gets into his cab when he hears the old woman singing in the London streets, Bernard searches for some way to articulate the ear-con himself, integrating both Rhoda and the series of singers' cries in the process and aligning it with the formation of art. When he describes his inability to marry the "'woman who made me Byron'" (*TW* 200), as noted in chapter 1, he exclaims, "'here again there should be music. Not that wild hunting-song, Percival's music; but a painful, guttural, visceral, also soaring, lark-like, pealing song to replace these flagging, foolish transcripts'" (*TW* 200–1). This description overtly denotes the linkage between the aural domain and the artistic subject's capacity to make meaning. Bernard now distinguishes between a wild hunting-song – suggesting gun violence and shooting for sport – and a larklike but harsh sound. Again, Woolf maintains the resilient and unruly asso-ciations of the earlier earcons.

In his final soliloquy, in which he integrates Rhoda's (and the others') attributes, Bernard continues to search for an adequate way to make sense of death. He sits in a tavern with an unnamed dinner companion, often interpreted by critics as the reader him- or herself. He comes to the conclusion that perhaps a howl or a cry might produce the effect he seeks:

"By what name are we to call death? I do not know. I need a little language such as lovers use, words of one syllable such as children speak when they come into the room and find their mother sewing and pick up some scrap of bright wool, a feather, or a shred of chintz. I need a howl; a cry. When the storm crosses the marsh and sweeps over me where I lie in the ditch unregarded I need no words. Nothing neat. Nothing that comes down with all its feet on the floor. None of those resonances and lovely echoes that break and chime from nerve to nerve in our breasts, making wild music, false phrases. I have done with phrases. (*TW* 236)

Bernard searches for a mode of communication that will simultaneously signify and dislodge the socially constructed mechanisms of meaning; he yearns for a cry to articulate this desire. The exceptional prose aptly reflects this by specifying the need for such a "howl." The fundamental difference in *The Waves* is that the articulation of this earcon is not only received and elaborated by main "characters" but is also longed for and acknowledged as an important process of signification. In addition, while Rhoda ascultates the sound, Bernard attempts to articulate it himself, for a song (without words) is invoked at the zenith of *The Waves*: "'Let me now raise my song of glory. Heaven be praised for solitude. Let me be alone. Let me cast and throw away this veil of being, this cloud that changes with the least breath, night and day, and all night and all day'" (*TW* 236).

Bernard's cohesion of the novel's "voices" could be understood as being antithetical to Woolf's social argument of heterogeneity. But if Jessica Berman is correct, Bernard's "consolidation" is not achieved in fascist terms:

Woolf's work runs determinedly counter to the onward rush of fascism, presenting an oppositional cosmopolitan politics that resists the lure of the corporate state and that is prescient in this understanding of the danger of the fascist aesthetic. The gathering stages of fascism may produce rhythms, intonations, and oceanic feelings that hide its hard-booted political identity – but the waves of Woolf's novel, by moving according to another logic, uncover its masculinist, violent danger. (156)[3]

Moreover, the earcon is part of this critique – not over and above other sensory impressions but an integral part of many. It exposes gender imbalances, social injustice, and the implications of nationalistic fervour, asking its listeners to reflect on their own imbrication in social conditions. Its network pattern of reception and articulation provides "nothing neat," not even "lovely echoes" that become "false phrases." In addition, in *The Waves* such sounds are overtly linked with artistic praxis, performed in the novel itself, no less, as it traverses the minds of its community of main "characters."

II. Integrating the Earcon in *The Years*

Given the growing prevalence of music and sound in *The Waves*, it is fitting that Woolf contemplated entitling her next novel simply *Music*, among other possibilities.[4] *The Years* is concerned with the passage of time, the reciprocal interchange between traditional private and public spheres, and the dilemmas faced by women in England in the late nineteenth and early twentieth centuries. These issues are represented through the chronicles of an extended middle-class English family, the Pargiters. Despite the fact that the novel is Woolf's most overtly political, it was also the most popular of her writings during her lifetime.

The Years is a decidedly aural text, punctuated by voices in hallways, street calls and songs, overheard waltzes, the guns and sirens of war, funeral music, and the bells of various churches in urban spaces (both London and Oxford), to name just a few of its sonics. Music and ambient sounds mark the ceremonies as well as the daily experiences of the characters' lives. Indeed, the highly aural nature of the novel is evidenced by the number of critics who have explored urban sound in the text. Margaret Comstock's contribution about the significance of the loudspeaker to the reassessment of the novel in 1977 is a case in point. Rishona Zimring has argued intriguingly that "Woolf uses sounds to insist upon the alienating noise of a modern, urban existence (and its ideologies of progress)" (129), while Cuddy-Keane considers the novel in her exploration of aurality in the modernist period, proposing that "the city plays a formative role in stimulating this increased auditory awareness" ("Modernist Soundscapes" 382). Angela Frattarola also includes *The Years* in her analysis of "found sound" sampling in Woolf's works. As noted, the novel is unquestionably political in nature; thus, sound is crucial to this social critique and it is repeatedly intertwined with music in the text, particularly when the earcon is voiced. Recalling the aged women from the earlier novels, this time Woolf deploys the earcon through one of her main characters, Sara Pargiter, in the later stages of her life. In addition, the children's chorus sung at the family gathering in the "Present Day" chapter also contains the same characteristics as the earlier unintelligible earcons, now pluralized and vocalized in actual choral singing. The old and young both articulate this sound in *The Years*, suggesting that it is cyclic and connected to temporality.

Woolf gives the "battered woman" and her song new life in *The Years*, but Sara's position as a crucial character changes the reader's access to this singer's thoughts and experiences. Sara hears the cries, wails, and musics of the city, but she also produces the earcon herself, a combination of Rhoda's function as auscultator and Bernard's as enunciator. As Sara ages, she becomes more and more disenfranchised as she is no longer an eligible commodity on the marriage market. Thus, the reader is privy to the narrative of the "other life" the earlier homeless women might have had, if they had managed to avoid homelessness, through the history of Sara's upbringing. Although early in life she enjoys ruling-class circumstances, later she is subject to the material conditions of poverty produced by being one of the daughters of educated men, as Woolf argues in *Three Guineas*. Berman suggests that Woolf was able to "think 'women' and 'women's politics' without returning to the separate bodies of 'woman at the washtub' or 'woman in the parlor'" in *The Waves* (Berman 120); Sara accomplishes the integration of the latter two in *The Years*. In my reading, the utterance of the earcon marks and interrogates these social borders, calling for the reader to reexamine her role in such hierarchies.

The scenes from 1910[5] in which Rose Pargiter visits her cousins Maggie and Sara Pargiter (who are sisters) illuminate this commingling of previously separate and classed bodies. The meeting, during which Sara sings at the piano, bookends a section in which Lady Kitty Lasswade (née Kitty Malone) attends the opera. (Kitty is another cousin; she has married a lord, according to her mother's wishes.) Ambient sound and music are ubiquitous throughout the chapter. Noise pollution, for example, is noted immediately when Rose walks to Sara and Maggie's house for lunch; it is a marker of class: "The shabby street on the south side of the river was very noisy" (*TY* 146). Rose has proposed the get-together after hearing Maggie's *voice* in a shop. As she travels to the sisters' home, among the loud commotions of the street, "now and again a voice detached itself from the general clamour" (ibid.), in similar fashion to Mrs Ramsay's auscultation of a voice outside the window. Subsequently, traces of the earcon of unintelligibility introduce Sara, who sits at her piano:

> A woman shouted to her neighbour; a child cried. A man trundling a barrow opened his mouth and bawled up at the windows as he passed. There were bedsteads, grates, pokers and odd pieces of twisted iron on his barrow. But whether he was selling old iron or buying old iron it

was impossible to say; the rhythm persisted; but the words were almost rubbed out.

> The swarm of sound, the rush of traffic, the shouts of the hawkers, the single cries and the general cries, came into the upper room of the house in Hyams Place where Sara Pargiter sat at the piano. She was singing. (Ibid.)

The city pulses with rhythmic sonorities from which the meanings of words are difficult to glean. As in *Jacob's Room*, such single and general cries also permeate domestic spaces. Yet, although the periphery sonics cross the physical borders of the home in both novels, Sara's response to such noise is markedly different from Jacob's, who seems not to notice "the woman battering at the door crying 'Let me in!'" (*JR* 149). Zimring argues that city sounds "provide Sara with a sort of raw material for verbally producing the city" (145). Sara is able to create a "new kind of poetic speech" (Zimring 146) out of the street's sonics. Thus, unlike Jacob's silence, which is unresponsive, Sara contributes her own music to the soundscape. The resultant pattern of movement crisscrosses from one sphere into the other, from an exterior acoustic arena into interior places and vice versa.

Indeed, an assemblage of sonics continues to flood the chapter, illustrating the social and cultural circumstances of both the characters and the specific time period. During her discussion with her sister about Rose's impending visit, Sara begins to compose a nursery rhyme about her cousin's name that will function as a metamorphosing leitmotif – Richard Wagner's operatic earcon – throughout the rest of the text: "Rose of the flaming heart; Rose of the burning breast; Rose of the weary world – red, red Rose!" (*TY* 148). Thus, Sara conceives of her cousin (and many others in the novel) in song. Rose is also introduced by her voice before the sisters see her: "A door slammed below; they heard footsteps mounting the stairs. 'There she is,' said Maggie. The steps stopped. They heard a voice saying, 'still further up? On the very top? Thank you.' Then the steps began mounting the stairs again" (ibid.). Conversation over lunch is interrupted repeatedly by jarring sounds outside the window – the iron collector, but also a roaring dray, increasing the intensity of urban noise throughout the passage. The various clatters and cries seem to declare the city's obsession with the consumption of goods, underscoring the sisters' "poverty-stricken" (ibid.) apartment but also the omnipresent destitution, yet pulsating energy, of the street sellers of the city. Lastly, when Sara and Rose go to a suffrage meeting later in the chapter, the segue is again a vocalizing street vendor; this time he sells violets, misspelled in the text – "vilets" (*TY* 157) – to evoke the accent and actual sound of his voice. (Sara is neither as giving nor even as sympathetic as one might assume; she takes the violets without paying for them. The novel, therefore, often exposes Sara's failings.)[6]

The segment, then, via reverberated sonics, traces the associations among various human and nonhuman heterogeneous and material things. The connections made by the urban sounds and resonating bodies, both in their diffusion and auscultation, do not suggest an already perceived and homogenous map. Instead, I would suggest, as Latour argues, that the passage evokes a "network-tracing activity" ("On Actor-Network" 14). As is often the case for Woolf, the random movement of sound is showcased, an unsystematic dynamic that is essential to Latour's thinking as well. Thus, as Jon Murdoch has summarized, "space is an effect of network activity. It emerges from within heterogeneous networks and its shape and its form is given by the shape and form of the various networks" (75). This sonic-laden chapter abstracts space in such a manner, questioning the limits of the built environment's borders and rearranging its shapes and forms by creating new networks. Woolf accomplishes this reconfiguration of human relations through the mechanism of the "wandering waves of sound," to use Walter Pater's apt phrase for sonic movement (Pater 113).

The concern to disclose social stratification through sound also carries into the scene during which Kitty attends the opera. As Emma Sutton has argued in her book on Woolf and classical music, Wagner's significance to Woolf is substantial. This "exceptional section of the novel," Sutton contends, "although it describes only one Act of the third part of Wagner's tetralogy … is one of the longest uninterrupted passages and a unique depiction of art music, to which this novel (like *Between the Acts*) gives little overt attention. And it is a scene that draws together *The Years'* attention to music, Jews and anti-Semitism" (*Virginia Woolf* 127). Sutton ably focuses on Woolf's indebtedness to, and critique of, Wagner in this section. In addition, I submit that it reveals Woolf's understanding of music as a socially constructed and structuring art form. The music, and, specifically, the singing voice instantly causes Kitty to reflect on her life. But in this novel, aligned no doubt to what Sutton views as Woolf's critical stance on "Hitler's 'cult of Wagner'" (ibid.), the narrative suggests that the sonorous art can create an almost obsequious version of the past: "the music made her think of herself and her own life as she seldom did. It exalted her; it cast a flattering light over herself, her past.

But why did Martin laugh at me for having a car? she thought. What's the good of laughing? she asked" (*TY* 165). Similar to the gramophone in *Between the Acts*, as I shall discuss, music is capable of persuading its listeners, even if it unsettles fixed linguistic meaning.

As sonic signifiers multiply in the chapter and novel, sounds reach into social spheres to remind those within their acoustic arenas to reassess their assumptions. If Sara responds by making up songs and playing the piano, Kitty provides another perspective through the reception of sound. Yet, she is not simply a passive listener. Woolf utilizes the scene at the opera to demonstrate the forgetfulness that can come with economic security. Kitty begins to contemplate her life critically, but ultimately stops short of any new understanding. She cannot remember precisely what Siegfried (the eponymous hero of Wagner's opera) and his hammering recall from her past:

> Hammer, hammer, hammer he went. She leant back again. What did that make her think of? A young man who came into a room with shavings in his hair … when she was very young. In Oxford? She had gone to tea with them; had sat on a hard chair; in a very light room; and there was a sound of hammering in the garden. And then a boy came in with shavings in his hair. And she had wanted him to kiss her. Or was it the farm hand up at Carter's, when old Carter had loomed up suddenly leading a bull with a ring through its nose? (*TY* 165)

Class implications undergird the scene, remembered perhaps by the reader if not by Kitty. The episode recalled by Woolf's redeployment of Wagner's leitmotif technique with the repetition of "hammer, hammer, hammer" is the scene just before Mrs Malone (Kitty's mother) establishes for the reader that she prefers Lord Lasswade to Edward Pargiter as a match for her daughter, a wish she has obviously managed to manifest. Now that Kitty is Lady Lasswade, goes to suffrage meetings in her operatic dress, and travels the city in her new motor car, she misremembers earlier desires for men of whom her mother would not have approved. Her thoughts commingle the son of an educated man (Jo Robson) with the unnamed farmhand at old Carter's. Thus, this earcon is redeployed by Woolf to trigger the issue of convenient ruling-class amnesia.

The hammer motif will resound at the end of the chapter as well and be recollected one final time in the "present day" when the reader learns that Kitty lives alone in the North of England; only a boy who chops wood interrupts her solitude. But first the narrative returns to Hyams Place, Sara, and Maggie. As I have suggested, Sara is attuned, inimitably, to the cries from the street, but she also articulates the unintelligible earcon herself. In addition to performing her own leitmotif for Rose, she accompanies herself on the piano and sings, despite her "reedy" voice. Although Sara explicitly wonders, "'What's the good of singing if one hasn't any voice?'" (*TY* 167), a poignant statement given the poverty of their situation, she does continue to sing and play throughout the scene. Interestingly, and in contrast to the opera Kitty has just attended, Sara vocalizes a combination of marching songs and nursery rhymes, music that will be foregrounded in *Between the Acts*. The songs in this instance, however, suggest that high art, military music, and folk tunes are all part of the same cultural matrix – they can create both unthinking allegiance to authoritarian governmental policies and also new possibilities for signification in their associational heterogeneity.

Sara's performance of a "pompous eighteenth-century march" in which she sings of "'brandishing, flourishing my sword in my hand'" (*TY* 167) recalls the climactic actions of Siegfried detailed during Kitty's visit to the opera, in addition to what Anna Snaith has identified as quotations from Edmund Spenser's *The Faerie Queen*.[7] Simultaneously, as Snaith details, sing-song nursery rhymes in Sara's rendering belie her commingled allusions to two of Shakespeare's greatest orations on death: Ariel's well-known air in *The Tempest* that begins "Full fathom five thy father lies; / of his bones are coral made" (1.2.396–410) and Clarence's dream from *Richard III* (1.4.24–33), a prophetic (and verbally stunning) incubus of another watery demise. Sara vocalizes: "'Running water; flowing water. May my bones turn to coral; and fish light their lanthorns; fish light their green lanthorns in my eyes'" (*TY* 168). All the while, she accompanies herself on the piano as she "hummed, in time to the music" (ibid.). Thus, the section after Kitty's experience at the opera provides myriad associational poetic and rhythmical references in the form of an accompanied, improvisational song – a sort of Woolfian opera in language.

Subsequently, when Sara tells Maggie more about the suffrage meeting, she literally acts it out for her, dramatizing the sights and sounds that, previously, the reader has only had access to through Eleanor (another cousin who was at the assembly): a woman hanging clothes in a back garden and someone rattling a stick on the railings outside. In her performance, Sara imitates the voice of Mr Pickford, who welcomes Kitty to sit down when she arrives at the meeting: "here she changed her voice and imitated the tones in which a middle-class man might be supposed to welcome a lady of fashion" (*TY* 169). This vocal mimicry is then followed by Sara's imitation of Lady Lasswade seated in her chair, and then again by the nursery rhyme about "withered Rose, spiky Rose, tawny Rose, thorny Rose," a phrase that mutates, eventually, into an allusion to W.B. Yeats's poem "To the Rose upon the Rood of Time."

But finally, these sonic snippets assemble in an uncanny but now familiar figure, if one is attuned to the earcons of the novels: during her reenactment of *Siegfried*, Sara transforms into an old woman. The moment is triggered by loud voices from the public house outside their flat:

> Sara got up and went to the window. A crowd had gathered outside the public house. A man was being thrown out. There he came, staggering. He fell against a lamp-post to which he clung. The scene was lit up by the glare of the lamp over the public house door. Sara stood for a moment at the window watching them. Then she turned; her face in the mixed light looked cadaverous and worn, as if she were no longer a girl, but an old woman worn out by a life of childbirth, debauchery and crime. She stood there hunched up, with her hands clenched together.
>
> "In time to come," she said, looking at her sister, "people, looking into this room – this cave, this little antre, scooped out of mud and dung, will hold their fingers to their noses" – she held her fingers to her nose – "and say 'Pah! They stink!'"
>
> She fell down into a chair. (*TY* 169–70)

Sara is called a "girl" in the scene, but somehow she looks near death's door, compressing the present moment with glimpses of the future, yet simultaneously evoking an ancient crone. The description of the prospective room is also simultaneously outside and inside, public and private (Sara imagines the home becoming fodder for potential historians or archaeologists happening upon it as they would Roman ruins or Anglo-Saxon tomb mounds). The subterranean description of the battered woman who conspicuously sings outside the underground station in *Mrs. Dalloway* is also educed by the description of the cavern. With Sara, therefore, periphery personages from the other novels are given more of a voice, although still shown to be marginalized in society. Historians yet to come will chronicle her ancient and anonymous life story of childbirth, debauchery, and crime, but it remains to be seen whether or not they will hear her "invincible thread of sound" (*MD* 74), which has morphed into songs with words, but with so many overlapping and unfixed allusions (a reader without explanatory notes might be at a disadvantage) and improvisatory elements that fixed meaning is as elusive as the unidentified "Allerseelen" of *Mrs. Dalloway* or the singer's "Ah!" in Wigmore Hall.

Fittingly, the chapter ends with one last statement of an earcon – another cry from the street by the man carrying iron scraps:

> Far off a voice was crying hoarsely. Maggie leant out [of the window]. The night was windy and warm.
> "What's he crying?" she said.
> The voice came nearer and nearer.
> "Death ...?" she said.
> "Death ...?" said Sara. They leant out. But they could not hear the rest of the sentence. Then a man who was wheeling a barrow along the street shouted up to them:
> "The King's dead!" (*TY* 171–2)

Historically, the King's death came as a surprise to the British people in 1910, as his failure to attend the performance of *Siegfried* on 5 May was blamed on a bout of bronchitis (his absence is noted during Kitty's attendance at Wagner's opera). The chapter ends, therefore, not only by reiterating a cry that permeates the domestic space of Maggie and Sara but also by making a connection to the end of the Edwardian age. In this version of 1910, eerily, a perceptible cry of death is uttered; it echoes the call of Jacob's name in Woolf's novel of 1922, the allusion to All Souls' Day and the old woman's remembrance of her deceased lover in *Mrs. Dalloway*, the lament for Prue and Andrew Ramsay in *To the Lighthouse*, but also Rhoda's and Bernard's cogitations in *The Waves*. The magnitude of what this particular utterance means, however, is left for the reader to discern as these words close this enigmatic and aurally saturated chapter.

In addition to Sara's theatrical transformation into an old woman who lives in a cave, the children's vocalizations at the end of *The Years* also evoke the "battered woman" from *Mrs. Dalloway* and, especially, her "ee um fah um so" (*MD* 72). Again, Woolf includes the incomprehensible "words" of a song; they are not English, nor are they clearly another known language.[8] But if one thinks of the passage as Woolf's attempt to utter the postlinguistic singing voice, they become more understandable, not for what they "mean" but for how they *do not contribute to making sense*, to recall Dolar. Similar to the subterranean figures in the other novels, the children have specifically been brought "up from the basement into the drawing-room" (*TY* 386) by Delia (one of Rose's sisters), who is hosting the party. Their words are conspicuously inscrutable, raising more questions about their denotation than providing answers:

> [The children] swept their eyes over the grown-up people for a moment, then, each giving the other a little nudge, they burst into song:
>
> > Etho passo tanno hai,
> > Fai donk to tu do,
> > Mai to, kai to, lai to see
> > Toh dom to tuh do –
>
> That was what is sounded like. Not a word was recognizable. The distorted sounds rose and sank as if they followed a tune. They stopped.
>
> They stood with their hands behind their backs. Then with one impulse they attacked the next verse:
>
> > Fanno to par, etto to mar,
> > Timin tudo, tido,
> > Foll to gar in, mitno to par,
> > Eido, teido, meido –
>
> They sang the second verse more fiercely than the first. The rhythm seemed to rock and the unintelligible words ran themselves together almost into a shriek. The grown-up people did not know whether to laugh or to cry. Their voices were so harsh; the accent was so hideous. (*TY* 386–7)

The description of this chorus as unintelligible, fierce, harsh, and almost "a shriek" is now familiar from the various incarnations of earcons I believe Woolf elaborates. Notably, this utterance and its social circumstances in *The Years* hark all the way back to the first articulation of the "cry" in *The Voyage Out*. This time, however, the English bystanders seem to engage in a critical process of understanding, albeit in complex and unstable terms.

The words of the song, then, are conspicuously ambivalent; the narrator and the party auscultators elaborate this for the reader. "'But what the devil were they singing?' said Hugh Gibbs. 'I couldn't understand a word of it, I must confess'" (*TY* 387). However, Eleanor, one of the central characters, tentatively ponders the significance of the song as Rhoda and Bernard have done before her:

> "But it was ..." Eleanor began. She stopped. What was it? As they stood there they had looked so dignified; yet they had made this hideous noise. The contrast between their faces and their voices was astonishing; it was impossible to find one word for the whole. "Beautiful?" she said, with a note of interrogation, turning to Maggie.
>   "Extraordinarily," said Maggie.
>   But Eleanor was not sure that they were thinking of the same thing. (*TY* 387–8)

Eleanor and Maggie seem to appreciate the "hideous" sounds, but both of their observations are couched in terms that dislodge fixity. The interrogative after Eleanor's remark that the song is "'Beautiful?'" and her uncertainty that Maggie is thinking the same thing when she says "'Extraordinarily'" leave the reader with little hope of defining or clearly interpreting the song. Yet, a few of the party's community of auscultators do actively engage in interrogating this "unintelligible" earcon (unlike the English visitors to the South American village). Despite the extreme flux of the novel's ending – Comstock argues, for example, "no one will sum up the party or *The Years*; not Nicholas, not Peggy, who is asked to speak 'for the younger generation' but who refuses; not even the caretaker's children, who sing their song for sixpence" (262) – some of these auscultators are at least beginning to engage with uncertainty. In this way and in this novel in particular, the earcon encourages anti-fascist modes of thinking.

The lack of fixity performed by the fragmented and now communal earcon memorably marks this musical event. In this instance, children, often part of the female-centred communities in the novels, now utter the earcon in song, a shift, I would suggest, that marks Woolf's hope for the future, even amid the horrifying atmosphere of Hitler's growing power in the late 1930s. They are the offspring of the working class, labouring for the middle classes who do not fully comprehend the significance of the sounds (or their exertions). Nevertheless, they interrupt the party of the present-day closing scene with sound, "bursting" into the acoustic arena of an interior, domesticated space. In other words, those who voice the earcon are no longer on a different continent, asking to be let in, disenfranchised outside on the street, isolated in an abandoned house, or even segregated on a recital stage; they are a small, and young, collective, a literal musical chorus, situated inside a family gathering surrounded by the city soundscape, and this time they have an informal audience. Having children voice the earcon suggests a tempered renewal of what the earcon signifies: a persistent cry that will carry on despite being largely unheard. Although the old attitude persists in Martin, who, like Peter before him in *Mrs. Dalloway*, reestablishes the class pecking order when he "slip[s] coins into their hands" (*TY* 387), in *The Years* the earcon, at least, grows in volume and consequence – it can no longer be ignored by the characters in the novel, or the reader.

III. Aural Multiplicity in *Between the Acts*

By the 1930s, acousticians and noise abatement societies in New York City were "exerting control over the soundscape of private life," according to Emily Thompson (167), because of the lack of success they had with the regulation of noise in the public, exterior spaces of city streets. Blesser and Salter explain that over the twentieth century, "in many countries, a series of legal battles attempted to regulate the right to generate sound, but most attempts proved futile. From the struggle to combat noise, the concept of the private acoustic arena gained prominence among the professional classes" (106). Woolf's novels document and resist this development: *The Waves* and *The Years* repeatedly foreground sound in interior, social spaces and represent the intrusion into the traditional private sphere of the cityscape in negative but also positive terms. By the end of the decade, however, Woolf shifts the acoustic arena once more, not just back to brief scenes of exterior, public space – such as those featured in *The Voyage Out, Jacob's Room*, and *Mrs. Dalloway* – but to an entire novel set largely outside. In addition, because *Between the Acts* incorporates a pageant, the issue of sound (both organized in the form of music and unregulated in the form of "noise") is foregrounded as the audience that hears it also grows. Correlatively, the unintelligible earcon proliferates, splintering even further and multiplying. In this final section of chapter 2, I explore what happens to the earcon in the exterior and social acoustic arena of *Between the Acts*.

Describing the stage for the pageant, which occurs on the grounds outside Pointz Hall, the narrator suggests that the trees surrounding the terrace create an al fresco theatre:

Waiting for Mr. Streatfield, she [Miss La Trobe] paced between the birch trees.

The other trees were magnificently straight. They were not too regular; but regular enough to suggest columns in a church; in a church without a roof; in an open-air cathedral, a place where swallows darting seemed, by the regularity of the trees, to make a pattern, dancing, like the Russians, only not to music, but to the unheard rhythm of their own wild hearts. (*BA* 47)

Miss La Trobe, the pageant's creator, notes,

"The very place for a pageant!" The lawn was as flat as the floor of a theatre. The terrace, rising, made a natural stage. The trees barred the stage like pillars. And the human figure was seen to great advantage against a background of sky. (*BA* 55)

Both of these descriptions foreground the outdoor circumstances of the play about to take place, describing it in terms very similar to ancient, Elizabethan, and eighteenth-century performance spaces.

As Woolf was well aware, open-air amphitheatres symbolized and even furthered the democratic principles of ancient Greece. Although this stage does not emulate the Dionysian Theatre at the Acropolis, for example, I would argue that its al fresco environment harks back to it. And Woolf did visit the Acropolis on her trip to Greece in 1906 and again later in 1932. Moreover, Blesser and Salter suggest, "the ancient Athenians have been described as a critical and demanding audience, both emotionally and intellectually" (95). Correspondingly, in *Between the Acts*, the reader is given access to the myriad thoughts and conversations of often disparaging and exacting listeners. According to Blesser and Salter, the ancient Greeks were unique in connecting open-air theatres to social democracy (albeit a gendered one that privileged Athenian males). In addition, "given their strong interest in all forms of aural activities, including music, oration, rhetoric, and religion, the ancient Greeks were likely to have been aware of how these activities were influenced by spatial acoustics" (94). Thus, the open-air aspect of the makeshift stage in the novel suggests the aurality of theatrical space and its practices from ancient Greece, in addition to its Grecian comic modes, as Cuddy-Keane argues.

But the outdoor "theatre" also recalls the Elizabethan period (as does the pageant itself),[9] with the raised thrust stage of the Shakespearean playhouse and its open roof, at least in the manner that the audience is situated below the patio area. The sixteenth-century English stage, in contrast to the ancient Greeks,

> emphasized small interior spaces, with improved intelligibility and great aural intimacy, in their theaters. Given the English climate, enclosing theater spaces was mandatory. And given that theaters served as entertainment, rather than as political expression of open democracy, they did not need to be large. English theaters of this period were one of the earliest documented examples of customized aural architecture – acoustic spaces intended for a single use. (Blesser and Salter 97)

It is significant, therefore, that the performance takes place in an "open-air cathedral," for it signals Woolf's combination of a democratically focused theatrical space with the artistic value ascribed to the Elizabethan stage. Acoustics in such a space would be notoriously difficult to control, even unwieldy, and Woolf takes full advantage of displaying this in the novel.

The platform acting area with the trees on the side is, of course, perhaps visually closest to a proscenium stage, which gained dominance during the eighteenth century and was the most common type throughout the nineteenth and twentieth, except for the fact that the sky fills the top part of the arch and there is, embarrassingly, no curtain, just bushes to hide behind on the side. This type of stage has its roots in the versions of it from ancient Greece and Rome. The primary difference would still be the raked viewing position of a Greek or Roman audience, yet the elevated acting platform and out-of-doors atmosphere of the ancients would be akin to this version at Pointz Hall.

Thus, delimited spatial boundaries are questioned and fundamentally disrupted in this partly natural, partly built, environment that barely contains this pageant. Indeed, the aural architecture of several historically specific theatrical spaces is loosely assembled: ancient Greece and Rome, the Elizabethan period, the eighteenth and nineteenth centuries, and even, of course, then-contemporary versions of the English country pageant (a format with which Woolf would have been familiar: E.M. Forster's *England's Pleasant Land* (1940) was published by the Hogarth Press while she was writing *Between the Acts*, which she started in 1938).[10] This theatrical trajectory is also akin to the time periods of the pageant's content. Bookended by the domesticated sphere of Pointz Hall, "a middle-sized house" (*BA* 5), bits and pieces throughout the history of drama and its consequent spatial acoustics are superimposed in this heterogeneous patchwork of a "theatre."

Furthermore, Miss La Trobe is an outsider to her community: in addition to being of non-English descent, she is also a lesbian. Her exclusion because of these subject positions speaks to the dominant cultural codes of nationality and sexuality, demonstrating that she is doubly outcast from her society. Hence, she encapsulates the Outsiders' Society Woolf articulates in *Three Guineas*, not only because she is a bit of a social pariah but also because she dynamically creates and directs a play in which the whole village will be included, either as performers or as audience members (even this distinction is blurred in the novel). In the later 1930s Woolf returns to creative characters who perform, much like her first heroine, Rachel Vinrace. But unlike *The Voyage Out*, the artists in the later novels generate their own works rather than enacting the efforts of others. In so doing, Woolf suggests that "we are not passive spectators doomed to unresisting obedience but by our thoughts and actions can ourselves change that figure" (*TG* 365).

Miss La Trobe's pageant is also a multidisciplinary artefact. Her play (similar to Sara's compositions) consists of poetic speech, live song, recorded music, off-stage barks from a megaphone in the bushes, technological noises (the chuffing of the gramophone, car horns), natural sounds (birds, dogs, cows, etc.), rain, the voices of the audience, and airplanes, if we include Reverend Streatfield's interrupted summation as part of the pageant. Indeed, Cuddy-Keane has noted the polytextural quality (the incorporation of different media into the notion of many-voiced sounds, or polyphony) of much of Woolf's later work.[11] All combine in ways that they could not in an interior public performance space. In addition, those who work in the local village are the amateur performers, who enact Miss La Trobe's script for the local merchants and gentry, although this hierarchal class division is also questioned by the relentless parody in the book and the audience's participation (through the novel's detailing of their incessant comments). Combined with the space of this makeshift, reflexive, and exterior stage, La Trobe's springtime pageant functions to "find[] new words and creat[e] new methods" (*TG* 366), as Woolf recommends in *Three Guineas*.

Perhaps inevitably, then, given the rhizomatic associations of the theatrical space, the actors, the audience, and the performance of the pageant, the earconic cries splinter and are voiced by a variety of human and nonhuman bodies and mechanisms. Again, the possible meaning of words is at issue throughout the text, particularly when the earcon emerges during the pageant. But this time it is because the acoustics of this open space wreak havoc on direct, fixed meaning. Right from the start, the singing of the chorus – this time perform- ing the commentary function of ancient Greek drama – is repeatedly inaudible to the audience because of the wind. While the gramophone chuffs instead of playing its assigned music, "A long line of villagers in shirts made of sacking began passing in and out in single file behind her [Miss La Trobe] between the trees. They were singing, but not a word reached the audience" (*BA* 57). Shortly thereafter, the reader is informed again,

> The villagers were singing but half their words were blown away.
> Cutting the roads ... up to the hill top ... we climbed. Down in the valley ... saw wild boar, hog, rhinoceros, reindeer ... Dug ourselves in to the hill top ... Ground roots between stones ... Ground corn ... till we too ... lay under g – r – o – u – n – d ... (Ibid.)

And lastly, in this opening scene about England's earliest history,

> all the time the villagers were passing in and out between the trees. They were singing; but only a word or two was audible "... wore ruts in the grass ... built the house in the lane ..." The wind blew away the connecting words of their chant, and then, as they reached the tree at the end they sang:
> "To the shrine of the Saint ... to the tomb ... lovers ... believers ... we come ..." (*BA* 59).

A largely unintelligible song, therefore, is an integral part of the pageant at its beginning. What seeps through the blowing wind is the mention of an ancient history,[12] similar to Sara's cave, Mrs McNab, or the sub- terranean allusions attached to the old women who sing in London's streets. The commonality is again that of a song with inscrutable (and now even inaudible) words, earcons that will crescendo as the play con- tinues. Woolf's deployment of these ineffable utterances asks readers to hear what seems to be an irrelevant cry, lost on the wind. Yet, I would argue, Woolf is after something else with her use of song in *Between the Acts*. Indeed, as Dolar claims, the singing voice "is endowed with pro- fundity: by not meaning anything, it appears to mean more than mere words" (31). The epigraph with which I started chapter 2 suggests as much and reveals the stakes: to listen to "no language but a cry, Ay, ay, ay, ay" (*TG* 362), as she argues in *Three Guineas*, might prevent disaster in the future.

At the end of the first act, the gramophone accompanies the reprieve of the disbanding audience: "And then, as they raised themselves and turned about, the music modulated. The music chanted: Dispersed are we. It moaned: Dispersed are we. It lamented: Dispersed are we, as they streamed, spotting the grass with colour, across the lawns, and down the paths: Dispersed are we" (*BA* 69–70). The words used to describe this initial refrain of "Dispersed are we" – wailed, chanted, moaned, lamented – also recall the descriptions of the earcon from the earlier novels. A technological manifestation of a bodiless voice, something I discuss further in Part 2, the gramophone grieves the same circumstances that La Trobe does, the scattering of the community and the consequent fracturing of emotion: "Here was her downfall; here was the Interval" (*BA* 68–9). As in the earlier novels, and despite its ambiguity, the earcon of *Between the Acts* does evince participation from its confused auditors: self-reflection, something that will also be foregrounded in the visual sphere by the fragmented mirrors in the "Present Day" portion of the play. But the bemused responses of the audience members echo the lack of understanding articulated even in *The Voyage Out* when Rachel and Terence hear the "unintelligible cry" of the women in the village.

In the middle of Act 2, Miss La Trobe experiences another kinetic crisis. An anonymous voice cries out, in the midst of the eighteenth-century play,

> "All that fuss about nothing!" a voice exclaimed. People laughed. The voice stopped. But the voice had seen; the voice had heard. For a moment Miss La Trobe behind her tree glowed with glory. The next, turning to the villagers who were passing in and out between the trees, she barked:
> "Louder! Louder!"
> For the stage was empty; the emotion must be continued; the only thing to continue the emotion was the song; and the words were inaudible. (*BA* 100).

Miss La Trobe "glow[s] with glory," but not because someone understands the "message" in the play, for it is unclear what it is one could have gleaned. The song, regardless of its words, is "the only thing" to continue the emotion of the moment; it is the "place where what cannot be said can nevertheless be conveyed" (Dolar 31). In *The Years* this sort of response and potential self-reflection occur after the children sing their uncanny chorus. In *Between the Acts* the reader witnesses the expansion of such questions and retorts, which are uttered throughout the pageant. Indeed, they produce much of the content of the novel.

Once the pageant breaks for the interval, Miss La Trobe experiences another potential disaster: "And the stage was empty. Miss La Trobe leant against the tree, paralysed. Her power had left her. Beads of perspiration broke on her forehead. Illusion had failed. 'This is death,' she murmured, 'death'" (*BA* 101). Although satirical, the connections between artistry and the pain of demise recall Bernard's solemn pairing of the two issues as he searches for some way to articulate his anguish in writing. Correspondingly, albeit farcically, and enabled by the open-air, rural venue, a cry, or in this case "bellow," issues from the mouths of cows:

> Then suddenly, as the illusion petered out, the cows took up the burden. One had lost her calf. In the very nick of time she lifted her great moon-eyed head and bellowed. All the great moon-eyed heads laid themselves back. From cow after cow came the same yearning bellow. The whole world was filled with dumb yearning. It was the primeval voice sounding loud in the ear of the present moment. Then the whole herd caught the infection. Lashing their tails, blobbed like pokers, they tossed their heads high, plunged and bellowed, as if Eros had planted his dart in their flanks and goaded them to fury. The cows annihilated the gap; bridged the distance; filled the emptiness and continued the emotion.
>
> Miss La Trobe waved her hand ecstatically at the cows.
>
> "Thank Heaven!" she exclaimed. (*BA* 101–2)

At the nadir of artistic collapse, a "yearning," "primeval voice" reiterates a pluralized chorus of earcons, an invitation to "shut off the wireless and listen to the past" (*TG* 362). The cry of the women in the village in South America is for their children. In *Jacob's Room*, Woolf's first novel about world war, there are several scenes in which the earcon emerges in a female-centred, communal space situated outside. Similarly, the old woman who clutches her child with her back to the bank and the cry heard by Fanny outside Hampstead Garden Suburb foretell the Greek women who cry for their children at the end of this novel. All mirror the loss of Betty Flanders, the mother who unwittingly raises a son to serve as military "wastage."[13] The articulation of the earcon out of the mouth of a bawling cow because it has lost its calf, therefore, links the losses from wartime violence and national interests with their consequences to the private sphere. As she informs the addressee in

Three Guineas: "For such will be our ruin if you, in the immensity of your public abstractions forget the private figure, or if we in the intensity of our private emotions forget the pubic world. Both houses will be ruined, the public and the private, the material and the spiritual, for they are inseparably connected" (*TG* 365). This time nature, another guttural voice, is enlisted to utter this cry. In "The Moment" (my second epigraph) a similarly sombre, and profound, version of such an earcon suggests urgently that it is "more difficult for the voice to carry through this dark" (Woolf, "Moment" 8).

Thus, La Trobe's gesture of relinquishing control of her work, taking what comes out of the mouths of cows, runs contrary to the notion that she is solely dictatorial – despite her officiousness. Indeed, Rosenfeld indicates, "to rescue her audience from their subconscious Hiterlerism is Miss La Trobe's quest in *Between the Acts*" (173). Cuddy-Keane concurs, arguing further that her performance "is democratic rather than authoritarian and a model of community that, as I have argued, is not a hierarchical ranking but a 'dynamic inhabiting of mutual space' ('Politics' 284) ... an egalitarian conjunction of respect for difference and apprehension of the whole" ("Virginia Woolf, Sound Technologies, and the New Aurality" 93). Thus, it is fitting that at this moment, the playwright's relief and thankfulness that nature has "taken up the burden" counterbalances her abrupt and autocratic commands. Moreover, as Sultzbach observes, "Woolf's inclusion of the cows that save the pageant play ... acknowledges the presence of nonhuman actors in a larger environmental historical drama" (14). The cry from the natural world also links this earcon with artistry in a new way, as a potential alternative to physical violence. As Woolf states in the essay "Thoughts on Peace in an Air Raid" (published in 1940): "if we are to compensate the young man for the loss of his glory and his gun, we must give him access to the creative feelings" (*E6*: 245).

By the time of the third Interval, just before the "Present Day," the audience is no longer merely unsettled, it is immobile: "No one moved. There they sat, facing the empty stage, the cows, the meadows and the view, while the machine ticked in the bushes" (*BA* 127). Miss La Trobe, although she will experience a third kinetic crisis, will again resign control of the subject matter as the audience and the material world become the play: "'After Vic.' she had written, 'try ten mins. of present time. Swallows, cows etc.'" (*BA* 129). She has forbidden music, and allowed instead "the horns of cars on the high road [...] and the swish of the trees" (*BA* 127), combining the technological and natural worlds.

The effect of this experiment in potential self-reflection on the audience is one of fear: "All their nerves were on edge. They sat exposed. The machine ticked. There was no music. [...] They were neither one thing nor the other; neither Victorians nor themselves. They were suspended, without being, in limbo. Tick, tick, tick went the machine" (*BA* 127–8). The gramophone now emulates a ticking time-bomb, an ominous intoning of the novel's political concerns. Something, La Trobe fears, has gone wrong:

> "Reality too strong," she muttered. "Curse 'em!" She felt everything they felt. [...]
>
> And then the shower fell, sudden, profuse.
>
> No one had seen the cloud coming. There it was, black, swollen, on top of them. Down it poured like all the people in the world weeping. Tears, Tears. Tears.
>
> "Oh that our human pain could here have ending!" Isa murmured. Looking up she received two great blots of rain full in her face. They trickled down her cheeks as if they were her own tears. But they were all people's tears, weeping for all people. [...]
>
> "That's done it," sighed Miss La Trobe, wiping away the drops on her cheeks. Nature once more had taken her part. (*BA* 129–30)

The unthinkable sounding of time in the play invokes dread in the audience, but La Trobe understands that the unknowable is a precondition of reality (or the present-day moment), for she allows another event, in this case the rainstorm, to add to her play. Indeed, rain is a particularly fascinating element to employ here. It certainly traverses the visual and the tactile worlds but it is also an aural occurrence of multiplicity, one that obviously could not be experienced in such a tangible and effective way indoors. Sultzbach rightly argues, "Woolf's representations of Miss La Trobe's 'unrehearsed blessings,' ... refuses to translate the moo of the cows into human language. The affect is to suggest the ways in which the nonlinguistic sound carries a meaning which – far from diminishing its significance to the human script – exceeds the 'failing' moments of the human speech" (14). Although a retreat, perhaps, from the postlinguistic singing voice, it is fitting that the natural world articulates the cry in Woolf's novel written during the Second World War, as the totalizing scale of networked associations was illuminated to her by the terror and magnitude of another global conflict of violence. Enunciating the communal "weeping for all people," the cry that has elicited self-reflection by resisting specificity throughout the novels nevertheless crescendos to end the "Present Day" section of the pageant and insists on being heard, as well as being seen and felt.

Listening to these earconic cries throughout Woolf's fiction brings the novels together in new ways. Although I have explored these sonics in the novels chronologically, a variety of nonlinear and fresh connections reveal that Woolf's methods themselves are rhizomatic. The critical reflection induced, albeit somewhat unsuccessfully, in the British travellers of *The Voyage Out*, for example, reverberates in Lucrezia Warren Smith's response to the old woman opposite Regent's Park tube station and the respondents who listen to the children's chorus at the end of *The Years*. Speculative moments echo in *Between the Acts* also, but perhaps more despairingly and futilely, as in her very first book, in terms of penetrating the class-based and imperialist mindset of its English listeners – two novels that are also notably indebted to the art of music. The associations among spatial expanses of greenery and the natural world are also illuminating, connecting the unbuilt environment of the village scene in *The Voyage Out* with the urban parks of *Jacob's Room* and *Mrs. Dalloway*, as well as the rural environments of *To the Lighthouse* and *Between the Acts*. Lastly, tracing the thread of the singing, postlinguistic voice makes linkages between the physicality of the vocal mechanism and its ineffability in *Mrs. Dalloway*, *To the Lighthouse*, *The Waves*, *The Years*, and *Between the Acts*, as the urgency of the sound foments because of the Second World War. Yet, although the earcon grows in volume, it is not because of hypothetical social progress; on the contrary, I would suggest the sound increases in intensity because of collective regression. Thus, in Part 2 of this book, I shall explore what is implied by the Woolfian earcon: how can we learn to listen more ethically and effectively?

PART 2

Profound Listening and Acousmatics

Chapter Three

Initial Apperceptions

… freedom of listening is as necessary as freedom of speech.

Roland Barthes, *The Responsibility of Forms* 260

Now the human voice is an instrument of varied power; it can enchant and it can soothe; it can rage and it can despair; but when it lectures it almost always bores.

Virginia Woolf, "Why?" (1934), 229

In an essay entitled "Why?" (1934), Woolf questions lecturing as a fruitful practice for education because of its one-way mode of communication. Throughout the text she recounts the sound of a speaker's voice – the means of signification – as opposed to the content of the language he articulates. Although the voice can express many moods, she argues, if interactions are one-sided, as is often the case during a lecture, not only is it boring, but it also "incites the most debased of human passions – vanity, ostentation, self-assertion, and the desire to convert[]" (*DM* 231). Put another way, such imbalanced utterance is irresponsible. Instead, she asks, employing the interrogative pattern set up by the title,

> Why encourage your elders to turn themselves into prigs and prophets, when they are ordinary men and women? Why force them to stand on a platform for forty minutes while you reflect upon the colour of their hair and the longevity of flies? Why not let them talk to you and listen to you, naturally and happily, on the floor? Why not create a new form of society founded on poverty and equality? Why not bring together people

of all ages and sexes and all shades of fame and obscurity so that they can talk, without mounting platforms or reading papers or wearing expensive clothes or eating expensive food? Would not such a society be worth, even as a form of education, all the papers on art and literature that have ever been read since the world began? Why not abolish prigs and prophets? Why not invent human intercourse? Why not try? (Ibid.)

The insistent repetition of the interrogative creates a rhythm in the reader's or auditor's ear, foregrounding the material qualities of sound. But to employ such an imitative aurality in an essay, a form traditionally dependent on proven statements and, essentially, one-way conversation is itself innovative, demonstrating her quip to the composer Ethel Smyth that she writes "to a rhythm and not to a plot" (*L4*: 204), even in what seems to be a polemic.

In addition, "Why?" explores a significant issue for Woolf that often manifests in her fiction when she thinks across art forms: the novels consistently investigate, interrogate, and reveal the importance of the reception of speech, sound, and music, in addition to representing and performing sonorities in the form of earcons, for example, which is the focus of Part 1.[1] But Woolf not only performs such active listening in her novels by documenting aural perceptions, she also theorizes such issues by depicting characters who auscultate the world around them, in addition to focalizing it. Woolf recognizes that listening is a productive, indeed ethically crucial, mode of social interaction. In this part I shall employ a model of layered listening posited by the film theorist Michel Chion to uncover the multifaceted nature of aural reception in Woolf's novels.

But Mikhail Bakhtin also understood the value of listening to "human intercourse." Indeed, he theorized that an apperceptive listener – an auditor who is conscious of hearing – is integral to the process of social interaction. As Bakhtin would describe the practice, "understanding and response are dialectically merged and mutually condition each other; one is impossible without the other" (282). Woolf's dissatisfaction with the lecture mode acknowledges precisely this dynamic. The latter does not mean, however, that there are no dissonances between the sender and the receiver of sound. On the contrary, the speaker, according to Bakhtin, optimistically anticipates both consonance and discord. The subject's orientation, therefore, is "toward the specific world of the listener; it introduces totally new elements into his discourse ... The speaker breaks through the alien conceptual horizon of the listener, constructs his own utterance on alien territory, against his, the listener's, apperceptive background" (ibid.). The willingness of an amenable auditor, then, is vital to human interchange. Woolf believed similarly, that listening to others, perhaps even because of their differences, is indispensable for new possibilities and methods.[2]

Moreover, as Bakhtin maintains, an utterance produces an active role for the listener as well as the speaker, thereby reconfiguring the subject/object relationship:

> In the actual life of speech, every concrete act of understanding is active: it assimilates the word to be understood into its own conceptual system filled with specific objects and emotional expressions, and is indissolubly merged with the response, with a motivated agreement and disagreement … Understanding comes to fruition only in the response. (Ibid.)

Or as Roland Barthes demonstrates in his essay "Music's Body" from *The Responsibility of Forms*, there is an exchange between sounding and hearing: *"listening speaks,"* he argues, and active listening "assumes the responsibility of taking its place in the interplay of desire, of which all language is the theater" (259). Aptly, then, in Woolf's work, I argue, an interchange occurs between the act of making sounds (even those disruptive of speech) and the reciprocation of those sounds, so that "free listening is essentially a listening which circulates, which permutates, which disaggregates, by its mobility, the fixed network of the roles of speech" (Barthes 259).

Thus, although Woolf's novels detail the positive "understanding" gleaned from the listening process for the subject, they also critique its reception (or the lack of it) by disclosing the consequences of the loss of an interlocutor – someone who takes part in a conversation. For Woolf, fundamental to the power-knowledge relations of the utterance (verbal and non-verbal) is the willingness of and necessity for an apperceptive auditor. As Barthes suggests, "it is not possible to imagine a free society, if we agree in advance to preserve within it the old modes of listening: those of the believer, the disciple, and the patient" (259). Ultimately, as noted in the first epigraph to Part 2, "freedom of listening is as necessary as freedom of speech" (Barthes 260). Analysing the various modes of listening Woolf employs in the novels, therefore, reveals that her concentration on sound and music is deeply rooted in her political and social concerns.

To help unpack the various levels and experiences of listening in Woolf's novels, I shall use the work of the sound theorist and composer Michel Chion, providing a brief introduction here to terms I shall use throughout Part 2. He argues "there are at least three modes of listening, each of which addresses different objects. We shall call them *causal listening, semantic listening,* and *reduced listening*" (*Audio-Vision* 25). Although Chion focuses on the cinema, the material nature of his project – the fact that he is concerned with everyday objects as represented on screen (in addition to non-diegetic music) – is applicable to similar depictions of life in written narratives. (Woolf, of course, underscores such assumptions about realism in the novel, but she consistently concerns herself with the circumstances of daily private and public lives even as she reinvents what constitutes the "novel.") Consequently, I find all three modes at work in her texts, on the narratorial level, on the level of character, and as experienced by the reader's inner audition.[3]

As Chion defines it, "causal listening, the most common, consists of listening to a sound in order to gather information about its cause (or source). When the cause is visible, sound can provide supplementary information about it ... When we cannot see the sound's cause, sound can constitute our principal source of information about it" (*Audio-Vision* 25–6). Correspondingly, exploring scenes of hearing in Woolf's novels often uncovers a search for sources. Chion identifies semantic listening as "that which refers to a code of a language to interpret a message: spoken language, of course, as well as Morse and other such codes. This mode of listening, which functions in an extremely complex way, has been the object of linguistic research and has been the most widely studied" (28). One of the most fruitful findings of Part 2 is the repeated disruption of this mode in Woolf's novels. Lastly, from Pierre Schaeffer's lexicon, the French composer and developer of *musique concrète*, Chion determines a third mode of listening: "Schaeffer gave the name *reduced listening* to the listening mode that focuses on the traits of the sound itself, independent of its cause and of its meaning. Reduced listening takes the sound – verbal, played on an instrument, noises, or whatever – as itself the object to be observed instead of as a vehicle for something else" (*Audio-Vision* 29). Perhaps the most innovative use of sound in Woolf's novels corresponds to this type of audition – something Melba Cuddy-Keane has explored from a different angle with the concept of sonicity (see Introduction). This layer of hearing is particularly prevalent in the novels, and, ultimately, another of Woolf's groundbreaking components as a modernist experimentalist.[4] In addition to intermingled and overlapping ties among the three modes of listening, the causal has a particular relationship to the third type that focuses on sound for its own sake. In turn, this link often facilitates the disruption of the meaning-making process. In fact, the reduced level is consistently foregrounded in her works, even in *The Voyage Out*; I argue that this is part of her continuing project to disclose the intersection of gender and knowledge.

But some musical theorists have been dissatisfied with Schaeffer's terms, upon which Chion relies heavily, particularly those of reduced listening and *l'objet sonore* (or "sound object," the word applied to the sounding body in his exploration of *musique concrète*). Francisco López, a nature recording artist, for example, prefers the term "profound" to the term "reduced" "because the latter connotes simplification" (85). I utilize López's word in Part 2 because it more accurately describes Woolf's deployment of sound. Indeed, the word "profound" illustrates better the expansiveness and significance she often enacts through this type of listening. Moreover, according to López, "the richness of this sound matter in nature [as well as in urban space, one should add where Woolf is concerned] is astonishing, but to appreciate it in depth we have to face the challenge of profound listening. We have to shift the focus of our attention and understanding from representation to being" (86). I believe Woolf would agree.

Lastly, out of these three modes of listening emerges another practice in regard to sonority, one that sequesters sound from its source: the acousmatic circumstance, which is the other side of Schaeffer's argument concerning the effect of the radio (and recording technologies) on the modern ear. As Chion summarizes,

> Schaeffer emphasized how acousmatic listening, which we shall define further on as a situation wherein one hears the sound without seeing its cause, can modify our listening. Acousmatic sound draws our attention to sound traits normally hidden from us by the simultaneous sight of the causes – hidden because this sight reinforces the perception of certain elements of the sound and obscures others. The acousmatic truly allows sound to reveal itself in all its dimensions. (*Audio-Vision* 32)

The three modes of listening I have discussed are not mutually exclusive – they often overlap and commingle, as the following analysis will demonstrate. Nonetheless, Woolf's incorporation of these three modes reveals a particular interest on her part in the bodiless voice, something several critics have noted about the gramophone in *Between the Acts*.[5] Indeed, from *Jacob's Room* (1922) onward, the disembodied voice is a key trope that enables Woolf to unpack the power-knowledge relationships of her society.

In addition, Woolf's employment of what Chion terms the *acousmêtre* – "when the acousmatic presence is a voice, and especially when the voice has not yet been visualized" (*The Voice* 21) – focuses the reader's attention not only on what (or who) might be responsible for particular utterances (the bodiless voice of Evans in *Mrs. Dalloway*, for example) but also on what or who might be responsible for the related events in the social sphere. As Chion explicates, the *acousmêtre* has four specific attributes: "the ability to be everywhere, to see all, to know all, and to have complete power. In other words: ubiquity, panopticism, omniscience, and omnipotence" (*The Voice* 24). Woolf not only intuited such capacities in her depictions of disembodied voices, but also worked to dislodge or reconfigure them to imagine new possibilities for such investments in authority. She often de-acousmatizes them, thereby "dooming the *acousmêtre* to the fate of ordinary mortals" (Chion, *The Voice* 27). Time and again, what seems to be an insubstantial voice of authority is revealed to have a sounding body, a material existence. Counter to early twentieth-century trends concerning sonic purity (see Part 1) and what Jonathan Sterne argues is a bias in favour of fidelity at the heart of sound reproduction technology (which I shall discuss in more detail in chapter 4), Woolf's deployment of sonority, often in musical form, and its reception, dislodges its presumed transcendence, grounding it in bodies but also in technologies.

I. Materialized Sonics and Listening Subjects in *The Voyage Out*

In *The Voyage Out*, as expected, both the narrator and the characters employ the first two more common modes of listening: causal and semantic. Perhaps surprisingly, however, individual characters also practise profound listening – audition for the sake of sound. Moreover, music is not the only aurality to elicit such auscultation, as one might suppose in this, albeit atypical, female bildungsroman whose protagonist is a pianist. The Clarissa Dalloway in this novel (Woolf's first incarnation of her) has a keen sense of aurality, for example; indeed, she responds to the sonicity of words when she explains that she enjoys the *sound* of Greek rather than its meaning:

"I own," she said, "that I shall never forget the Antigone. I saw it at Cambridge years ago, and it's haunted me ever since. Don't you think it's quite the most modern thing you ever saw?" she asked Ridley [...] "I don't know a word of Greek, but I could listen to it for ever – " (*VO* 44)

At this point, insufferable Mr Pepper recites in Greek the second chorus from *Antigone*, an apposite intertext to *The Voyage Out* as it chronicles a woman's resistance to social and political oppression that ends in her death. (Woolf will refer to *Antigone* again in *The Years* in the "1907" chapter, which I shall discuss in Part 3.) After the recitation, Clarissa laments, "'I'd give ten years of my life to know Greek'" (*VO* 44). Understanding the language is a loaded issue for Woolf, intimately tied to gender, class, and the exclusionary system of early twentieth-century education, as she argues in her essay "On Not Knowing Greek." The scene demonstrates Mr Pepper's gendered privilege, as well as Mrs Dalloway's exclusion from such advantage.[6] In the process, however, Clarissa learns to listen differently, a moment of profound audition to the sounds of language rather than their semantic content.

Yet the other characters in *The Voyage Out* (and perhaps the reader too) think Clarissa is rather odd for her mode of listening. Helen comments to Rachel that Clarissa does not understand what is said to her:

"She was quite nice, but a thimble-pated creature," Helen continued. "I never heard such nonsense! Chitter-chatter-chitter-chatter – fish and the Greek alphabet – never listened to a word anyone said – chock-full of idiotic theories about the way to bring up children – I'd far rather talk to him any day. He was pompous, but he did at least understand what was said to him." (*VO* 88)

These observations from Helen come directly after Rachel explains that Richard Dalloway has kissed her (inappropriately) and Rachel's realization that the women in Piccadilly are sex-trade workers. Ominous sexual overtones communicated through the technique of juxtaposition suggest several uncommonly linked social mechanisms: the education system, art and the canon, the marriage market, and colonialism – all of which combine to imply that the Dalloways' social status perpetuates a system of authoritarianism on the world stage. As Kathy Phillips has argued, Woolf's comminglings often illuminate the ideological workings of Empire, pointing to "consistent social criticism" in which "domestic details seem to comment indirectly, through implied metaphor, on issues of world-wide scope" (xiii). Here, such imbalances are shown to function within marriages and among class distinctions. Sound for its own sake – Clarissa's desire to listen to Greek – is used as social critique. Nonetheless, while Clarissa seems to listen differently from the others, she does so selectively, leaving the impression that her arrogance overwhelms her respect for and experience of being othered.

But unlike Clarissa, Rachel is repeatedly described as being content in the position of listener, even though she, too, sometimes seems to struggle to understand what is being said. During a scene at a church in Santa Marina, Rachel drifts into profound listening, not just because she is musical, but because she does not discern significant meaning from the religious sermon. The scene is auscultated by the third-person narrator first, but then more directly from Rachel's perspective:

> From their faces it seemed that for the most part they made no effort at all, and, recumbent as it were, accepted the ideas that the words gave as representing goodness […].
>
> Whatever the reason might be, for the first time in her life, instead of slipping at once into some curious pleasant cloud of emotion, too familiar to be considered, Rachel listened critically to what was being said. By the time they had swung in an irregular way from prayer to psalm, from psalm to history, from history to poetry, and Mr Bax was giving out his text, she was in a state of acute discomfort. Such discomfort she felt when forced to sit through an unsatisfactory piece of music badly played. (*VO* 264)

The passage continues to describe the sound of poorly performed music in which the "stress" is "put on the wrong places" (ibid.). The experience of listening semantically, apparently for the first time in her life, produces discomfort for Rachel. But the narrative compares Rachel's experience of the words as equivalent to the non-verbal sound of music rather than discussing the religious or philosophical concepts being espoused with which Rachel might have issues. The analogy speaks to Rachel's "ear," certainly, and to her receptiveness as being thoroughly imbued with her musical sensibility. She not only hears words as music but understands her discomfort with their meanings as sonorous, as though it were the same as listening to a "piece of music badly played." Woolf is making an indirect argument, I would suggest, about the significance of critical alternatives to inactive, and complacent, audience reception.

Yet, at other times, the issue of Rachel's capacity to listen is fore-grounded in particularly negative terms in the novel. Her fiancé, Ter-ence, notices when she is *not* listening, for example, especially when she plays the piano; repeatedly, he interrupts her to realign her focus in chapter 22, preferring that she write responses to their engage-ment congratulations. Her resistance to his expectation is to practise both causal and profound listening as opposed to semantic, all the while performing her music. The novel documents that there is an, albeit fleeting, freedom in such listening techniques for Rachel, and an anonymity she gains by being ignored – the kernel of Woolf's sub-sequent musical figure, "Anon," and a marker of the argument for necessary isolation that will occur in *A Room of One's Own*. Rachel comments, for instance, during a discussion with Terence about his novel of silence that "'a girl is more lonely than a boy. No one cares in the least what she does. Nothing's expected of her. Unless one's very pretty people don't listen to what you say … And that is what I like'" (*VO* 248).

After she becomes ill, however, things change. Indeed, by uncover-ing the novel's utilization of the modes of listening, one finds that the consequences for asymmetrical aural practices – Barthes's "old modes of listening: those of the believer, the disciple, and the patient" (Barthes 259) – are dire. The scene at the start of her sickness illuminates the process. Terence reads aloud to her from John Milton's masque, *Comus*, originally titled *A Mask presented at Ludlow Castle, 1634: on Michelmas night, before the Rt Hon. Iohn Earl of Bridgewater, Viscount Brackly, Lord President of Wales, and one of His Majesties most honourable privie coun-cil*. The lengthy title implies the monarchical politics typically involved in court masques of the Caroline period (1625–49). Historically full of spectacle, music, and entertainment to laud the King and Queen, the work by the Puritan Milton takes a more critical tack towards court culture. His plot, about the thwarted rape of a quite outspoken and boldly resistant Lady, ends with the help of a water nymph, Sabrina, who frees the Lady who has been magically confined to a chair – a moral about female chastity rather than lionizing the King. Woolf crit-ics usually, and understandably, maintain that this allusion evokes the themes of female sexuality and violence embedded in both texts. Molly Hite argues, "When Rachel moves from *Comus* to coma, she thus brings together a group of ideas not only about male sexual conquest, but also about female suicide. And in this context chastity becomes an issue to Rachel herself" (540). But conversely, Lisa Low observes that this read-ing misjudges Milton's resilient heroine:

> *Comus* does not represent the patriarchal plot feminist critics have claimed. Rather, Woolf must go as far back as Milton's *Comus* ... to find an alternative in which the heroine is made mighty ... Woolf turned to *Comus*, in other words, because she found Miltonic chastity – the Lady's enormous self-confidence, her steely ability to withstand sexual interference – both psychologically therapeutic and politically prescriptive. (255)

Rachel's resistance to the marriage script through aurality and the deployment of the poem's request to listen at this poignant moment in Woolf's text lends support to Low's claims. But Woolf's choice of a masque, for her most overtly musical protagonist, is also significant: it is a precursor to early opera that thoroughly incorporates music in and around its poetic text, more akin to the performative, intermedial art form of the pageant that will be incorporated into *Between the Acts* than a strictly literary reference.[7]

Indeed, the words Woolf chooses to cite directly are taken from the "song" that the Attendant Spirit (originally played by Henry Lawes, who composed the music for the masque) sings to persuade Sabrina to help the Lady. The textual content is infused with aurality as the Spirit beckons to Sabrina to listen:

> Sabrina fair,
>   Listen where thou art sitting
> Under the glassy, cool, translucent wave,
>   In twisted braids of lilies knitting
> The loose train of thy amber dropping hair,
> Listen for dear honour's sake,
>   Goddess of the silver lake,
>   Listen and save! (*VO* 381)

By this point in the novel, Rachel has difficulty performing the role that she has been assigned. The strain of being the receiver of others' thoughts, at the expense of profound attentive hearing (a skill that is the result of her musical training, I would propose), seems to be one of the factors that lead her away from life. After hearing the first part of the poem that introduces the nymph, Rachel can no longer listen semantically because of her illness:

> The words, in spite of what Terence had said, seemed to be laden with meaning, and perhaps it was for this reason that it was painful to listen to

them; they sounded strange; they meant different things from what they usually meant. Rachel at any rate could not keep her attention fixed upon them, but went off upon curious trains of thought suggested by words such as "curb" and "Locrine" and "Brute," which brought unpleasant sights before her eyes, independently of their meaning. (*VO* 380–1)

As Septimus Warren Smith will experience after her, Rachel can no longer trust what she hears. The connections between signifiers and what they signify are distorted. And the solace she used to find in her capacity to appreciate even the sound of words – such as "Locrine" – has turned sinister.

Importantly, Terence is beginning, at this point, to understand the audition of language in similar terms to Rachel. He "was reading Milton aloud, because he said the words of Milton had substance and shape, so that it was not necessary to understand what he was saying; one could merely listen to his words; one could almost handle them" (*VO* 380). He begins to appreciate profound listening to language, similar to Clarissa, albeit for different reasons and with contrary connotations of education and empire. (Conceivably, Terence is familiar with *Comus* from his education – and all that it implies in terms of gender, class, and nation – not exactly light reading, despite his comments.) Indeed, throughout the chapter, the function of receiving sound gradually passes to Terence. As Rachel drifts deeper and deeper into her illness, Terence begins to feel the burden of listening that has been incumbent upon Rachel: "the strain of listening, and the effort of making practical arrangements and seeing that things worked smoothly, absorbed all Terence's power. Involved in this long dreary nightmare, he did not attempt to think what it amounted to" (*VO* 390). As the tension and anxiety of Rachel's last days take hold of him, Terence becomes more and more depleted.

In the final pages of this penultimate chapter, Rachel has one last moment of connection with Terence: she simply says, "'Hullo, Terence'" (*VO* 411). His relief is palpable, but in the interim he has learned not to fill the silence with talk. Instead, he has discovered how to listen, although it is clearly too late:

An immense feeling of peace came over Terence, so that he had no wish to move or to speak. The terrible torture and unreality of the last days were over, and he had come out now into perfect certainty and peace. His mind began to work naturally again and with great ease. The longer he sat there the more *profoundly* was he conscious of the peace invading every corner of his soul. Once he held his breath and *listened acutely*; she was still breathing; he went on thinking for some time; they seemed to be thinking together; he seemed to be Rachel as well as himself; and then he *listened again*; no, she had ceased to breathe. [...] They had now what they had always wanted to have, the union which had been impossible while they lived. (*VO* 412; my emphasis)

As my italics suggest, "profoundly" seems an especially apposite adjective to describe the process, albeit admittedly coincidental, as the stakes are high in this scene: these are Rachel's last gasps before passing away. When Terence finally slips into the mode of attentive, profound audition, listening for the quality of her breath rather than her words, he experiences the union (even in terms of subjectivity) which seemed unattainable under their previous social conditions. But for Woolf, the answer, even in this first novel, is not to replace one method of speaking/listening with another, but to dislodge the oppositional nature of such processes. Unsure whether or not he is talking aloud – an important strategy at this point, as he usually almost lectures with certainty and authority – he has finally learned to listen. The semantic meaning of the words he may or may not be voicing is much less important than the experience of this moment produced by profound listening. After he hears her last breath, they both seem to experience "perfect happiness" (ibid.). Of course, it is no accident on Woolf's part that Rachel will not be alive to enjoy this potential matrimonial contentment. Ultimately, marriage seems to go hand-in-hand with death for the musical protagonist of Woolf's first novel.

II. Involuntary, Yet Profound, Listening in *Night and Day*

In *Night and Day* (1919) courtship rituals within the patriarchal marriage market are interrogated similarly to *The Voyage Out*, and also through sound, perhaps because this novel is equally concerned to critique the English social hierarchy and its consequences for women. *Night and Day* is the story of Katharine Hilbery and her eventual marriage. First engaged to William Rodney, she realizes that a relationship based on social conventions and expectations will not satisfy her. Instead, she discovers that Ralph Denham also desires a marriage based on mutual trust and respect. All ends tidily in that William finds a more suitable match in Katharine's musical cousin, Cassandra Otway, and Mary Datchet, Ralph's potential partner, resolutely commits herself to her feminist work in the city. Perhaps Woolf's most thematically and formally conservative novel, it is, nevertheless, concerned to question the strictures of social conventions.

One instance in which sound intersects with societal expectations is brought to the fore with the technological device that separates the body from the voice to isolate sound in new ways: the telephone, which became a relatively common apparatus in upper-class residences in London from 1912 onward.[8] The exact date for the setting of the novel is ambiguous, but it is prior to 1914.[9] Chapter 24 (of 34), in which Katharine answers three telephone calls, from Mary Datchet, William Rodney, and lastly, Ralph Denham, is a pivotal one in the novel. By the end of it, Katharine will have escaped an unwanted union with the rather vapid William that has been imposed upon her by family obligations. Woolf's rendering of Katharine's reception of the calls to her home illuminates what Sterne would call the plasticity of sound media, of which a distinguishing characteristic is the "malleability of sound itself and the malleability of practices of hearing and acoustic space" (182). Woolf's depiction of the acousmatic circumstance created by telephony reveals the historical moments prior to its socio-cultural crystallization so that "it is the mutability as opposed to the eventuality of form that is at stake" (Sterne 182). Each time someone calls, for example, the "telephone-bell" is used to describe the directive, rather than just the word telephone, suggesting that the sound it makes is still distinguished in the Edwardian/Georgian mind from the actual mechanism of communication. The ring of it is also particularized by Woolf: "the sharp call of the telephone-bell still echoed in her ear, and her body and mind were in a state of tension, as if, at any moment, she might hear another summons of greater interest to her than the whole of the nineteenth century" (*ND* 323–4)

As I have shown elsewhere,[10] when Katharine answers Ralph's call (the only one to which the reader is privy), she ponders the nature of how people communicate, acknowledging that this relatively newly accessible technological device plays a part in *how* she hears. What does the absence of the body attached to the voice, Katharine contemplates, do to the transmission and reception of sound? The occasion is another instance in which a character listens profoundly, not for the content of the *acousmêtre*, but for it sonicity. In addition, Woolf describes the particularities of the physical environment around the phone that are shown to affect the reception of the voice on the other end:

> The alcove on the stairs, in which the telephone was placed, was screened for privacy by a curtain of purple velvet. It was a pocket for superfluous

> possessions, such as exist in most houses which harbour the wreckage of
> three generations. [...] The thread of sound, issuing from the telephone,
> was always coloured by the surroundings which received it, so it seemed
> to Katharine. Whose voice was now going to combine with them, or to
> strike a discord? (*ND* 324–5)

The Victorian period is encased in this sequestered, telephonic recess,
metaphorically indicating the weight of obligations under which Katharine has been suffering throughout the novel. Yet, into this crevasse
seeps the, as yet, unsolidified concepts of what this new sound medium
portends, as though it enables some disruption of Katharine's matrimonial fate. And indeed it does, because the voice is Ralph's asking for
a meeting at Kew Gardens. In positive terms, then, the scene implies a
crucial question: what might a subject be capable of if he or she were
not attached to a physical (and gendered) body? As Katharine ponders,
"the unfamiliar voice now asked for Miss Hilbery. Out of all the wel-
ter of voices which crowd round the far end of the telephone, out of
the enormous range of possibilities, whose voice, what possibility, was
this?" (*ND* 325).

But as John Picker has shown, a gendered understanding of the act of
listening pervades much of the discourse concerning sound and noise
in late nineteenth- and early twentieth-century London. In reference to
the hated barrel organs of street musicians, Picker suggests part of the
consternation of male Victorian elites was perpetuated by the perception that the hearer had no control over his aural faculty: "The 'organ-
grinding nuisance' in part appeared a threat to professional identity
because it violated 'the terms of human physicality' and the 'sense of
social and material order.' Barrel organs preyed on their middle-class
victims through the involuntary faculty of hearing" (65). The femi-
nized circumstances of not being able to close one's ears as one would
one's eyes foments much of the vitriol levelled at street musicians. In
the scene described above, Woolf reveals how very vulnerable any listener is on the receiving end of the telephone. Indeed, in *Night and Day*
Ralph's call is shown to encroach upon Katharine's domestic sphere in
intimidating ways. When he calls her, Katharine feels "more than the
usual sense of being impinged upon the point of a bayonet" (*ND* 325).
The military association is not incidental, for the brief scene is quickly
followed by references to colonial struggles: Katharine "dropped the
machine, and looked fixedly at the print of the great-uncle who had not
ceased to gaze, with an air of amiable authority, into a world which, as

yet, beheld no symptoms of the Indian Mutiny" (ibid.). Nevertheless, Woolf also demonstrates that the stakes in the domestic sphere are different for women than they are for men. In fact, Ralph's phone call is explicitly not by invitation and Katharine is acutely aware of the fact that this device leaves her vulnerable to intrusion in new ways, despite the privacy promised by the curtains.

The description of Katharine's aural experience also accentuates the acousmatic circumstance of telephony. When Ralph asks Katharine if Saturday will work for a meeting, she hears his voice, "gently swinging against the wall, within the black tube" (*ND* 325):

> She watched the oscillation of the tube, and at the same moment became conscious of the individuality of the house in which she stood; she heard the soft domestic sounds of regular existence upon staircases and floors above her head, and movements through the wall in the house next door. (*ND* 325)

This scene of profound listening – the phone triggers thoughts about the sonics inside and outside of Katharine's home – exhibits a new conception of aurality produced by the telephone. As Picker demonstrates in his fascinating chapter on George Eliot's *Daniel Deronda* (published in 1876, the same year Bell patented the invention), Eliot's prescient understanding of "'separateness with communication'" is an idea that is inspired by the telephone; it "can be considered an acoustic process, a distillation of the essence of sympathetic vibration" (Picker 99). The simultaneous intimacy and distance of Ralph's voice pervades Katharine's reception of it. Moreover, the swinging tube, almost magically, captures the sound of a voice and turns it into a physical, separated sound object (albeit with sleight-of-hand, as the dangling receiver is the trumpeted body that only enables the reception of the sound). As Chion explains in his book *Sound: An Acoulogical Treatise* (2016), "radio, telephone, and recording systemized the acousmatic situation and provided it with a new meaning by dint of insinuating it automatically and mechanically" (loc. 2959). Schaeffer's twined concepts of the *acousmêtre* and *l'objet sonore* are here revealed in Woolf's novel of 1919, therefore, some time before Schaeffer started formulating his ideas while he was working for Radiodiffusion Française in the late 1930s.

In addition, the acousmatic circumstances triggered by the telephone ricochet in the content that follows, for Katharine is haunted by the ubiquity, panopticism, and omniscience of acousmatic voices described subsequently. Running an errand for her mother, she brings a letter to mail that she has written inviting Cassandra to stay with her, although she thinks better of sending it when the time comes to slip it in the post-box:

> The longer she held the letter in her hand, however, the more persistently certain questions pressed upon her, as if from a collection of voices in the air. These invisible people wished to be informed whether she was engaged to William Rodney, or was the engagement broken off? Was it right, they asked, to invite Cassandra for a visit, and was William Rodney in love with her, or likely to fall in love? Then the questioners paused for a moment, and resumed as if another side of the problem had just come to their notice. What did Ralph Denham mean by what he said to you last night? Do you consider that he is in love with you? Is it right to consent to a solitary walk with him, and what advice are you going to give him about his future? [...]
>
> "Good Heavens!" Katharine exclaimed, after listening to all these remarks, "I suppose I ought to make up my mind." (*ND* 327)

When Katharine returns home to host tea with William, these insistent ancestors materialize as her guests: William's American aunt, Mrs Vermont Bankes; Mr Augustus Pelham – "the diarist" who "liked a calm atmosphere in which to tell his stories" (*ND* 331); her mother; and her intended. The pervasiveness and authoritarian capacity of the *acousmêtre* is foregrounded: "The voices of the invisible questioners were reinforced by the scene round the table, and sounded with a tremendous self-confidence, as if they had behind them the common sense of twenty generations, together with the immediate approval of Mr Augustus Pelham, Mrs Vermont Bankes, William Rodney, and possibly, Mrs Hilbery herself" (*ND* 332). Woolf elaborates this pinnacle moment in Katharine's life by infusing the weight of Victorian, patriarchal obligations with the power of the acousmatic circumstance, activated by the transience of telephony. Notably, Katharine is listening semantically to these voices in the air, as they are characterized, even though they are only in her head. The chapter demonstrates, however indirectly, that the difference between possibility and subjection in terms of the *acousmêtre* is just as much about *how* one listens (profoundly when triggered by the telephone and Ralph's voice, semantically when heeding her overburdened conscience) as it is about to whom one listens.

III. International Acousmatics: War and Its Veterans
in *Jacob's Room* and *Mrs. Dalloway*

In *Jacob's Room* the critique of the marriage plot that has been the focus of the first two novels is fundamentally disrupted: the attention shifts to the consequences of war on social relations in the private sphere. Significantly, with the excision of a central male-female courtship narrative comes a change in the function of listening in the novel. Indeed, the text demonstrates that war happens because people are not concerned to listen to each other. Simultaneously, as Todd Avery has discussed in relation to Bloomsbury's various involvements with the British Broadcasting Company (later Corporation), "the ontological fact of radio's existence brought into being a new kind of audience, the listener, whose emergence coincided with the moment of modernism's heyday in the 1920s and 1930s" (8). More specifically, broadcasting began in the US in 1920 and in Britain in 1922, Pamela Caughie documents, primarily "as a means of connecting dispersed populations and isolated individuals to one another and to the cultural life of the nation ... Building on the technology of the telephone and telegraphy, wireless broadcasting was less a technological revolution, like the phonograph, than a social revolution. A modern mass public dates from the inception of broadcasting" ("Virginia Woolf: Radio, Gramophone, Broadcasting" 337, 338). Woolf herself noticed the effect of the wireless on everyday life, Caughie notes, or, I would add, at least chronicles George Bernard Shaw's experience of it, detailing how mass communication is concurrently both private/personal and public/collective. Writing an account of "the Shaws" in her diary as a first-person recollection in George Bernard's voice, Woolf dramatizes what he says about his own speech-making abilities for radio and his listening practices as a music critic: "The great pleasure of the Broadcasting to me is that I can sit at home & conduct The Meistersinger myself. I sit with the book of the score & conduct & I'm furious when they don't follow me. That way one finds how often the singers make howlers – come in a bar early or late. Beecham – (here he sang a piece of the Magic Flute) turned *that* – which is solemn, slow, processionly[?] – into a hornpipe" (*D4*: 107). In what looks to be an oversight, Caughie cites only the first sentence and seems to attribute these words to Woolf herself, omitting that they are a ventriloquized version of Shaw, but her point still remains that Woolf, along with other readers of *The Listener* (the BBC's magazine), was coming to a new understanding of audition "as an *active* form of listening;

highly attentive to technique; sensitive to nuances of voice; selective in tuning in certain kinds of programmes and tuning out distractions, including the sound of the technology itself" (Caughie, "Virginia Woolf: Radio, Gramophone, Broadcasting" 338).

Jacob's Room, published in 1922, reflects these social transformations in its expanded reach of sound. Although the wireless is evoked, its actual capabilities are portrayed ambiguously in the novel, yet the sheer distance it travels and the impossible reception of it by various Londoners is striking, and more wide-ranging than the telephone episode in *Night and Day*. In addition, the narrator functions as an overarching auscultator, but not, as is often the case in the earlier novels, as only a veil for the various thoughts and experiences of the main characters. Instead, this ironically distanced voice, occasionally in the first person, auscultates city space and the sounds of war somewhat like an *acousmêtre* herself whether or not a character reflects on such sonorities. In Woolf's first extended experimental narrative, the narratorial voice searches for new approaches to hearing.

In the penultimate chapter, for example, the narrator updates the reader on Jacob's status (and his effect on those who love him) after returning from Greece: Bonamy is jealous over Jacob's affection for the woman he met on his journey, Sandra Wentworth; Clara Durrant is pointedly not this woman; Florinda is pregnant by another man; Fanny Elmer is still in love with Jacob but he is clearly not thinking about her; and his mother, Betty Flanders, can hear the guns of war across the English Channel, as discussed in chapter 1. Just before the scene with Betty, Jacob sits "under the plane tree" in Hyde Park; at the same time, in another part of the city, a "procession with its banners passed down Whitehall" (*JR* 239, 241), a street that is the bastion of British government, military defence, and the monarchy. The parade enables the narrator to generalize the experiences of seeing and hearing but then also shift to the noisy, pulsating traffic that "spun to a smooth continuous uproar; swerving round the curve of Cockspur Street; and sweeping past Government offices and equestrian statues down Whitehall to the prickly spires, the tethered grey fleet of masonry, and the large white clock of Westminster" (*JR* 240) – a description that foretells similar, oft-cited moments in *Mrs. Dalloway*.

Thus, the passage begins by identifying an earcon very familiar to Londoners. But then it quickly moves to an anonymous voice acousmatized by the new technology of the wireless:

Five strokes Big Ben intoned; Nelson received the salute. The wires of the Admiralty shivered with some far-away communication. A voice kept remarking that Prime Ministers and Viceroys spoke in the Reichstag; entered Lahore; said that the Emperor traveled; in Milan they rioted; said there were rumours in Vienna; said that the Ambassador at Constantinople had audience with the Sultan; the fleet was at Gibraltar. The voice continued, imprinting on the faces of the clerks in Whitehall (Timothy Durrant was one of them) something of its own inexorable gravity, as they listened, deciphered, wrote down. (*JR* 240)

Katharine's ancestral voices have turned even more malefic and ubiquitous. Here, a bodiless, ominous radio communication, introduced by the sonority of Big Ben (connoting official timekeeping and the order invoked by the parliament buildings), details the international beginnings of the large-scale conflict that will become the First World War. As Michael Whitworth has argued, "the anonymity of the voice stands in stark contrast to the physical frailty of the politicians" (163). Understandably, Whitworth interprets the inscrutability of these voices in *Jacob's Room* as connoting patriarchal authority: "this paragraph anticipates the grey car scene in *Mrs. Dalloway*, where the 'greatness' of the figure in the car is a function of its invisibility. The figure is powerful exactly because it cannot be identified as Queen, Prime Minister, or Prince of Wales. The 'voice' speaks with the authority of the marble statesman [of Whitehall], but cannot be identified with any named individual" (ibid.). Although he does not use the word, his categorization of the voice's authoritarianism suggests the *acousmêtre*. Indeed, Woolf's description again denotes its four "powers." The clerks are busy "deciphering" the voice's catalogue of events; global imperial ambitions are articulated: "Papers accumulated, inscribed with the utterances of Kaisers, the statistics of ricefields, the growling of hundreds of workpeople, plotting sedition in back streets, or gathering in the Calcutta bazaars, or mustering their forces in the uplands of Albania, where the hills are sand-coloured, and bones lie unburied" (*JR* 240). But as is customary with Woolf, technology is depicted both positively and negatively. The social and ethical awareness of the people who wield such means determines its munificence or malevolence.

But how one listens to the acousmatic circumstance is also again at issue. All three of Chion's types are deployed in the segment, but in new ways that largely resist both causal and semantic listening. The strokes of Big Ben are allocated causally, as is the Admiralty on the other end of the wires of "some far-away communication." Yet, causative attribution is disrupted as the ability to hear such distant sounds is foregrounded. An even more generalized "voice" repetitively verbalizes statements about a variety of world events (soliciting semantic listening) but does not make the connections between them (therefore resisting it at the same time). The voice's connection to humanity is dislodged as it is at least once removed from the corporeal, emitted from a machine rather than a human being. Later it reverberates "in the square quiet room with heavy tables, where one elderly man made notes on the margin of type-written sheets" (*JR* 240). Woolf is concerned to document such ontologically ambiguous circumstances in her narrative. The voice's body remains undesignated, or at least diffused across the globe. The result is vocal anonymity, and, ultimately, capriciousness.

Yet, Woolf often employs acousmatics to foreground the issue of social responsibility. It is no accident that links are made among Big Ben; the Admiralty; Prime Ministers, Viceroys, Emperors, Ambassadors, Sultans, Kaisers, and workpeople; military deployments; riots; geographical locations across the world; the British naval stronghold of Gibraltar; and lastly, in a return to London, the clerks in Whitehall (personalized through Jacob's friend Timothy Durrant). The circuit returns back to London to reveal the connections within such grids, crossing the public spheres of this particular metropolis. As noted, these various situations are sounded by an acousmatic voice spoken "plainly" (*JR* 240) over the wireless. According to Chion, "Schaeffer thought the acousmatic situation could encourage reduced listening, in that it provokes one to separate oneself from causes or effects in favor of consciously attending to sonic textures, masses, and velocities" (*Audio-Vision* 32). In *Jacob's Room*, on the narratorial level, this is often the result of the acousmatic voice. Rather than focusing on the meanings attached to signifiers (the list above), or even on more information about the source of these very significant sonorities, the narrator simply juxtaposes statements. Thus, the deciphering work is left to the reader/listener; the narrative insists upon it. Because acousmatics encourage auditors to practise profound listening, Woolf's narratorial employment of them asks the same of her audience.

A similar situation occurs in the segments that describe an aural version of war on distant shores (as discussed in Part 1). Betty Flanders's search for the source of the sound she hears from across the English

Channel – an acousmatic circumstance described as nocturnal women beating carpets or perhaps "someone moving downstairs? Rebecca with the toothache?" (*JR* 246) – heightens the imperious nature of the booming guns. Showing the risk and potential fear that can be invoked by not knowing the source of a sound (an issue at the forefront of the air raid in *The Years*, to which I shall return), the passage reveals an unsuccessful search for the cause of this strange but startling noise, which Chion suggests is often a component of the acousmatic situation. This shift to causal listening, in the larger context of the novel, is a search for responsibility – not to assign blame, but to involve the reader in the social conditions of the globe. It is profound listening – Woolf's exploration of sound for its own sake materialized here in the metaphor of the nocturnal women – that generates this process.

Big Ben is, almost infamously, sounded in *Mrs. Dalloway* as well, of course. But in addition to the city sounds auscultized by the narrator, there is a crucial character who is an attuned and acute listener in the novel, although he is rarely understood in such terms: Septimus Warren Smith. The shell-shocked First World War veteran provides another striking example of Woolf's capacity to elucidate the intersection of the private and public spheres, and the consequences for the subject when interconnections are ignored. Through Septimus's illness, Woolf explores the limits of condoned modes of social behaviour that govern daily interactions. His experiences, like Katharine's, are both positive and negative. In addition to the fear and panic that eventually induce his suicide, Septimus has the most heightened and perhaps emotionally significant experiences in the novel.

As Hermione Lee has argued, Woolf's portrayal of illness is often revelatory: "in her writing she transforms illness into a language of power and inspiration" (194). But illness can also represent the despair of solitude, largely because of the seclusion created by the breakdown in understanding with other human beings. Septimus's wife, Lucrezia (Rezia), also suffers greatly from her isolation and lack of an interlocutor. Her loneliness is palpable: "I am alone; I am alone! She cried, by the fountain in Regent's Park" (*MD* 22). Lee contends,

> Septimus and Rhoda (in *The Waves*) are imprisoned alone inside their violent feelings of horror at the human race and their inability to communicate. They act out the frightening solipsism of mental illness. There is a ludicrous, awful gap between Septimus' manic inspiration, and the banal unintelligibility of his utterances and scribbles. (Lee 194)

The senses seem to over-stimulate Septimus. He is unable to see or hear the world as others know it; this isolates him. Yet, importantly, for my purposes, more than any other character to this point in the novels (except perhaps Rachel, the musician), he practises profound listening. Indeed, he rarely listens semantically or causally, and when he does, he cannot trust the connection between cause and effect or signifier and signified (also similar to Rachel during her illness).

Woolf demonstrates, nevertheless, that perhaps Septimus's interpretations and experiences are, to a certain extent, simply different from those around him. He does understand and appreciate, for example, the significance of sound and often construes aural experiences musically, creating art out of sonorities usually classified as "noise" or insignificant conversation. When a nursemaid tells Rezia that the aeroplane in the sky is advertising toffee,

> Septimus heard her say "Kay Arr" close to his ear, deeply, softly, like a mellow organ, but with a roughness in her voice like a grasshopper's, which rasped his spine deliciously and sent running up into his brain waves of sound, which, concussing, broke. A marvelous discovery indeed – that the human voice in certain atmospheric conditions (for one must be scientific, above all scientific) can quicken trees into life! (*MD* 20)

Septimus is an astute listener, and here a specific woman's voice is separated from her body in his head, almost like the hanging receiver of Katharine's telephone. Because he is less concerned to assign meaning to the nursemaid's words, he hears their sonicity, exhilarated by the experience of sound waves in his body. The vocality of the utterance carries such "life," and, indeed, seems to have the ability to make inanimate objects sentient through its vibrations. Thus, Woolf physicalizes sound (an issue I shall return to in Part 3), adding density to what is typically dismissed as ephemeral and meaningless aural hallucinations. The employment of sonic tropes of matter suggests that Septimus has access to an aesthetic capacity unacknowledged by the likes of Drs Holmes and Bradshaw – with their ludicrously delimiting cures of porridge and proper Proportion – but akin to Rachel's piano playing.

Correspondingly, Septimus subsequently imagines transforming invisible music into physical substance. As the following extended quotation reveals, his profound listening enables him to come to imperative conclusions about the materiality of what he hears, sees, and feels:

He lay very high, on the back of the world. The earth thrilled beneath him. Red flowers grew through his flesh; their stiff leaves rustled by his head. Music began clanging against the rocks up here. It is a motor horn down in the street, he muttered, but up here it cannoned from rock to rock, divided, met in shocks of sound which rose in smooth columns (that music should be visible was a discovery) and became an anthem, an anthem twined round now by a shepherd boy's piping (That's an old man playing a penny whistle by the public-house, he muttered) which, as the boy stood still, came bubbling from his pipe, and then, as he climbed higher, made its exquisite plaint while the traffic passed beneath. This boy's elegy is played among the traffic, thought Septimus. Now he withdraws up into the snows, and roses hang about him – the thick red roses which grow on my bedroom wall, he reminded himself. The music stopped. He has his penny, he reasoned it out, and has gone on to the next public-house. (*MD* 61–2)

Septimus experiences music – the "old man playing a penny whistle" – in spatial terms as sound waves meet and rise in a sort of dance. The symphony of traffic noise (motor horns) penetrates into his reverie to provide a respite that generates highly imaginative comminglings of sight, space, and sound, even while the trace of death still intrudes upon the Arcadian moment, for the "shepherd boy" plays an elegy. Repeatedly, Woolf attempts to make music visible in the novels; here Septimus confirms such a "discovery." This material realization reorganizes the association between sounds and their sources. If the *acousmêtre* is about sonorities that disrupt sight, the materialization of sound waves adds the corporeal to the ephemeral, but here in a reassembled form. In the process, new possibilities are enabled in the "real" world.

As with Clarissa Dalloway in *The Voyage Out*, Septimus – often thought of as her double in this novel – recognizes the value of Greek more for its melodic sonority than for its propositional content. In the earlier work, Clarissa's capacity to practise profound listening calls attention to a system of education that excludes some and admits others along the lines of gender. Similarly, nondescript acousmatic voices and sounds call attention to the "guns of war" and positions of social authority (Prime Ministers, Emperors, Kaisers, etc.) in *Jacob's Room*. Septimus's experience combines the issues highlighted in the previous novels and adds another layer to them, revealing a lack of comprehension (and a consequent abuse of power) regarding illness and sanity in the medical sciences.

Despite Septimus's condition as a victim of shell-shock, the sounds of birds enable him to make important discoveries. As noted, music is capable of animating objects: wave vibrations "quiver" them into animation, to use a verb from *The Waves*. After commenting that the human voice can "quicken trees into life!" Septimus assures himself he will not go mad. Instead, "he would shut his eyes; he would see no more" (*MD* 20). Closing his eyes leaves him more attuned to the sounds around him:[11]

> The sparrows fluttering, rising, and falling in jagged fountains were part of the pattern; the white and blue, barred with black branches. Sounds made harmonies with premeditations; the spaces between them were as significant as the sounds. A child cried. Rightly far away a horn sounded. All taken together meant the birth of a new religion. (*MD* 20)

As is often the case, sound represents and enacts the linkage between unseen things, and here even seems to do so purposefully, with "premeditations." Notably, the gaps between the sounds are simply part of a system of differences; the absence of sonic resonance still suggests its presence. Because Septimus listens in a profound manner, he hears more than the source or the meaning: he hears the overall pattern the sounds make, an assemblage, in Gilles Deleuze's terms, or a network in Bruno Latour's, as I explore in Part 1.

The sparrows are also capable of *speaking* Greek to Septimus. But again, the pitch of the spoken Greek (its sonicity) is the important component of the language for Woolf. While talking aloud to himself, "in his shabby overcoat, his legs crossed, staring," he has another disturbing revelation:

> Men must not cut down trees. There is a God. (He noted such revelations on the backs of envelopes.) Change the world. No one kills from hatred. Make it known (he wrote it down). He waited. He listened. A sparrow perched on the railing opposite chirped Septimus, Septimus, four or five times over and went on, drawing its notes out to sing freshly and piercingly in Greek words how there is no crime and, joined by another sparrow, they sang in voices prolonged and piercing in Greek words, from trees in the meadow of life beyond a river where the dead walk, how there is no death. (*MD* 22)

The segments I have quoted document the inspirational side of Septimus's experiences. Heightened sonic moments express the vibrancy of existence by combining notions of spirituality with the natural and physical worlds, although both are also notably held in check by the mention of death. Nonetheless, my point is that the disruption of causal and semantic listening enables Septimus to experience such finely tuned moments.

Yet, the disturbance of the two modes of listening most commonly produced in social circumstances also has its negative effects and, indeed, perpetuates Septimus's distance from others. He either feels too much or too little, and the sonic world is significant in both situations. Although the dislodgment of causal and semantic relationships between sounds and the bodies that produce them elicits some of Septimus's most aesthetically rewarding moments, therefore, it also creates his most alarming ones. But the important difference in terms of the threat is the disembodied voice, in addition to the menace of Drs Holmes and Bradshaw. The inability to assign a body to Evans's voice (Evans was an officer killed in the war with whom it is implied Septimus was in love) leads Septimus to imagine he can no longer function in his society.

Previously, Woolf combined the acousmatic voice with technological innovations – such as the telephone (*Night and Day*) and the wireless (*Jacob's Room*) – but in *Mrs. Dalloway*, during the Septimus passages that are inundated with allusions to ancient Greece,[12] she employs a sort of Pythagorean "curtain" to elucidate the voice of Evans. According to Schaeffer, the word *acousmatic* comes from the Greek philosopher most associated with music: Pythagoras. Schaeffer clarifies his definition in *Treatise on Musical Objects*:[13] "*Acousmatic*, the *Larousse* dictionary tells us, is the: '*Name given to the disciples of Pythagoras who, for five years, listened to his teachings while he was hidden behind a curtain, without seeing him, while observing a strict silence.*' Hidden from their eyes, only the voice of their master reached the disciples" (Schaeffer 76–7). The issues at stake for Woolf, however, have everything to do with social responsibility, a rejection of the "old modes of listening" (259) in Barthes's terms. Septimus's experiences in war expose the consequences of blind obedience to a master's voice.

The reader's first introduction to Evans comes directly after the birds speak in Greek to Septimus. In an evoking of the *acousmêtre*, the reader is informed: "Evans was behind the railings!" (*MD* 22). In a subsequent passage a strange death-dream is recounted in which, "before waking, the voices of birds and the sound of wheels chime and chatter in a queer harmony, grow louder and louder, and the sleeper feels himself drawing to the shores of life" (*MD* 62). As Septimus stirs he again witnesses

birds: "up in the sky swallows swooping, swerving, flinging themselves in and out, round and round, yet always with perfect control as
if elastics held them. [...] Beauty was everywhere" (*MD* 62–3). Evans is
subsequently described as a bird, instigated by Rezia's comment "'it is
time'" (*MD* 63):

> The word "time" split its husk; poured its riches over him; and from
> his lips fell like shells, like shavings from a plane, without his making
> them, hard, white, imperishable, words, and flew to attach themselves to
> their places in an ode to Time; an immortal ode to Time. He sang. Evans
> answered from behind the tree. The dead were in Thessaly,[14] Evans sang,
> among the orchids. There they waited till the War was over, and now the
> dead, now Evans himself –
>   "For God's sake don't come!" Septimus cried out. For he could not look
> upon the dead. (Ibid.)

The allusions proliferate, a strategy that encourages distance from the
semantic level of listening. In addition to the ancient Greek ode – a
segment sung by the chorus after an episode that usually comments on
what has been done in a play – the poems of John Keats and T.S. Eliot
are evoked. Overlapping references recall Keats's "Ode on a Grecian
Urn," which ends with the statement "'Beauty is truth, truth beauty,' –
that is all / Ye know on earth, and all ye need to know" (ll. 49–50)
just implied in the previous passage with the comments "all of this
[...] was the truth now; beauty, that was the truth now" (*MD* 62–3).
Similarly, Keats's "Ode to a Nightingale" is also alluded to; that poem
closes with the questions "Was it a vision, or a waking dream? / Fled is
that music: – Do I wake or sleep?" (ll. 79–80). Correspondingly, Septimus is in a liminal state between waking and dreaming. Lastly, Eliot's
violated and "inviolate" nightingale, who sings the "'Jug Jug' to dirty
ears" (l. 103) in *The Waste Land*, is also suggested in the bird/cityscape
commingling.
    Yet, responsibility is key to the passage on the levels of both content
and narrative. As Woolf notes in her essay "On Not Knowing Greek,"
the dramatic chorus supplies

> comment, not action [...] the old men and women who take no active
> part in the drama, the undifferentiated voices who sing like birds in the
> pauses of the wind; who can comment, or sum up, or allow the poet
> to speak himself or supply, by contrast, another side to his conception.
> Always in imaginative literature, where characters speak for themselves

and the author has no part, the need of that voice is making itself felt. (CR1: 29)

The birds (their pauses were noted earlier), Evans, who even becomes a bird, and Septimus's experience of both are the choral voices that comment on the social conditions of post-war London, similar to the chorus sung by the caretaker's children in *The Years*, as discussed in Part 1. But with so much indirection, the question still remains: what are such interspersed utterances suggesting? The literary associations provide a partial answer: the evocations of the nightingale myth connote violence, rape, and the abuse of power (Eliot's association), as much as truth, beauty, and music (Keats's).[15]

Evans seems strangely capable of answering Septimus's cries from "behind the railings!" (*MD* 22), "behind the tree" (*MD* 63), or "singing behind the screen" (*MD* 125). The voices of the dead converse with Septimus more clearly than the living: "A voice spoke from behind the screen. Evans was speaking. The dead were with him" (*MD* 83). Yet Evans's acousmatic circumstances do not lead Septimus to search for the body that is producing the sound or for meaning from the words he speaks. One point of Septimus's role in the novel is to demonstrate the consequences of the lack of responsibility on the national level. In fact, although the reader is told that "a voice spoke from behind the screen," what the voice says is not specified, even despite Septimus's repetition of the phrase, "communication is health; communication is happiness. Communication, he muttered" (*MD* 84). As Evans continues "singing behind the screen" (*MD* 125), Septimus experiences more and more sound: "hearing something new; listening with his hand up [...] Or he was hearing music. Really it was only a barrel organ or some man crying in the street. But 'Lovely!' he used to cry, and the tears would run down his cheeks [...] And he would lie listening until suddenly he would cry that he was falling down, down into the flames!" (*MD* 126). In contrast, Rezia "heard nothing" (ibid.). Septimus seems not to hold to Victorian class assumptions about illness-inducing barrel organs either, as Picker has shown. Instead, he hears the "noise" as lovely music.

But significantly, something changes shortly before Dr Holmes arrives: Evans stops responding. Septimus has lost his interlocutor in reality because of the war; when he is unable to find his imagined apperceptive listener as well, he loses all hope:

As for the visions, the faces, the voices of the dead, where were they? There was a screen in front of him, with black bulrushes and blue swallows.

> Where he had once seen mountains, where he had seen faces, where he
> had seen beauty, there was a screen.
>
> "Evans!" he cried. There was no answer. A mouse had squeaked, or a
> curtain rustled. Those were the voices of the dead. The screen, the coal-
> scuttle, the sideboard remained to him. Let him, then, face the screen the
> coal-scuttle and the sideboard ... but Rezia burst into the room chattering.
> (*MD* 130)

Evans's sonicity is repeatedly described as the voice of the dead, an
ominous reminder of the carnage of war. Although Septimus cries out,
as he has previously, this time "there was no answer." Moments later
Dr Holmes pushes his way into the large Bloomsbury lodging-house –
he "was a powerfully built man" (*MD* 133) – and Septimus, who is
perched on the windowsill, flings himself "vigorously, violently down
on to Mrs. Filmer's area railings" (*MD* 134).

Thus, Woolf utilizes the *acousmêtre*, as she does in *Jacob's Room*, to
mark the lack of responsibility produced by the social and political
situation. In *Mrs. Dalloway*, the voice behind the curtain, reminiscent
of those authoritative Pythagorean lectures, exposes the unbalanced
power-knowledge relations of such positions: its four attributes of
ubiquity, panopticism, omniscience, and omnipotence. But inexora-
bly, the narrative poignantly illustrates when Dr Holmes comments
after Septimus's suicide, "no one was in the least to blame" (*MD* 134).
Woolf's irony is arresting. Subsequently, ethical responsibility is foregrounded even more forthrightly in the employment of the disembodied voice in the novels that follow, the focus of chapter 4.

Chapter Four

Bodies and Voices

We must learn to listen, for listening is acting.

Chion loc. 5063

In *The Audible Past*, Jonathan Sterne argues that theories of acousmatic sound tend to hold a set of assumptions that reveal investments in ahistorical notions of transcendence, ultimately presuming that human experience and the human body are outside history. This creates a number of problems that hinge upon a faulty notion of fidelity. It presumes that face-to-face interaction and bodily presence are the privileged arenas of all communication, which leads to a negative understanding of the seemingly bodiless voice, a "disorienting effect on the senses that are otherwise oriented or grounded in coherent bodily experience" (21). It also presumes that the body is wholly intact, undamaged, and phenomenologically coherent prior to technological separation. And, lastly, these assumptions imply the neutrality of sound-reproduction technologies themselves, as though they are not part of social relationships (21–2). Sterne's historical approach, particularly in his fifth chapter, reveals how this notion of fidelity in the sound/body duality is, indeed, constructed by socio-cultural confluences.

Michel Chion's employment of Pierre Schaeffer's *acousmêtre*, Sterne would argue, does partake in the aforementioned presumptions, but fascinatingly, as I have discussed throughout chapter 3 and shall explore further in chapter 4, Woolf's employment of the bodiless voice rarely does. Although she alludes to its ubiquity and authoritarian character, particularly in the novels that deal more overtly with war (*Jacob's Room* and *Mrs. Dalloway*), she discloses not only that the anonymity and

generalization on which the acousmatic condition relies are key components for the authority it evokes, but also that there are consequences
for this totalizing gesture. Moreover, she is at pains to ask ethical questions about responsibility. One of the ways by which she strengthens
her concern to disclose accountability is by showing how the bodiless
voice *is* actually attached to a body, despite the perception that it might
not be. In addition, technology is revealed, Sterne has shown, to be
socially constructed and not entirely negative as a marker or lament for
a lost bodily presence. For Woolf, technologies are ultimately another
fallible component of our very imperfect human existence, not ahistorical machines that create, outside of socio-cultural dynamics, a "wholly
disorienting modern existence" (Sterne 21).

I. *To the Lighthouse* and Family Acousmatics

In *To the Lighthouse* another particularly astute listener inhabits the text:
Mrs Ramsay. Indeed, after her death is bluntly declared in chapter 3 of
"Time Passes," the action of listening is mentioned only one more time,
in chapter 7 of the same section, perhaps a result of the novel's realigned
focus on Lily Briscoe and visual art in the third section, "The Lighthouse." Lily's refusal to play the same domestic role as Mrs Ramsay –
the consummate auscultator of her family, friends, and especially her
husband – provides the inspirational conclusion to this work, often
understood as a female künstlerroman. Hence, the dinner scene in section 1 of the novel, during which Mrs Ramsay is able to gather everyone to her table to enjoy the delectable *boeuf en daube*, contains the most
references to listening in the text, the majority of which are performed
by Mrs Ramsay, who also has a special capacity for profound listening.

Mrs Ramsay's practice of acute audition usually begins with perceiving sonicity, as opposed to causes or semantics. When she sympa-
thizes with Charles Tansley, for example, despite his pretensions, she
hears the sound of his voice rather than the meaning of his words. The
pitches and tone of his speaking voice tell her more about his personality than what he says:

> She could see how it was from his manner – he wanted to assert himself,
> and so it would always be with him till he got his Professorship or married
> his wife, and so need not be always saying, "I – I – I." For that was what his
> criticism of poor Sir Walter, or perhaps it was Jane Austen, amounted to.

"I – I – I." He was thinking of himself and the impression he was making, as she could tell by the sound of his voice, and his emphasis and uneasiness. (*TL* 143–4)

This once-removed technique of observation, for it is characterized in visual terms also, is described as *not listening*: "At any rate they were off again. Now she need not listen" (*TL* 144). Yet simultaneously, "so she saw them; she heard them" (ibid.). Not listening, therefore, does not describe deafness, but a different kind of hearing – listening for the sake of sound and what it reveals about the material world, not for meaning in the conventional sense. Mrs Ramsay's ability to see/hear past the surface enables her to hold the moment in suspension: "and the whole is held together; for whereas in active life she would be netting and separating one thing from another; she would be saying she liked the Waverley novels or had not read them; she would be urging herself forward; now she said nothing. For the moment she hung suspended" (ibid.). Mrs Ramsay listens causally and profoundly, to delay and transform the semantic level. Such methods promote an understanding of an alternative – and unspoken – discourse below/beside the surface of linguistic communication.

The detailing of filtered sonics is reiterated in the relationship between Mrs and Mr Ramsay. Mrs Ramsay is brought back to the present moment of the conversation around the table by a question from an unassigned "somebody" – "'Ah, but how long do you think it'll last?'" (*TL* 144):

It was as if she had antennae trembling out from her, which, intercepting certain sentences, forced them upon her attention. This was one of them. She scented danger for her husband. A question like that would lead, almost certainly, to something being said which reminded him of his own failure. How long would he be read – he would think at once. (Ibid.)

Here, Mrs Ramsay does enact causal and semantic listening as she prepares to protect her husband, but interestingly, Woolf describes the moment in highly aural terms. In the process of "half listening" (*TY* 215) to the conversation, some important phrases seep through her meditative state. Indeed, the reader experiences a comprehensive representation of hearing during the dinner. To this point in the section, all three modes of listening have been revealed to intersect, but worthy of note is that the profound level is equally, if not more, important.

Moreover, the dinner segment also ends with an acousmatic scene that intermingles all three types of listening. As with Katharine and Septimus, the *acousmêtre* can be positive and negative, revelatory and imposing; in *To the Lighthouse*, the constructive side is emphasized to represent art and life, elements Woolf often calls upon to suggest alternatives to patriarchal institutions and ways of being. Again, the scene begins behind a sort of screen, as I discuss in regard to Septimus. Mrs Ramsay looks out the window, which is opaque and reflective because it is dark outside:

> She looked at the window in which the candle flames burnt brighter now that the panes were black, and looking at that outside the voices came to her very strangely, as if they were voices at a service in a cathedral, for she did not listen to the words. The sudden bursts of laughter and then one voice (Minta's) speaking alone, reminded her of men and boys crying out the Latin words of a service in some Roman Catholic cathedral. She waited. Her husband spoke. He was repeating something, and she knew it was poetry from the rhythm and the ring of exaltation and melancholy in his voice:

> Come out and climb the garden path,
>   Luriana Lurilee.
> The China rose is all abloom and buzzing with the yellow bee. (*TL* 148–9)

The experience of sound takes precedence over semantic content until it lands in poetry, an aurally infused display of language. But her auditory experience continues to foreground a bodiless voice: "The words (she was looking at the window) sounded as if they were floating like flowers on water out there, cut off from them all, as if no one had said them, but they had come into existence of themselves" (*TL* 149). Mrs Ramsay hears the voices as separated from the bodies that produce them so that sound takes on its own agency and "come[s] into existence."

The trigger for such inspiration is poetry, a form of writing Woolf also associates with the commentary of the Greek chorus ("On Not Knowing" *CR*1: 28). Fittingly, these utterances are subsequently described as music:

> She did not know what they meant, but, like music, the words seemed to be spoken by her own voice, outside her self, saying quite easily and

naturally what had been in her mind the whole evening while she said different things. She knew, without looking round, that everyone at the table was listening to the voice saying:

> I wonder if it seems to you
> Luriana, Lurilee

with the same sort of relief and pleasure that she had, as if this were, at last, the natural thing to say, this were their own voice speaking.

   But the voice stopped. She looked round. She made herself get up. (*TL* 150)

This *acousmêtre* reverberates in each individual mind at the same time, as if this "were their own voice speaking" (notably, a simultaneously singular and plural grammatical construction, both private/public and individual/communal). Such simultaneity is highly sonic in nature, omnidirectional and omnipresent, yet experienced internally by those seated around the table. Triggered by the laughter and voices and then Mr Ramsay's recitation of this poem that is pointedly not explicated, semantic and causal listening are alluded to but quickly dislodged. While profound listening enables Woolf to capture a collective onto-logical occurrence, the finale to the dinner scene illustrates what she declares in "A Sketch of the Past": "we are the words; we are the music; we are the thing itself" (*MB* 72). The passage commingles the processes of listening with artistic and ontological realization. Similar to Septi-mus, Mrs Ramsay is capable of hearing acousmatic voices that are dis-tinct from the "reality" others confirm, yet the voices do not lead to the question of her sanity. Nevertheless, also like Septimus, she seems to have an especially musical capacity for audition, turning noises, voices, and ambient sounds into sonorous art.

   But one of the primary differences between Mrs Ramsay's and Sep-timus's aural experiences is that the bodiless voice is de-acousmatized. The *acousmêtre* begins as a singular utterance – which does suggest Mr Ramsay's authoritarian and patriarchal approach to life – but is quickly separated from his body and pluralized (this will also hap-pen on a larger scale in *Between the Acts*). The final moments of the passage, however, detail the grounding of the voice in the body of Mr Carmichael, the poet, who "chant[s]" the final words of the poem and turns to Mrs Ramsay, "as if he did her homage" (*TL* 150). This reconnection of the voice with a body enables the scene to end "with a feeling of relief and gratitude" (ibid.). Subsequently, the tableau "vanish[es] even as [Mrs Ramsay] looked, and then, as she moved and took Minta's arm and left the room, it changed, it shaped itself differently; it had become, she knew, giving one last look at it over her shoulder, already the past" (ibid.). Such aural revelations also reveal, therefore, Woolf's concern to attach a body – the material domain – to charged utterances.

II. The Gender of Listening in *The Waves*

If *To the Lighthouse* documents the simultaneity and interrelation of listening practices from an initially singular point of view (Mrs Ramsay's), *The Waves* chronicles a variety of auditory experiences from multiple perspectives. The novel begins, for example, with the awareness of hearing (as well as the other senses) – the auscultation of birdsong and animals by three characters follows the first italicized interlude. Rhoda imitates the sonorous, blank melodies of the birds – "'I hear a sound,' said Rhoda, 'cheep, chirp; cheep chirp; going up and down'" (*TW* 5) – and, Susan notes, they "'are singing up and down and in and out all round us'" (*TW* 6). In addition, Louis auscultates another sound and rhythm: "'I hear something stamping,' said Louis. 'A great beast's foot is chained. It stamps, and stamps, and stamps'" (*TW* 5). Profound listening, coupled with enunciations signalled by onomatopoeic words, alternates with causal attribution that establishes what makes the sound. Woolf's opening pages of the novel emulate how children might take in their environment through their senses, without much concern for semantic content. The sonicity of the situation helps to enliven the reader's sensory experience as well.

Perceptual processes shift, understandably, more towards semantics as the children grow into adulthood. Indeed, during another pivotal dinner scene, this time in the penultimate segment of the book, the different layers of listening are foregrounded; several of the personalities (Neville, Louis, Rhoda, and Bernard) specifically beckon others to listen, more so than in any other episode (the word itself occurs six times). An echo of Mrs Ramsay's apperceptive practice while the family enjoys the *boeuf en daube*, the reunion supper at Hampton Court gathers all six "characters" together after they have been apart in the previous episode. The various monologues uncover particular – but now familiar – patterns concerning the reception of sound for Woolf. Notably, the gathering begins with a description of profound listening, the sonority of Bernard's voice, which establishes his middle age:

> "Hampton Court," said Bernard. [...] "The tone of my voice as I say 'Hampton Court' proves that I am middle-aged. Ten years, fifteen years ago, I should have said 'Hampton Court?' with interrogation – what will it be like? Will there be lakes, mazes? Or with anticipation, What is going to happen to me here? Whom shall I meet? Now, Hampton Court – Hampton Court – the words beat a gong in the space which I have so laboriously cleared with half a dozen telephone messages and post cards, give off ring after ring of sound, booming, sonorous. (*TW* 168)

Bernard's keen awareness of his own aurality becomes significant again in his final soliloquy when he experiences silence instead of an echo of his own voice; he ponders silence in this supper segment also. During the supper, however, as with Mrs Ramsay's capacity to auscultate those around the table, the *sonicity* of Bernard's voice produces more information about his life experiences than the words that "beat a gong in the space" cleared for daily interactions. Woolf resurrects the day-to-day toil of the cityscape by suggesting that verbal communication can sound similar to Big Ben's leaden circles. All of these associations demonstrate heightened listening that disrupts both the causal and semantic levels of attribution. Ultimately, throughout the section, Bernard practises apperceptive listening, in Bakhtin's sense, as interested in receiving sound as much as he is in making it.

Neville, on the other hand, requires others to listen to him. In contrast, his method of social interaction is not dialogic:

> "There is always somebody, when we come together, and the edges of meeting are still sharp, who refuses to be submerged; whose identity therefore one wishes to make crouch beneath one's own. For me now, it is Susan. I talk to impress Susan. Listen to me, Susan. (*TW* 170)

Neville, concerned as he is with his lineage and leaving an impact on the world, his "papers," can be compared to Mr Ramsay. He asks others to hear him and describes his own sounds in exceptionally aural terms: "'These papers in my private pocket – the clamour that proves that I have passed – make a faint sound like that of a man clapping in an empty field to scare away rooks. Now it has died down altogether, under Susan's stare (the clapping, the reverberation that I have made), and I hear only the wind sweeping over the ploughed land and some bird singing – perhaps some intoxicated lark'" (*TW* 169). His effort to "impress" Susan leaves him largely unaware that "understanding and response ... mutually condition each other" (Bakhtin 282), despite the reverberations he has made. When he wonders if the waiter has heard of him, however, he realizes, "no, the sound of clapping has failed" (*TW* 170). He is shown to be disappointed when he listens only for semantics, what applause implies for his sense of superiority.

Louis auscultates both urban space and the natural world in profound terms: "'Listen', I say, 'to the nightingale,¹ who sings among the trampling feet; the conquests and migrations. Believe – ' and then am twitched asunder" (*TW* 175). Later in the episode he implores again:

> "But listen," said Louis, "to the world moving through abysses of infinite space. It roars; the lighted strip of history is past and our Kings and Queens; we are gone; our civilization; the Nile; and all life. Our separate drops are dissolved; we are extinct, lost in the abysses of time, in the darkness." (*TW* 180)

Louis hears, impossibly, the infinite space of (his)tory, yet his version of it includes only "civilization," a one-sided account of the past as far as Woolf is concerned, empty because no response is even sought. Woolf demonstrates here that the same sort of acousmatic authority is evoked in the history of civilizations as in the wires of the Admiralty in *Jacob's Room*. The cost of such one-way communication is the loss of intersubjectivity.

Nevertheless, Louis also, uniquely for this novel, engages with Rhoda in one of the most dialogic moments in *The Waves* during this episode: a section in parentheses in which they seem to talk with each other. He appears to respond to her address to him:

> ("Yet, Louis," said Rhoda, "how short a time silence lasts. [...] Susan, who feels scorn and fear at the sight of these preparations, fastens the top button of her coat, and unfastens its. What is she making ready for? For something, but something different."
>
> "They are saying to themselves," said Louis, "It is time. [...] And going with them, Rhoda, swept into their current, we shall perhaps drop a little behind."
>
> "Like conspirators who have something to whisper," said Rhoda.)
> (*TW* 181)

Although a meaningful moment, given the novel's radical excision of conventional dialogue, the pattern of interaction is still a gendered one in which a woman asks a question, and a man answers with certainty and direction.

Susan, according to Bernard, "'hears the breathing of all her children safe asleep'" (*TW* 180), and she acknowledges the poignancy of silence – "'In this silence,' said Susan, 'it seems as if no leaf would ever fall, or bird fly'" (ibid.). Yet, she does not ask the others to listen to her, unlike Neville, Louis, and Bernard. Correspondingly, Jinny's listening practices are minimized and conjoined with a lover's tryst in this section: "'as we murmured all the secrets of our hearts as into shells so that nobody might hear in the sleeping-house, but I heard the cook stir once, and once we thought the ticking of the clock was a footfall'" (*TW* 177–8). She is particularly tied to the visual domain and to the tactile sense. One of her monologues in the Hampton Court section begins, "'I see what is before me'" (*TW* 176), and elsewhere, "'I like what one touches, what one tastes'" (ibid.), a consequence of her orientation towards the male gaze and her occlusion in the body. She also comments that her "'imagination is the body's'" (ibid.) and mentions how she has "'sat before a looking glass'" (*TW* 177). She is more akin to a voiceless body than a bodiless voice, revealing the gendered dynamics at play in acousmatics. Thus, these two women enact listening without responding. They receive but they do not partake in the other side of dialogic exchange, and Jinny's practice of looking at herself is less about empowerment than it is about conforming to socially prescribed gender norms.

On the other hand, the male characters are emboldened by being listened to, a gendered situation that John Picker has shown arises in the Victorian period particularly in response to the rising middle-class disdain for urban noise. Discussing Thomas and Jane Carlyle's differing responses to sound inside and outside of the domestic abode, Picker suggests, citing the cultural historian Peter Bailey, that Victorians were

> beginning to endorse gendered conceptions of levels of sound. Women were increasingly "socialised as the quieter if not silent sex," while "bravura noise-making was an essential signal of masculine identity for much of this era" [Bailey 209]. The middle-class Victorian man who embarked on a home-based occupation requiring silence had, it would seem, quite an uphill battle if he were to convey the separateness and, indeed, noisiness of masculinity. (55)

Both sides of the dialogic relation of speaking and listening are shown in *The Waves* to be necessary for understanding, but the roles the "characters" play in the dynamic depend on the assumptions that adhere to male and female minds and bodies.

Rhoda, however, is somewhat of an exception to this pattern. Unlike Neville, but like Bernard and Louis, Rhoda does auscultate those around her. She is also the only woman in the text characterized as being distinct from her body. In fact, she transforms and sometimes rejects the material or corporeal world altogether. When describing the gathering, for example, she uses highly intangible terms: "'the still mood, the disembodied mood is on us,' said Rhoda, 'and we enjoy this momentary alleviation (it is not often that one has no anxiety) when the walls of the mind become transparent'" (*TW* 183). At times an *acousmêtre* herself, she nevertheless perceptively auscultates the sounds of her companions:

> "'Waiter!' says Bernard. 'Bread!' says Susan. And the waiter comes; he brings bread. [...] Your voices sound like trees creaking in a forest. So with your faces and their prominences and hollows. [...] Behind you is a white crescent of foam, and fishermen on the verge of the world are drawing in nets and casting them. A wind ruffles the topmost leaves of primeval trees. (Yet here we sit at Hampton Court.) Parrots shrieking break the intense stillness of the jungle. (Here the trams start.) The swallow dips her wings in midnight pools. (Here we talk.) (*TW* 178–9)

Rhoda (like Septimus) transforms the city soundscape into other aural and tactile imaginings. The parenthetical comments repeatedly ground the descriptions of her abstract oceanic and arboreal environment in the present moment. Rhoda, more than any other personage in the novel, practises profound listening, also drawing on pre-(his)story – a time before Louis's "civilization" – to do so.

When Rhoda hears music, also similar to Septimus, it materializes into matter. Earlier in the narrative, Rhoda's description of music's effect recalls Septimus's aural revelations in Regent's Park. After describing an ineffable "'Ah!'" of a singer in Wigmore Hall (analysed in Part 1), Rhoda contemplates,

> "There is a square; there is an oblong. The players [of a quartet] take the square and place it upon the oblong. They place it very accurately; they make a perfect dwelling-place. Very little is left outside. The structure is now visible; what is inchoate is here stated; we are not so various or so mean; we have made oblongs and stood them upon squares. This is our triumph; this is our consolation. (*TW* 128–9)

Converting sound waves into matter, Woolf attempts to represent substantiality when music sounds. Now, the players simply "'make a perfect dwelling-place.'" In addition, the "'building'" of sound produced by a quartet of "'beetle-shaped men come with their violins'" (*TW* 128) is at once round and square, two shapes that do not typically fit together, yet somehow "'very little is left outside.'" Neither matter nor sound has the luxury of solidity in Rhoda's rendering.

In the Hampton Court section, Rhoda mentions the oblong again, making the connection between place and sound even more explicit. Rhoda speaks of an oblong and a square, now referring to Hampton Court Palace (several rooms were designed by Christopher Wren, who was, even more famously, also the architect for St Paul's Cathedral in London). The string quartet is again used as a simile for these shapes: "'Wren's palace, like the quartet played to the dry and stranded people in the stalls, makes an oblong. A square is stood upon the oblong and we say, 'This is our dwelling-place. The structure is now visible. Very little is left outside'" (*TW* 183). To reverse the figure of speech, the quartet performed for the parishioners, like Wren's palace, creates an actual place in which to gather as a community, fittingly so, given that music is a highly social art form and the quartet is one of its representative groups. Sound and matter are, one way or another it seems, dissolved into each other. Intriguingly, Steven Connor argues, "the self defined in terms of hearing rather than sight is a self imaged not as a point, but as a membrane; not as a picture, but as a channel through which voices, noises and musics travel" (206–7). Such a protean and porous subjectivity is reminiscent of many seemingly contradictory comminglings in the novel. Rhoda's profound listening further enables such paradoxical ontological modes. But she, like Septimus, hears too much. Sonority ultimately dissolves the corporeal, leaving her unable to function in the material world.

Only the writer in the novel seems able to strike the balance because he understands the reciprocal nature of the utterance. Bernard auscultates the present moment, bringing his friends, and the reader, back to the material world:

> "Silence falls; silence falls," said Bernard. "But now listen; tick, tick; hoot, hoot; the world has hailed us back to it. I heard for one moment the howling winds of darkness as we passed beyond life. Then tick, tick (the clock); then hoot, hoot (the cars). We are landed; we are on shore; we are sitting, six of us, at a table." (*TW* 180)

It is left to self-reflexive Bernard, the writer, to de-acousmatize these sounds of (his)story, to beckon the others to come back to the table and the shore, to reattach the material circumstances using simple causal associations (the "tick" is established as the clock; the "hoot," as the cars) in the present moment. This mooring is one responsibility of the artist for Woolf.

Bernard seems aware, as Bakhtin argues, that "primacy belongs to the response, as the activating principle … it prepares the ground for an active and engaged understanding" (282). His discussion of mortality in the final soliloquy suggests that death is the absence of his voice, the moment when there is no longer an echo of his own vocality:

> 'This self now as I leant over the gate looking down over fields rolling in waves of colour beneath me made no answer. He threw up no opposition. He attempted no phrase. His fist did not form. I waited. I listened. Nothing came, nothing. I cried then with a sudden conviction of the waste of this immeasurable sea. Life has destroyed me. No echo comes when I speak, no varied words. This is more truly death than the death of friends, than the death of youth. (*TW* 227)

Vividly, Woolf portrays the refractory nature of the voice, the simultaneity of making sound and hearing one's own utterance. The passage enacts the necessity of the apperceptive listener, for it is the lack of echo – "No echo comes when I speak" – that Bernard laments, the lack of a receiver of his sounds. Bernard bewails the absence of the "other" (here, even within himself). Hence, he exclaims that even though he may produce "a cry; a howl," if no one hears him, art and life are meaningless.

III. "Hush! … Somebody's listening": *The Years*

In contrast to *The Waves*, which mines the depths of subjectivity and inner consciousness and is, therefore, largely remote from the physical world, *The Years* is overtly political and historical in nature. Yet dialogic exchange is integral to Woolf's critique of gendered scripts in both books. Written during the late 1930s as the rise of fascism encroached on the everyday lives of Europeans, and Britons, the novel represents the effect of subconscious Hitlerism (as Woolf calls it in "Thoughts on Peace in an Air Raid") on the forgotten and surplus "odd women" prevalent during the early twentieth century. Significantly, as Margaret Comstock documents, new sound technologies enabled international conflict to "invade[] civilian life" (253) in frightening and imminent ways. Because of the wireless, Adolf Hitler's amplified, broadcast voice was as audible in Monks House, Sussex, as it was in Nuremburg.

Hitler's speeches heard over the wireless and given in the late 1930s hark back to the threatening acousmatic experiences enabled by new technologies that Woolf details in her earlier novels *Jacob's Room* and *Mrs. Dalloway*. But additionally, to a listener in London, Hitler's orations in German might have sounded like a melody of words – now a violent, forceful, and terrifying one – detached from propositional content. R. Murray Schafer has elaborated on such circumstances in works that explore the interdisciplinary terrain of words and music. In his book *When Words Sing*, he suggests that "foreign languages, too, are music when the listener understands nothing of their meaning" (25). Of course, the words were anything but meaningless in German, and Woolf, who could understand some of the language, was keenly aware of their import.[2] Nevertheless, in her diaries from the decade, Woolf often documents her own profound listening to the sound of Hitler's voice as she heard it over the wireless. Indeed, on 13 September 1938, she notes his vociferous sounds: "Hitler boasted & boomed but shot no solid bolt. Mere violent rant, & then broke off. We listened in to the end. A savage howl like a person excruciated; then howls from the audience; then a more spaced & measured sentence. Then another bark. Cheering ruled by a stick. Frightening to think of the faces. & the voice was frightening. But as it went on we said (only picking a word or two) anti-climax" (D5: 169). As her employment of music and sound often reveals, disrupting linguistic meaning does not void it of its gravity. Woolf often heightens the sonorous component of language by transforming it into music (as in the children's chorus in *The Years*) or enacts profound listening to uncover other layers of significance (as Mrs Ramsay does in *To the Lighthouse* or Bernard in *The Waves*).

Furthermore, as her essay "The Leaning Tower" details, Woolf was also critical of the political poets of the 1930s who adopted – albeit with different words and anti-fascist politics – a similar tone and rhetoric in their poetry. Correspondingly, the novels document more and more urgently that listeners can be manipulated. Far from being transcendent and beyond worldly reproach, sound is an instrument of humanity's atrocities just as much as its aesthetic beauty. It is neither mystical nor benign. In most cases, Woolf implies that it is the method of balanced interchange and reception, in addition to its meaning, that needs to change.

An episode that explores the fruitlessness of the mode of lecturing (an issue Woolf writes about in her essay "Why?," with which I began this chapter), of one-way communication, occurs in the "1914" chapter of *The Years*. Martin and Sara Pargiter (who are cousins) meet by accident on the steps of St Paul's Cathedral, have lunch in a "City chop house," and then travel to Hyde Park to meet Maggie, Sara's sister. The chapter's opening passage (each one begins with a description of the weather and the environment, in similar fashion to the Interludes of *The Waves*) describes both rural and urban landscapes; the aurality of church clocks connects the two spaces with parallel sonorities:

> In the country old church clocks rasped out the hour; the rusty sound went over fields that were red with clover, and up went the rooks as if flung by the bells [...]
>
> In London all was gallant and strident; the season was beginning; horns hooted; the traffic roared; flags flew taut as trout in a stream. And from all the spires of all the London churches [...] the hour was proclaimed. The air over London seemed a rough sea of sound through which circles travelled. But the clocks were irregular, as if the saints themselves were divided. There were pauses, silences.... Then the clocks struck again."
> (*TY* 202)

The aural backdrop to daily life in the country and the city is both old and new, rusty and rough, pleasant and harsh, and irregular – in a word, polyphonic. Moreover, one cannot help but think, in a chapter set on the eve of the First World War, of John Donne's decree in Meditation 17 – "any man's death diminishes me, because I am involved in mankind, and therefore never send to know for whom the bell tolls; it tolls for thee" (109) – a fitting start to this chapter that also foregrounds listening as an act. Appositely, to add to the association, Sara and Martin meet on the steps of St Paul's; Donne, of course, was made Dean of the famous Cathedral in 1621 by King James I, a position Donne held until his death in 1631. A near-death illness he suffered in 1623 occasioned his writing of the Meditation from *Devotions upon Emergent Occasions* (penned in December 1623 and published in 1624). Woolf employs sonicity for the apperceptive reader/listener to make these connections as the characters do not, but the links are telling: they ask, as Donne had before her, for critical self-reflection and personal accountability.

Indeed, a lack of dialogic exchange is exposed in the chop house in which Martin and Sara have lunch. This is a particularly homosocially identified place (as Anna Snaith documents, the City chop house would find a woman to be out of place),[3] yet Martin brings her unthinkingly to this "hot and crowded" (*TY* 206) restaurant explicitly because "he wanted to make her talk" (*TY* 207). He asks her numerous questions while he attempts to impress those around him. First, what was she doing at St Paul's? She replies, "'listening to the service'" (*TY* 206) – as I argued in Part 1, and will return to in Part 3, Sara is the novel's most aurally attuned character – but she gets preoccupied by all of the tumultuous movements and sounds around her. He tries again: "'I didn't know you went to services'" (*TY* 207), but "she did not answer. She kept looking round her, watching the people come in and out" (ibid.). When she finally responds to his question, he is embarrassed and worried that someone will overhear her:

> "And what, Sal," he said, touching the little [prayer] book, "d'you make of it?"
>   She opened the prayer-book at random and began to read:
>   "The father incomprehensible; the son incomprehensible – " she spoke in her ordinary voice.
>   "Hush!" he stopped her. "Somebody's listening."
>   In deference to him she assumed the manner of a lady lunching with a gentleman in a City restaurant. (Ibid.)

The power of overhearing – not profoundly but for semantic content in order to judge presumed social conditioning – is illuminated in the exchange. Woolf drives the point home when Sara asks Martin the same question: "'And what were you doing,' she asked, 'at St. Paul's?' 'Wishing I'd been an architect,' he said. 'But they sent me into the Army instead, which I loathed.' He spoke emphatically. 'Hush,' she whispered. 'Somebody's listening.' He looked round quickly; then he laughed" (ibid.). Sara has, by repeating his own phrase about listening back to him, revealed, to the reader at least, how significant the act of listening can be in everyday life. The active component of listening is foregrounded: being overheard has the power to keep one in line, so to speak, adhering to social codes of behaviour, just as Martin himself acknowledges he is obliged to do with his occupation.

But when Martin and Sara stroll through Hyde Park looking for Maggie, they become the ones to *overhear* others: three passersby, this time, who mumble and talk to themselves. The scene also begins with Martin inadvertently rambling when Sara lags behind to tie her shoe: "'How

I like – ' he said aloud. He looked round. He had spoken to the empty air. […] But he felt as if he had missed a step going downstairs. 'What a fool one feels when one talks aloud to oneself,' he said as she came up. She pointed. 'But look,' she said, 'they all do it'" (*TY* 214). They proceed to pass a gesticulating "middle-aged woman" whom Martin engages in seemingly nonsensical conversation. Next a young man walks by, "muttering": "he scowled at them as he passed them" (*TY* 215). Lastly, another "lady passed them, talking to herself," after the narrator's auscultation of this spring day in the park: "The air puffed soft in their faces. It was laden with murmurs; with the stir of branches; the rush of wheels; dogs barking, and now and again the intermittent song of a thrush" (*TY* 216). This first grouping of three passersby, in addition to Martin, details a dilemma Woolf has been concerned to unpack before: the absence of an interlocutor, or lack of echo, as Bernard puts it in *The Waves*, as though they are all searching for an apperceptive listener. In addition, the date of the chapter, "1914," links the eve of the First World War with this aurally infused segment. A deficiency in listening leads to dire circumstances in both novels. Moreover, it is no accident that Woolf chooses the year 1914 as one of her salient chapters in *The Years*, as the buildup to another potential world war was fomenting in 1937, the novel's publication date.

The three grumblers are followed by three "orators" at Speakers' Corner. Martin and Sara have gone the wrong way and landed in "the bald rubbed space where the speakers congregate. Meetings were in full swing. Groups had gathered round the different orators" (*TY* 216). Interestingly, given Barthes's notion that "freedom of listening is as necessary as freedom of speech" (260), Woolf chooses this public space to demonstrate precisely this point, for the "orators" reveal the inadequacy of the lecture mode, despite Martin's suggestion to stop and hear them. In addition to signalling that Martin and Sara are physically mobile by mentioning such facts, Woolf uses the volume of sound to disclose the proximity of the characters to the various speakers. The narrator records:

> Mounted on their platforms, or sometimes only on boxes, the speakers were holding forth. The voices became louder, louder and louder as they approached.
>
> "Let's listen," said Martin. A thin man was leaning forward holding a slate in his hand. They could hear him say, "Ladies and gentlemen …" They stopped in front of him. "Fix your eyes on me," he said. They

fixed their eyes on him. "Don't be afraid," he said, crooking his finger. He had an ingratiating manner. He turned his slate over. "Do I look like a Jew?" he asked. Then he turned his slate and looked on the other side. And they heard him say that his mother was born in Bermondsey, as they strolled on, and his father in the Isle of – The voice died away. (*TY* 216)

Very little sense can be made of the orator's comments. What filters through, however, is the anti-Semitism of the speaker and his assumption that his listeners will share such prejudices, another contextual connection to the publication date of the novel.[4] His menacing manner is tyrannical and possessive as he demands that the listeners fix their eyes on him. The effect on Martin and Sara is to do exactly as he says and so they robotically obey him. Woolf captures their movement away from the speaker aurally, by noting the change in the volume of sound he is emitting.[5]

The result of the next speaker is comparable: "'Fellow citizens!' He was shouting. They stopped. The crowd of loafers, errand-boys and nursemaids gaped up at him with their mouths falling open and their eyes gazing blankly. His hand raked in the line of cars that was passing with a superb gesture of scorn" (*TY* 216–17). Martin joins in the admiration of his skill as an orator – "'But he's a jolly good speaker,' said Martin, turning. The voice died away" (*TY* 217) – and he imitates the speaker's accent: "'Joostice and liberty,' said Martin, repeating his words, as the fist thumped on the railing" (ibid.). The care Woolf takes to document the aural dimension is striking; it is a technique she uses throughout the novel to detail voices in hallways, sounds on the street, and lost conversations. Once again, the method serves to focus attention on the sounds of the speeches rather than the meaning of the words.

Lastly, they turn their attention to an "old lady" whose "audience is extremely small" (*TY* 217). Yet, "her voice was hardly audible. She held a little book in her hand and she was saying something about sparrows. But her voice tapered off into a thin frail pipe. A chorus of little boys imitated her. They listened for a moment. [...] The voices grew fainter, fainter and fainter. Soon they ceased altogether" (ibid.). Very little in the way of semantic listening takes place. Instead, in each case with the orators, the sound of the voice is assigned a source (a body), a short phrase of semantic import is mentioned, and then commentary on the sonic resonance is elaborated.

The segment ends with a short discussion Martin attempts to have with Sara about the orators. As usual, Sara is evasive and more concerned with imitating the sounds she has heard than engaging in debate, yet her comments, as always, are incisive:

> "Did you agree with him?" [Martin] asked, taking Sara's arm to rouse her; for her lips were moving; she was talking to herself. "That fat man," he explained, "who flung his arm out." She started.
>
> "Oi, oi, oi!" she exclaimed, imitating his cockney accent.
>
> Yes, thought Martin, as they walked on. Oi, oi, oi, oi, oi, oi. It's always that. There wouldn't be much justice or liberty for the likes of him if the fat man had his way – or beauty either.
>
> "And the poor old lady whom nobody listened to?" he said, "talking about the sparrows...."
>
> He could still see in his mind's eye the thin man persuasively crooking his finger; the fat man who flung his arms out so that his braces showed; and the little old lady who tried to make her voice heard above the catcalls and whistles. There was a mixture of comedy and tragedy in the scene. [...]
>
> What would the world be, he said to himself – he was still thinking of the fat man brandishing his arm – without "I" in it? (*TY* 217–18)

The reference to the "I" echoes Woolf's insistence in *A Room of One's Own*, the essay "Why?," *Three Guineas*, and elsewhere that the monolithic subject bars the way to fruitful dialogic exchange. As Natania Rosenfeld summarizes in reference to Woolf's complaint about the "I" in her first extended polemic, "the ego of the writer looms so large that all interest and all variety are obscured. There is no perspective apart from those of the author and his male protagonist – which are one and the same" (153). Martin's comments suggest that he at least ponders the issue after the lecturing of the orators. In addition, the tactic of "derisive mimicry" (Rosenfeld 154) Woolf utilizes in *Three Guineas* and the later works to "disrupt the litanies of the patriarchs, reactionaries, and dictators" (ibid.) is also deployed (problematically in terms of class assumptions) with the repeated cockney hail, "Oi," and Sara's imitation – a function, however, of her performative methods, I argue in Part 3. Woolf's characters' prejudices seep through their critical stance towards the authoritarian techniques of the speakers.

Moreover, recalling how the scene began, in which the importance of an apperceptive listener is illuminated, Sara mutters to herself, as Martin did at the start of the segment. After hearing the speakers, both Sara and Martin understand each other when they repeat the expletive "Oi." As noted, the connotations are pejorative and class-bound, as the word "Oi" signals London's working class. Yet, both Martin and Sara are characterized as performing the same actions as several of those they hear: they both talk to themselves in public, seeming to forget that "somebody's listening" (*TY* 207). Whether they are aware of their derogatory manner or not, the narrative puts them on the same level, despite the snobbish imitation of class lingo. The little semantic snippets that do make it through are exceptionally poignant: they mark the loss of justice, liberty, and beauty, certainly a "mixture of comedy and tragedy," when one-way communication is instantiated. Regardless of the content of the speeches, the lecture method is shown to ensure a lack of exchange – very little, if any, semantic substance from the orators gets through to their auditors.

Modes of listening are also foregrounded during another dinner party scene, this time in the chapter titled "1917," noticeably set *during* the First World War. The meal, however, is unlike the Ramsays' or the reunion supper in *The Waves* for one particularly poignant reason: its backdrop is an air raid. Those dining together are under physical threat, which obviously changes the dynamics of the conversations. In addition, an attack by aircraft is not only a visual encounter but also a conspicuously aural one. Connor argues, "in the twentieth century, the experiences of war and of urban life have been horrifyingly conjoined in the experience of the air-raid. The terror of the air-raid consists in its grotesquely widened bifurcation of visuality and hearing" (210). Woolf's air-raid scene shrewdly represents this very split and she utilizes the heightened effect of listening to capture the fear and terror the situation creates – the inability to discern precisely in which direction a bomb is coming, or when it will be dropped, yet the barrage of sonics that compel those on the ground to listen for its approach.

The fact that she chooses to set the moment during another supper scene – usually a life-affirming and revelatory situation in the novels – suggests the encroachment on and potential eradication of everyday human relations that the acousmatic circumstances can portend (and indeed will herald in the late 1930s and early 1940s). The chapter begins by foregrounding silence – here a tool to evoke stillness, stagnation, and trepidation. Visual images of pallid light and darkness combine to generate the mood of fear, as an ominous searchlight "rayed round the sky, and stopped, here and there, as if to ponder some fleecy patch" (*TY* 252). Similarly, Eleanor's fellow passengers – she takes the omnibus to her cousin Maggie's home – look "cadaverous in the blue light" (ibid.). Her apprehension is evoked further as she scurries among the "obscure little streets under the shadow of the Abbey" (ibid.). When she arrives, "she knocked and rang at the same moment, for the darkness seemed to muffle sound as well as sight. Silence weighed on her as she stood there waiting" (ibid.). The gothic descriptors that characterize the street are both imagistic and sonorous, creating a contrast with the warmth inside her cousin's home: "the sitting-room ablaze with light" (*TY* 253) and conversation.

Eleanor arrives in the midst of a discussion between Renny (Maggie's husband) and Nicholas (a friend of Sara's), one that underscores the thematics of war – they have been discussing Napoleon and the "psychology of great men" (*TY* 253). As Woolf and her readers would be keenly aware of Hitler's then-contemporary rise to power, the allusion to the earlier dictator is laden with exigency because of the potential loss of civil and personal liberties. A discussion about ontology bookends the chapter with the issue of individual and social responsibility, interrupted by the sound of guns booming and the threat of dropping bombs.

Correspondingly, the aurality of the passage is striking. Sara, the most musical character in the novel, and Eleanor, its most discriminating listener, are playing and singing together. They are performing a waltz (a recollection from an episode ten years earlier) when they are cut short by a threatening sound:

> "Dancing …" Sara repeated. She began drumming on the table with her fork.
> "When I was young, I used to dance," she hummed.
> "All men loved me when I was young.… Roses and syringas hung, when I was young, when I was young. D'you remember, Maggie?" She looked at her sister as if they both remembered the same thing.
> Maggie nodded. "In the bedroom. A waltz," she said.
> "A waltz …" said Eleanor. Sara was drumming a waltz rhythm on the table. Eleanor began to hum in time to it: "Hoity te, hoity te, hoity te …."
> A long-drawn hollow sound wailed out.

"No, no!" she protested, as if somebody had given her the wrong note.
But the sound wailed again.
    "A fog-horn?" she said. "On the river?"
    But as she said it she knew what it was.
    The siren wailed again.
    "The Germans!" said Renny. (*TY* 260)

The sounds of music performed by the makeshift trio of the three women are interrupted (three times) by the wail of another sonority: the sirens of war. The musical prelude creates an atmosphere of playfulness and song – Eleanor even imitates the rhythm of the waltz ("hoity te" emulates the three-four time signature required for the dance) – but this is abruptly cut short by the mechanical *acousmêtre* that interposes. Causal and semantic listening, rather than making and hearing music, become paramount as the group reluctantly relocates to the basement.

The new noise – as Maggie notes, "another raid" (*TY* 260) – threatens and contrasts what is initially a lighthearted moment. While the listeners search for the source of the acousmatic sound in an effort to establish its meaning, fear mounts; the characters demonstrate for the reader the effect that detached, bodiless noises can have on one's sense of safety. The visual domain also diminishes in intensity, a clue to the cadaverous images at the start of the chapter. Once in the basement, "[Eleanor] felt as if some dull bore had interrupted an interesting conversation. The colours began to fade. She had been looking at the red chair. It lost its radiance as she looked at it, as if a light had been extinguished underneath" (ibid.). The notion of boredom speaks more to the guests' attempts to maintain decorum, I would suggest, and to refuse to change their habits under the threat of violence than to actual tedium. The images seem to counteract the effort, however, as the wilting colours connote the vampirism of war rather than ennui. Simultaneously, sounds escalate: "They heard the rush of wheels in the street. Everything seemed to be going past very quickly. There was the sound of feet tapping on the pavement. Eleanor got up and drew the curtains slightly apart. The basement was sunk beneath the pavement, so that she only saw people's legs and skirts as they went past the area railings" (*TY* 260–1).

As the group attempts to converse, they are repeatedly interrupted by the boom of the guns now, rather than the warning sirens, a threatening increase in intensity owing to proximity by comparison to Betty Flanders's auscultation of explosions across the channel in *Jacob's*

Room. Eleanor asks if the children are asleep; she can hear the anxiety in the tone of Maggie's voice. Maggie replies, "'Yes. But if the guns ...' she began, helping the pudding. Another gun boomed out. This time it was distinctly louder" (*TY* 262). Nicholas understands the sounds better than most at the gathering. He is adept at listening for the cause of the noise and understanding its import, in this case essential for survival. Yet, although he is able to make the connections to causal and semantic listening, his conclusions are terrifying: "'They've got through the defences,' said Nicholas" (ibid.). They all attempt to "eat their pudding" (ibid.), but, not surprisingly, they are immediately disrupted:

> A gun boomed again. This time there was a bark in its boom.
>
> "Hampstead," said Nicholas. He took out his watch. The silence was profound.[6] Nothing happened. Eleanor looked at the blocks of stone arched over their heads. She noticed a spider's web in one corner. Another gun boomed. A sigh of air rushed up with it. It was right on top of them this time.
>
> "The Embankment," said Nicholas. Maggie put down her plate and went into the kitchen. [...]
>
> "On top of us," said Nicholas, looking up. They all looked up. At any moment a bomb might fall. There was dead silence. In the silence they heard Maggie's voice in the kitchen. [...]
>
> Then a gun boomed again. It was fainter – further away.
>
> "That's over," said Nicholas. He shut his watch with a click. And they all turned and shifted on their hard chairs as if they had been cramped. (*TY* 262–3)

Thus, the scene enacts the power-knowledge relations implied by the acousmatic circumstances. But here it compels a shift away from profound listening, actively attending to the sonics of the sirens and timed explosions no longer for the sake of sound but to discern their cause and meaning – lives now depend on it. Once the source is determined, the terror evoked is revealed to manifest the four aspects of the *acousmêtre*, even though the sonics are mechanical not vocal. The threatening sounds are certainly ubiquitous – everywhere and nowhere, as they can fall any place in an indistinct sonic range. The planes have complete advantage in terms of sight, pervasive and panoptic control that performs omniscience and omnipotence. In *The Years*, therefore, Woolf demonstrates the linkages between a lack of inclusive methods in discourse (in "1914") and the violence that proliferates into war (in "1917") through the reception of sound. In both chapters, listening – on the one hand, fears of being overheard and the lack of dialogic exchange in the lecture mode of oration, and on the other, the aurally heightened and horrifying experience of an air raid – reveals that both societal relations and national interests are unbalanced and even tyrannical. The methods by which power is acquired in the first place are disclosed and critiqued by exploring the disjunctions between sounds and the bodies from which they issue.

IV. Heterogeneous Reattachments in *Between the Acts*

Several critics have disclosed the relations between sound and social order in *Between the Acts*.[7] Although they do not employ Chion's framework, such studies demonstrate the importance of the three modes of listening for the novel. Woolf deploys sound and music in the text to dislodge the master/slave dichotomies of internalized Hitlerism, to "break the rhythm and forget the rhyme" (*BA* 134). After all, "a tyrant, remember, is half a slave" (ibid.). But she also thoroughly examines the reception of these sonorities to explore the very nature of discourse. Repeatedly, profound listening is enacted in the novel to reveal the machinations of acousmatics, as well as to critique them.

While in *The Years* active audition is covertly, but comprehensively, encouraged (as becomes apparent in the "1914" chapter), in *Between the Acts* the processes of apperceptive and profound listening are explicitly promoted. Thus, as Lucy Swithin is keenly aware, "sheep, cows, grass, trees, ourselves – all are one. If discordant, producing harmony – if not to us, to a gigantic ear attached to a gigantic head [...] and so [...] we reach the conclusion that *all* is harmony, could we hear it" (*BA* 125). Although Lucy Swithin is, along with every character in the text, a parodic figure, and this mention of a giant head in the sky is playfully ludicrous, the notion of harmony articulated is integral to the novel, and, as Cuddy-Keane has suggested, it foregrounds the very act of listening ("Virginia Woolf, Sound Technologies, and the New Aurality" 92). Moreover, Lucy's notion of harmony encapsulated in the trope of a gigantic ear is inclusive of "the agony of the particular sheep, cow, or human being" (*BA* 125), not for the sake of semantic closure but to enable heterogeneity in its discord. But this "ear" is particularly significant given the deployment of acousmatics in the novel (and throughout Woolf's oeuvre): it provides an alternative to the authority-laden invocation of the *acousmêtre*. The gigantic ear is omnipresent yet aurally inclusive (as opposed to panoptic); it is all-knowing yet also individual, divinely inspired, it seems, yet fallible (especially given the humour).

In contrast, the negative acousmatic voice is expressly deployed throughout the text by the gramophone and the megaphone. Indeed, as Bonnie Kime Scott argues, "the gramophone, in the hands of La Trobe, is primarily a tool of manipulation" (109); it is "heard, but not seen, and so it is difficult to identify" (105). Thus its potential as an *acousmêtre* is magnified. The narrator details, for example, what happens when the audience hears the jingoistic music of the pageant that emanates from the unseen turntable: "The audience was assembling. The music was summoning them. [...] Voices chattered. The inner voice, the other voice was saying: How can we deny that this brave music, wafted from the bushes, is expressive of some inner harmony?" (*BA* 86–7). An earlier glimpse of this pluralizing function of anonymity and acousmatics can be found in *To the Lighthouse*, when the voice of Mr Ramsay (which seems to be detached from him at the same time) prompts the dinner guests to ponder if this is "their own voice speaking" (*TL* 150). But in *Between the Acts* this moment demonstrates the coercive side of the gramophone's tunes – it assembles the crowd with its militaristic melodies that seem to put listeners into a trance. Michelle Pridmore-Brown contends, therefore, that under La Trobe's guidance, the machine is capable of creating a false unity, functioning "like a 'harmonium' (a word Woolf considered using in the draft) that permutes and consolidates cultural material [*Pointz Hall* 138]. La Trobe uses rhythm to create a wave pattern that organizes (magnetizes) these bodies, to create, for instance, the 'we' of patriotism" (Pridmore-Brown 414).

It is no coincidence, then, that the audience listens semantically to the patriotic music, does not question the causal link, and ignores the profound layer of sound. Likewise, the outer world is shown to impose a constricting order that forces the subject into servitude:

The audience was assembling. The music was summoning them. [...] When we wake (some were thinking) the day breaks us with its hard mallet blows. The office (some were thinking) compels disparity. Scattered, shattered, hither thither summoned by the bell. "Ping-ping-ping" that's the phone. "Forward!" "Serving!" – that's the shop. So we answer to the infernal, agelong and eternal order issued from on high. And obey. Working, serving, pushing, striving, earning wages – to be spent – here?

Oh dear no. Now? No, by and by. When *ears are deaf* and the heart is dry.
(*BA* 86–7; my emphasis)

The tyrannical unassigned voice of the office marks this deadening (and *deafening*) experience of enforced social order and implicates the acousmatic sounds of the gramophone in this homogeneity.

Yet, similar to Miss La Trobe's methods, which, as I argue in Part 1, are also democratic given her willingness to let the natural world take up the burden of emotion in her pageant, neither is the gramophone a wholly negative instrument. Indeed, engaged listening elicits an appreciation of the musical sounds emanating from the device (sound for the sake of sound), as opposed to the words the machine generates, right after the passage cited above. When the audience listens to the sounds from it *as* music, the narrator describes a very different experience:

For I hear music, they were saying. Music wakes us. Music makes us see the hidden, join the broken. Look and listen. See the flowers, how they ray their redness, whiteness, silverness and blue. And the trees with their many tongued much syllabling, their green and yellow leaves hustle us and shuffle us, and bid us, like the starlings, and the rooks, come together, crowd together, to chatter and make merry while the red cow moves forward and the black cow stands still. The audience had reached their seats. (*BA* 87)

Sonics involve the perceiver in both listening and looking, and in understanding the hidden procedures that break apart and then repair the community. Although Pridmore-Brown contends that this moment reveals the herd mentality created by the gramophone, I would argue this sonically saturated moment is an invitation to listen (and indeed look) profoundly. Tellingly, the audience's momentary inspirational experience is similar to La Trobe's at the end of her pageant when she witnesses the starling-pelted tree, described as a "rhapsody, a quivering cacophony, a whizz and vibrant rapture" (*BA* 150). Aurality, music in this case, beckons to the many to listen differently, even as the novel questions whether or not the community hears this call.

In his discussion of the historical shift from the phonograph (which could record the voice), popular in the *fin de siècle*, to the early twentieth-century gramophone (which was mass produced and did not give the owner the capacity to record), John Picker suggests that modernists (including Woolf) were distressed by the device:

The needle-skip (or stick), with its connotations of immobility and hollow
repetition, recurs in the work of those who were themselves discomforted
by the successor to the cylinder phonograph, the more insidious
gramophone: in Eliot's "Love Song" (1917), with Prufrock's faint "Do I
dare? Do I dare?"; in Faulkner's *Absalom, Absalom!* (1936), with Quentin
Compson's tortured "I don't hate it! I don't hate it!"; and most explicitly
in Woolf's *Between the Acts*, with the chuffing machine's monotonous
"Dispersed are we…. Dispersed are we." (140)

Yet, I would suggest, Woolf is less disconcerted than the others, perhaps because she is writing in 1941, when a longer time of everyday
usage has taken the machine out of the realm of unknowable mys-
tery and fear. It is well documented, as noted in my Introduction,
that Virginia and Leonard owned an Algraphone (a cabinet gramophone) from 1925, purchased a gramophone in 1929, and listened to
music nightly by the fireplace at Monks House. In *The Years*, characters comment on the machine's quality as a sound reproducer. Delia,
who throws the final family party, suggests its fallibility: "'They're
going to dance,' she said, pointing at the young man who was putting another record on the gramophone. 'It's all right for dancing,' she
added, referring to the gramophone. 'Not for music.' She became simple for a moment. 'I can't bear music on the gramophone. But dance
music – that's another thing'" (*TY* 329). The remarks imply a seasoned
discrimination that denotes shifting conceptions about the initially
enigmatic mechanism: its reproduction quality is not very good for
listening closely to music. In Woolf's work, then, the earlier plasticity of the practices of hearing concerning the instrument is shown
to have crystallized by the 1930s. Its chuffing in the darkly farcical
Between the Acts is certainly ominous, but throughout the text it is also
de-acousmatized by the novel's documentation of profound listening.
The many mistakes, mishaps, missed cues, and skipped grooves the
narrative records reattach (an albeit mechanical) body to the sounds
that issue from its trumpet, taking it out of the domain of transcendence; its existence as an imperfect, humanly controlled instrument
becomes apparent in contrast to the terrifying, monolithic voice of
nationalistic agendas.

In addition, other human acousmatic sounds and voices are both
tested and shattered in the novel. Each time the pageant breaks for an
Interval, the narrative reports multiple, various snippets of dialogue
from the audience usually unassigned to any particular body. La Trobe
auscultates them: "over the tops of the bushes came stray voices, voices

without bodies, symbolical voices they seemed to her, half hearing, seeing nothing, but still, over the bushes, feeling invisible threads connecting the bodiless voices" (*BA* 109). Multiple and fragmented acousmatized voices recount the play from diverse, undesignated points of view, yet the "invisible threads" of sound keep the "symbolical voices" in the material world, "join[ing] the broken" (*BA* 87).

The variety of perceptions is encapsulated in the questions posed after the play has finished:

> Friends hailed each other in passing.
> "I do think," someone was saying, "Miss Whatshername should have come forward and not left it to the rector ... After all, she wrote it.... I thought it brilliantly clever ... O my dear, I thought it utter bosh. Did *you* understand the meaning? Well, he said she means we all act all parts...." (*BA* 141–2)

The text implicates its reader/listener by initiating the segment with the subject/object relation of conventional conversation. Both positions (enunciator and receiver) are shown to depend on each other because of Woolf's dislodgment of clear identifying markers for either the subject or the object of the discourse. The identities of the pluralized speakers are unknown; the speech also slips into the second person. In fact, the hailed interlocutor could very well be the reader in this construction. In the process, the four "powers" of the *acousmêtre* are also displaced, becoming multifarious, open-ended, and inquisitive bodiless voices with contrary opinions rather than a singular, panoptic god. All of this occurs while the subject matter foregrounds and destabilizes the issues of authorship and authority.

In addition, Woolf also de-acousmatizes a particular spectator's voice, "ignoring the conventions" (*BA* 110):

> [...] a head popped up between the trembling sprays: Mrs. Swithin's.
> "Oh Miss La Trobe!" she exclaimed; and stopped. Then she began again; "Oh Miss La Trobe, I do congratulate you!"
> She hesitated. "You've given me ..." She skipped, then alighted – "Ever since I was a child I've felt ..." A film fell over her eyes, shutting off the present. She tried to recall her childhood; then gave it up [...]
> She gazed at Miss La Trobe with a cloudless old-aged stare. Their eyes met in a common effort to bring a common meaning to birth. They failed; and Mrs. Swithin, laying hold desperately of a fraction of her meaning, said: "What a small part I've had to play! But you've made me feel I could have played ... Cleopatra!
> She nodded between the trembling bushes and ambled off. (Ibid.)

Although the villagers cruelly refer to Lucy Swithin as "'Batty' [...] the word for old Flimsy" (ibid.), La Trobe takes her seriously:

> "You've twitched the invisible strings," was what the old lady meant; and revealed – of all people – Cleopatra! Glory possessed her. Ah, but she was not merely a twitcher of individual strings; she was one who seethes wandering bodies and floating voices in a cauldron, and makes rise up from its amorphous mass a recreated world. Her moment was on her – her glory. (*BA* 110–11)

The invisible strings that connect human beings also link ideas that Woolf takes seriously – aesthetics, life, and the cost of war. These are all concerns delicately and painstakingly articulated in the novels. In *Between the Acts*, however, the humour used throughout the text underscores the pretensions of ruling-class modes of behaviour. Lucy Swithin's comments and her inability to enunciate them dislodge any certainty that might be gained by de-acousmatizing the bodiless voices of the audience, but they do, nonetheless, take the assembly out of the realm of acousmatic omnipotence. In this book, Woolf finds a way to divest acousmatic circumstances of their authority, yet repudiate simple reversals. She does not replace one tyrant with another. Instead, she transforms and pluralizes the previously disembodied voice and reattaches material circumstances through the notion of human connection, the invisible threads – a metaphor she repeatedly employs to describe music throughout her oeuvre. As Eleanor ponders for a fleeting moment at the final party in *The Years*, for example, "Does everything then come over again a little differently? She thought. If so, is there a pattern; a theme, recurring, like music; half remembered, half foreseen? ... a gigantic pattern, momentarily perceptible? The thought gave her extreme pleasure: that there was a pattern. But who makes it? Who thinks it? Her mind slipped. She could not finish her thought" (*TY* 333).

But a potentially monolithic *acousmêtre* – the loudspeaker – is also deployed alongside the often de-acousmatized voices of the audience. The final verbal enunciation of the pageant follows ten minutes of "present time": the splintered mirrors employed by La Trobe to reflect back to the audience a fragmented vision of themselves. The scene makes them horribly uncomfortable: "Each tried to shift an inch or two beyond the inquisitive insulting eye. Some made as if to go" (*BA* 134). Self-reflection makes them squirm in their seats. But Woolf then employs the loudspeaker to create a similar effect to the mirrors. Replete with all of the connotations of authority it evokes, an *acousmêtre* is conjured: "but before they had come to any common conclusion, a voice asserted itself. Whose voice it was no one knew. It came from the bushes – a megaphonic, anonymous, loud-speaking affirmation" (ibid.).

Yet instead of producing an omnipotent utterance that simply reasserts control after several chaotic intervals and myriad critical comments from the audience, this *acousmêtre* intones a request:

> Look at ourselves, ladies and gentlemen! Then at the wall; and ask how's this wall, the great wall, which we call, perhaps miscall, civilization, to be built by (here the mirrors flicked and flashed) orts, scraps and fragments like ourselves? [...]
> All the same here I change (by way of the rhyme mark ye) to a loftier strain – there's something to be said: for our kindness to the cat; [...] There is such a thing – you can't deny it. What? You can't descry it? All you can see of your selves in scraps, orts, and fragments? Well then listen to the gramophone affirming....
> A hitch occurred here. (*BA* 135)

The nursery rhymish, nonsensical manner recalls Sara's imitative performances in *The Years*. Both women are artists in a sense, producing art forms that fundamentally question conventional generic and medial boundaries. The mode of rhyme and unanswered/unanswerable questions also undermines the author(ity) of the anonymous speaker, as she or he makes serious-minded comments about communal self-reflection. Thus, the powers of the *acousmêtre* are invoked by the bodiless loudspeaker but subverted by the novel's enactment of its use.

Mishaps continue to plague the performance. The questions cited above suggest that, if the audience members cannot discern (descry) what the speaker is requiring (to "Look at ourselves"), perhaps they should listen to the gramophone, which is set to play a musical hodgepodge of various tunes: "The records had been mixed. Fox trot, Sweet lavender, Home Sweet Home, Rule Britannia – sweating profusely, Jimmy, who had charge of the music, threw them aside and fitted the right one – was it Bach, Handel, Beethoven, Mozart or nobody famous, but merely a traditional tune? Anyhow, thank Heaven, it was somebody speaking after the anonymous bray of the infernal megaphone" (*BA* 135). But somehow,

Like quicksilver sliding, filings magnetized, the distracted united. The
tune began; the first note meant the second; the second a third. Then down
beneath a force was born in opposition; then another. [...] Compelled from
the ends of the horizon; recalled from the edge of appalling crevasses;
they crashed; solved; united. And some relaxed their fingers; and others
uncrossed their legs. (*BA* 134–5)

The narrator auscultizes the musical sounds and commingles the
effects with the movements of the audience as opposed to assigning
sources or semantics to the sounds. This act of profound listening (the
notes of a tune) moves the pageant's audience members to reflect on
themselves. The section then ends with them asking the question the
pageant has been implying the entire time: "Was that voice ourselves?
Scraps, orts and fragments, are we, also, that? The voice died away"
(*BA* 136). Correspondingly, the singular megaphonic voice becomes the
plural "ourselves," de-acousmatizing it in the process by grounding it
in the bodies of the community.

In *Between the Acts*, Woolf imagines alternative auditory practices
that encourage the profound level of listening. In addition, she reconfigures the typically singular and authoritative *acousmêtre* by assigning it multiple bodies to represent new, heterogeneous possibilities
and connections through the mechanisms of sound and music. In turn,
these strategies not only critique socio-political conditions depicted in
the novel and the representative spectators watching/hearing the play
but also implicate the community of readers absorbing the text, insisting, therefore, that sound is not simply or mystically transcendent but
grounded in the material world.

Thus, in Woolf's novels the apperception of sound is integral to ethical communal relations. By employing Chion's three modes of listening,
I uncover Woolf's multilayered representation of perceiving sound to
reveal another political function of exploring the aural domain. If Part
1 demonstrates that Woolf deploys musical methods to represent and
enact new ways to make meaning, Part 2 discloses that she is just as concerned with the reception of those practices, to reveal to the reader new
ways to listen. Moreover, Woolf's employment of acousmatics focuses
the reader's attention not only on what (or who) might be responsible
for particular utterances but also on what or who might be responsible
for the related events in both the private and public spheres. Repeatedly, the later novels, especially, counteract the powers associated with
the *acousmêtre* by grounding the ethereal voice in the tangible world,

attaching bodies to voices. In this way, Woolf's materialist feminism is shown to emerge effectively when the reception of sonority and music is foregrounded in the text. Indeed, as the epigraph to chapter 4 affirms, Woolf presciently understands that "we must learn to listen, for listening is acting" (Chion, *Sound* loc. 5063).

PART 3

Music *as* Performance in Woolf's Fiction

Chapter Five

Performing Women

In Part 3, I change the general focus from sound, as in the previous two parts, to the sonorous art form, more specifically, to explore what scenes of musical performance bring to Woolf's novels. I argue that in such representations Woolf portrays an artistic practice that is embodied, emphasizing material conditions. Moreover, Woolf's awareness of the efficacious nature of producing sound in various modes, especially music, makes a political claim about art and its crucial importance to life. The first section of chapter 5 concentrates largely on *The Voyage Out* (1915). As this is Woolf's only novel with a pianist as protagonist, it warrants considerable attention. I shall also briefly compare musical events in *Night and Day* and *Jacob's Room* to arrive at some conclusions about her three earliest novels. The rest of chapter 5 will investigate musical scenes in *The Years* (1937) and *Between the Acts* (1941). The last two works, particularly *Between the Acts* with its embedded countryside pageant, foreground the issue of performative reenactment; correspondingly, various musics and ambient sounds reverberate in their pages, illuminating the material conditions not just of music but also of sonority, more generally, in the service of art. If in Part 1 the voice represents the interruptive networks of sound that can exceed prescribed boundaries and in Part 2 profound listening helps to activate that disruptive potential, then in Part 3 the concept of performance brings the production and reception of the sonorous together, dynamically moving (both literally and emotionally) both producers and listeners.

In her novels Woolf often foregrounds the process of enactment as opposed to the product or the "work," to use the musicologist Nicholas Cook's schema.[1] Although the exact moment in music history when the notion of the score took precedence over the performative moment is debatable,[2] Lydia Goehr argues that around 1800 the "work" in Western art music was privileged over the performer in service to the composer's supposed intentions. Woolf's contemporaries Arnold Schoenberg and Igor Stravinsky, for example, although they diverged in their experimental methods and innovations, converged in their thinking about the performer's acquiescence to the composer and his presumably benign conduit, the musical score. But since at least the 1990s, musicologists have questioned the primacy of the notes on the page (a move similar to performance studies in the 1970s that critiqued the "textualist" imbalance in studies of drama), to demonstrate that "music was to be understood as in essence less a product than a process, an intrinsically meaningful cultural practice, much in the manner of religious ritual" (Cook, "Between Process" par. 3). Hence, Cook suggests thinking about music *as* performance to emphasize that it is a social praxis rather than a diaphanous and wholly abstract art. Furthermore, in a traditional model that privileges score/composer at the expense of the performer, the actant is routinely required to disappear. Indeed, as Cook contends with reference to Goehr, "the performer's only legitimate aspiration thus becomes one of 'transparency, invisibility, or personality negation'" (ibid.).[3] It is significant, therefore, that Woolf represents musical performances, as she has done with sound more generally, not as transcendent but as inseparable from the material world. This is prescient on her part and distinct from several contemporary composers as well as writers. T.S. Eliot's concept of the auditory imagination, for instance, is largely an intellectual and interior endeavour, albeit "below the conscious levels of thought and feeling" ("Matthew Arnold" 111).

Correspondingly, in performance studies, the concept of ephemerality has also been long debated. In her groundbreaking study *Performing Remains: Art and War in Times of Theatrical Reenactment* (2011), Rebecca Schneider maintains, contrary to Peggy Phelan's well-known argument that "performance's being ... becomes itself through disappearance" (146), that to read performance itself as vanishing, as "constitutively, that which *does not remain* ... and cannot reside in its material traces" (97) is to "reiterate[] performance as necessarily a matter of loss, even annihilation" (98). Chronicling this ephemerality in performance studies, Schneider demonstrates further that the binary equation of performance/loss depends on another age-old privileging: that of vision over the other senses.

Thus there is political promise in this equation of performance with disappearance: if performance can be understood as disappearing, perhaps performance can rupture the ocular hegemony ... And yet, in privileging an understanding of performance as a refusal to remain, do we ignore other ways of knowing, other modes of remembering, that might be situated precisely in the ways in which performance remains, but remains differently? The ways, that is, that performance resists a cultural habituation to the ocular – a thrall that would delimit performance as that which cannot remain to be seen. (98)

Hence, in her study, Schneider explores the possibilities of performance that endure, even persist, in ways other than the visual.

Woolf, as I have demonstrated, also finds alternative means of signification to the visual and language in music: it is a non-discursive process of meaning making in the aural domain. But her exploration of how to "remain[] differently" is not a simple reversal of sound over sight, or body over mind. I submit that in her writings she asks an indirect, but analogous, question to Schneider: "Should we not think of ways in which the archive [the written, the visual, the historical] depends upon performance, indeed ways in which the archive performs the equation of performance with disappearance, even as it performs the service of 'saving'?" (Schneider, *Performing Remains* 99). This emphasis on (not privileging of) the performatic – a word theorist Diana Taylor defines as the "nondiscursive realm of performance" (6) – manifests in Woolf's novels as musical scenes that accentuate the enactment of sounds embodied by the performers and often the listeners.

My incorporation of the term "nondiscursive," therefore, takes from Taylor's sense of it as encompassing all of the aspects that go into performance other than the written components, or a score where music is concerned. I use the word to refer to all of the corporeal, enigmatic, and unspoken or unscored components that do indeed occur when music is performed. I do not mean to suggest by deploying this word, however, that music is outside of or beyond discourse, as Michel Foucault would define the term; music, I believe, does contain, even nonlinguistically, ideas, attitudes, and emotions that are imbricated in relations of power and shared by its community of listeners. Remarkably, in Woolf's novels, the score/archive is not privileged over and above the performer or the musical event itself. While the earlier novels are somewhat more ambivalent about commingling the archive/history and the performatic, or, where Woolf is concerned, writing/history and musical performance, *The Years* and *Between the Acts* give the *performance of history* proverbial centre stage. This combination occurs in an attempt to intertwine the non-discursive and the archive, I argue, to critique the damaging effects of the patriarchal dismissal of the body that loomed large as another world war approached (a palpable awareness for Woolf, as I have disclosed in the previous parts). Indeed, Woolf's later novels reveal that history depends upon performance.

I. Women at the Piano in the First Three Novels

The Voyage Out, *Night and Day*, and *Jacob's Room* each contain moments in which women perform for informal gatherings. Indeed, Woolf's first protagonist is an accomplished amateur pianist. In addition to Rachel Vinrace, Cassandra Otway (in *Night and Day*) plays for her intended, William Rodney, and the Hilberys. Similarly, Clara, in *Jacob's Room*, plays piano "sonatas," and, at a soirée at the Durrants, Elsbeth Siddons sings Franz Schubert's "Who Is Silvia" (*JR* 118), the well-known *lied* based on Shakespeare's lines from *Two Gentlemen of Verona* (4.2.40–1), as noted in chapter 1. Although her accompanist remains unspecified, it could be Clara, as I shall discuss subsequently. The first three books also examine, either implicitly or explicitly, the shift from Victorian social values to modern ones, whether through an exploration and critique of the conventions of marriage or through the disclosure of the social dissolution and fragmentation that culminates in the First World War. Significantly, then, late nineteenth-century models of womanhood are interrogated. The gendered dynamics that pervade the musical education of young women are also under investigation.

As the novel indicates, for Rachel, "music goes straight for things" (*VO* 239). Correspondingly, her performances in *The Voyage Out* begin to challenge writing and language. Indeed, they counter what Taylor argues is "the centuries-old privileging of written over embodied knowledge" (8). After a frustrating discussion with Helen Ambrose and Mr and Mrs Dalloway, for example, Rachel seeks sanctuary in her room, a place in which she can produce sounds that do not contain the burden of words and, albeit in limited fashion, resist socially prescribed roles in a sequestered space. But Rachel's room also provides her with a place in which to perform sounds for her own ears, and the result is an early description on Woolf's part of sound materializing as matter, if only imagined by the narrator:

She slammed the door of her room, and pulled out her music. It was all old music – Bach and Beethoven, Mozart and Purcell – the pages yellow, the engraving rough to the finger. In three minutes she was deep in a very difficult, very classical fugue in A, and over her face came a queer remote impersonal expression of complete absorption and anxious satisfaction. Now she stumbled; now she faltered and had to play the same bar twice over; but an invisible line seemed to string the notes together, from which rose a shape, a building. (*VO* 58)

Although Woolf's description of Rachel commences with a typical "page to stage" scenario, describing the yellowed scores of well-known and lionized composers, the scene focuses on the process of Rachel's playing, her stops and starts, repetitions for the purposes of practising, and her complete "impersonal" absorption. Christine Froula argues that "music permits Rachel to be simultaneously highly accomplished and unworldly, even otherworldly; to dwell amid invisible 'Spirits'" (43). I would add that the reference to her loss of self speaks to the disappearance of the performer, tied, in this early novel, to a critique of restrictive codes of gendered behaviour for women. Getting lost in the music is figured as an escape for Rachel, a place where she can maintain some agency and not have to contend with social expectations.

But this early version of a room of Rachel's own in which she can avoid the expectations of the "angel in the house" is unceremoniously and abruptly interrupted by Mrs Dalloway: Rachel "was so far absorbed in this work, for it was really difficult to find how all these sounds should stand together, and drew upon the whole of her faculties, that she never heard a knock at the door. It was burst impulsively open, and Mrs Dalloway stood in the room. [...] The shape of the Bach fugue crashed to the ground" (*VO* 58–9). With the intrusion of Mrs Dalloway, what had begun to be embodied in a "shape," sound realized by the muscle memory of Rachel's hands, is still too fragile to stand against interference. It is striking that the rest of the scene describes this immersive experience in such physical terms. The musical sonorities are realized in architectural form so that the notes of Bach's fugue become a breakable physical shape, revealing the magnitude of Mrs Dalloway's intrusion. Thus, although the embodiment of music in the performer is not necessarily emphasized in this scene, the sounds of the music she enacts are.

In her study of Woolf and classical music, Emma Sutton adeptly examines the role of the female pianist and late nineteenth- to early twentieth-century conventions that circulate around the piano in Woolf's novels. Focusing primarily on Rachel (with some further exploration of Cassandra), Sutton compares E.M. Forster's Lucy Honeychurch's repertoire choices (both heroines play Beethoven's late piano sonata, Opus 111)[4] to reveal their significance in terms of gender autonomy. Sutton also contextualizes what the piano might signify in *Orlando* and *To the Lighthouse*. Suggesting that Woolf is attempting to "kill the pianist in the house," Sutton observes, "Forster's and Woolf's protagonists play repertoire that was, in effect, prohibited for women. The perception that this was 'masculine' music was the result not only of the technical and interpretative complexity of this late repertoire, but also for gendered discourses about Beethoven and his music more generally ... [he] was characterized as the exemplary Romantic 'genius' and 'hero'" (*Virginia Woolf and Classical Music* 61). Indeed, Phyllis Weliver, who has adroitly documented the significance of musical women in England from 1860 to 1900, observes, "the type of music played by prosperous daughters further illuminates music's meaning to respectable society. Serving social ends, music was an ornamental skill. Consumers wanted to play pieces that sounded more like concert hall repertoire than music hall tunes, but which did not require professional technique" (*Women Musicians* 34). Woolf's choices in terms of repertoire, therefore, are illuminating, as she was well versed in the class and gender politics that would be attached to seemingly benign "notes" for female musicians.

In addition, Weliver reveals how very integral playing the piano was to the marriage market for young women up to the twentieth century: "The performers who were most unambiguously appreciated in middle- and upper-class domestic settings were unmarried daughters. Because many lady musicians abandoned music-making after marrying, it seems that the greatest use of amateur music was to obtain a good marriage" (*Women Musicians* 33). Rachel and Cassandra can be contrasted not just because of their respective representations as characters who become engaged in the course of each novel and who happen to play piano, but by the type of music they perform and what their choices imply for their impending marriages, for it is highly likely that both will be expected to forego music making, except for the occasional entertainment for their husbands, families, or guests. Rachel's ability to play Beethoven's Opus 111 is in stark contrast, therefore, to Cassandra's simple and pleasing Mozart. The playing of the former suggests difficulty and (inappropriate) virtuosity, an autonomy that would most likely be sacrificed when Rachel marries, adding weight to Woolf's critique of the marriage market in her heroine's tragic and premature demise. As Sutton reveals, "the 1909 edition of Wilhelm von Lenz's monograph on Beethoven describes Op. 111 as 'very rarely performed', so Rachel and Lucy's choice of repertoire is even more unexpected and startling than it might now seem" (*Virginia Woolf and Classical Music* 60). Conversely, (unspecified) Mozart implies acquiescence or contentment with the status quo in terms of its potential difficulty and Cassandra's impending wifely success as William Rodney's fiancée. Woolf is keenly aware, therefore, of the social ramifications of musical performance.

Thus, Rachel Vinrace's facility as a pianist has everything to do with her prescribed innocence (and ignorance) as a young woman being groomed for marriage; it is no accident that Opus 111 is referred to in chapter 2 as Rachel daydreams and is most likely the piece she practises in chapter 22 while Terence repeatedly interrupts her in order to tell her that she "ought to be answering" their engagement letters while he should be "writing [his] book" (*VO* 344). Music is not simply a pastime for Rachel: it is both a refuge and a non-discursive mode of resistance. Indeed, although Woolf removes the phrases in the final version of *The Voyage Out*, in previous drafts of the novel, as one reads in Louise De Salvo's *Melymbrosia* (an earlier version, according to its editor), the fact that the narrator twice notes Rachel is "born to play" (*Melymbrosia* 65, 66), suggests that Woolf endows her character with more than the "ornamental skill" (Weliver, *Women Musicians* 34) required for the marriage market.

Unmistakably, then, Rachel's preference for her room is a self-imposed, voluntary confinement. Yet, this private space does not solely promote enclosure or limitation, for in it Rachel's sounds can be played and heard by and for herself, as opposed to the obligations outside her room to "reflec[t] the figure of man at twice his natural size" (*AR* 45), as Woolf will summarize later in *A Room of One's Own*. Indeed, in the earlier drafts of the novel, Woolf employs the now infamous looking-glass metaphor that will be crucial to *A Room* more directly to signal Rachel's potential self-scrutiny: "One wants to do something without an audience, Rachel was far away from all looking glasses" (*Melymbrosia* 66). Contrastingly, in *The Voyage Out* Terence is an inattentive but intrusive audience to Rachel's practising. In chapter 22 he attempts to elicit a response from her (after suggesting that women do not think), but she ignores his questions and continues playing her music:

Rachel said nothing. Up and up the steep spiral of a very late Beethoven sonata she climbed, like a person ascending a ruined staircase, energetically at first, then more laboriously advancing her feet with effort until she could go no higher and returned with a run to begin at the very bottom again. (*VO* 339–40)

Beethoven's late sonatas and quartets are significant throughout Woolf's oeuvre (see chapter 6); they often signify resistance to socially condoned modes of behaviour. The emphasis on the lateness of the sonata is also noteworthy in that the compositions are models of effort and experimental ingenuity. The exact movement Rachel is playing is not specified, but this sonata (Opus 111, No. 32 in C minor written between 1821 and 1822) has two highly contrasting parts, rather than the more typical three: 1. *Maestoso – Allegro con brio ed appassionato* (Majestic – brisk, with vigour and passion) and 2. *Arietta – Adagio molto semplice e cantabile* (A short aria – very simply and singingly). The second movement in C major is a set of eight variations on a sixteen-bar theme, with a short modulating interlude and a coda. Again, a particularly spatial (and aspirational) trope of physicality, mounting a staircase this time, is employed by Woolf to describe the sounds that emanate from the piano. This late Beethoven sonata is a testament to the staircase metaphor and to a spatial understanding of the piano keyboard.[5] Sutton has detailed the innovative fugue embedded in the development section of the rapid and frenetic Maestoso. In addition, variation 3, implanted in the second movement, is an arpeggiated descending and ascending passage marked *L'istesso tempo* (the same tempo) that enacts the extremes of a keyboard. In other words, it begins at the high end of the piano, descends to the bottom end, and then climbs its way back to the top only to tumble down again to the lowest notes played by the left hand (affectionately dubbed the "boogie-woogie" movement since it prefigures elements of jazz in its breadth and syncopated rhythms). My description is not as poetic as Woolf's, but it serves to show that the metaphor of the staircase is most likely a reference to this particular passage in this sonata, one that would require exceptional skill on Rachel's part and "repertoire that was, in effect, prohibited for women" (Sutton, *Virginia Woolf and Classical Music* 61).

Similar to the late string quartet, Opus 130 and 133, which I discuss in chapter 6, this sonata, Beethoven's last, was composed when he was completely deaf. The experimentation in the piece is remarkable in terms of tonal modulation (the exposition in the first movement shifts to the submediant – the sixth scale degree – instead of the more common mediant – the third); formal techniques such as the fugue (some argue a complex "double fugue") and variation form (Beethoven excelled at this improvisatory structure); melodic and rhythmic material, which, as noted, foretells ragtime approximately eighty years before its era; atypical time signatures (9/16 for the second movement) that stretch time per bar to provide fervent contrast with the first movement in terms of the tempo and mood and allow for the infamous "small notes" which divide the bar into twenty-seven beats (this is very uncommon); and even the overall form, which is irregular (the separation between the movements is indiscriminant in addition to the sonata's having two movements rather than three).[6]

Most important for my purposes, however, is the physical demand placed on the performer of this piece. Sutton notes, "for all the intangibility of sound, piano playing allows these women [Rachel and Lucy] to perceive their worlds as more orderly and more solid" (*Virginia Woolf and Classical Music* 63). Indeed, if ever a pianist is required to cover the entire territory of the keyboard, this sonata makes such a demand. Put another way, it forces the performer to stretch the limits of her own body, to *embody* the sonata in a way that performers before Beethoven had not been required to do. Contemporary pianist John Lill, for example, considered a leading interpreter of Beethoven as Tania Halban discusses, describes playing his "favourite" piece as physically challenging, citing even the opening downward leap of a seventh in the left hand as compelling the pianist to struggle to reach the notes. Hence, Rachel's playing of this piece as a response to the oblivious Terence is Woolf's indirect, but perhaps stubborn, statement of resistance to marriage in the domain of sound. Effectively, the metaphor conveys the effort it takes Rachel to "climb the staircase" of gendered assumptions about women's ability to think and subsequently produce and perform art. Although she plays in front of Terence, as the narrator notes, "there she was, swaying enthusiastically over her music, quite forgetful of him" (*VO* 339). Yet, the scene does even more than this. It is also an instance of the performatic, subtly but significantly captured by the staircase metaphor, an instance of a female piano player that necessitates embodied performance in the enactment of these particular notes composed by Beethoven. Woolf's choice of music accentuates the performer's corporeality and the sounds she creates instead of the primacy of the score or its composer. Ultimately, the scene describes her playing rather than lauding Beethoven or his archive.

Discussions between Rachel and Terence further distinguish the difference between writing and music. In her study of what constitutes the performatic, Taylor explains: "the strain between what I call the archive and the repertoire has often been constructed as existing between written and spoken language. The archive includes, but is not limited to, written texts. The repertoire contains verbal performances – songs, prayers, speeches – as well as nonverbal practices ... The repertoire, whether in terms of verbal or nonverbal expression, transmits live, embodied actions" (24). Furthermore, she contends, "the writing = memory/knowledge equation is central to Western epistemology ... That model continues to bring about the disappearance of embodied knowledge that it so frequently announces ... Part of what performance and performance studies allow us to *do*, then, is take seriously the repertoire of embodied practices as an important system of knowing and transmitting knowledge" (24, 26). Rachel's musical response to Terence questions this divide between archive and repertoire, during a scene, no less, in which they discuss the difference between their representative art forms.

Woolf's text suggests that Rachel's "system of knowing and transmitting knowledge" is in her performance, and this is pointedly contrasted to Terence's reliance on the writing = memory/knowledge binary that is exposed to be exceedingly gendered:

> While Rachel played the piano, Terence sat near her, engaged, as far as the occasional writing of a word in pencil testified, in shaping the world as it appeared to him now that he and Rachel were going to be married. [...] At last, having written down a series of little sentences, with notes of interrogation attached to them, he observed aloud, "'Women – under the heading Women I've written:
>
> "'Not really vainer than men. Lack of self-confidence at the base of most serious faults. Dislike of own sex traditional, or founded on fact? Every woman not so much a rake at heart, as an optimist, because they don't think.' What do you say, Rachel?" (*VO* 339)

Rachel then attempts again to delay *writing* the responses to their engagement congratulations by playing Beethoven. Moreover, as the scene continues, the staircase metaphor is employed to describe her embodied performance:

Attacking her staircase once more, Rachel again neglected this opportunity of revealing the secrets of her sex. She had, indeed, advanced
so far in the pursuit of wisdom that she allowed these secrets to rest
undisturbed. [...]
   Crashing down a final chord with her left hand, she exclaimed at last,
swinging round upon him:
   "No, Terence, it's no good; here am I, the best musician in South
America, not to speak of Europe and Asia, and I can't play a note because
of you in the room interrupting me every other second." (*VO* 340)

Her arrogance notwithstanding, her refusal to engage in the verbal
domain and the narrator's suggestion that she had "advanced so far
in the pursuit of wisdom" suggests that Rachel, who is typically rather
verbally vapid, nonetheless accesses and maintains a different type of
knowing. Indeed, she transmits "embodied cultural behaviour" (Taylor
26), which Woolf values as a productive mode of interaction, even in
her first novel.
   All told, the scene provides an early example of Woolf's employment of music to defamiliarize the medium of language. For, as Rachel
declares, speaking of the letters sent to them,

"They're sheer nonsense!" Rachel exclaimed. "Think of words compared
with sounds!" she continued. "Think of novels and plays and histories – "
Perched on the edge of the table, she stirred the red and yellow volumes
contemptuously. She seemed to herself to be in a position where she could
despise all human learning. (*VO* 340–1)

The divergences between the performatic and writing knowledge are
distilled lucidly in the passage, but so is the hopelessness of anyone
hearing or accepting Rachel's non-discursive mode of knowledge. This
bleakness is brought home to the reader when Rachel agrees to write
the letters, and the narrator notes, "Terence, meanwhile, read a novel
which someone else had written, a process which he found essential to
the composition of his own" (*VO* 344).
   Another musical performance in the novel provides an additional
instance in which the "score" is questioned and musical sound is corpo-
realized in linguistic metaphors and in the movement of actual dancing
bodies. Chapter 12 focuses on the engagement party of Susan War-
rington and Arthur Venning. Music is the backdrop for much of the
party, played first by a trio, piano, violin, and horn (*VO* 169), and then

by Rachel herself: "After a few minutes' pause, the father, the daughter, and the son-in-law who played the horn flourished with one accord. Like the rats who followed the piper, heads instantly appeared in the doorway" (ibid.). The passage that follows is striking for its depictions of sound as watery substance:

> There was another flourish; and then the trio dashed spontaneously into the triumphant swing of the waltz. It was as though the room were instantly flooded with water. After a moment's hesitation first one couple, then another, leapt into midstream, and went round and round in the eddies. The rhythmic swish of the dancers sounded like a swirling pool. By degrees the room grew perceptibly hotter. The smell of kid gloves mingled with the strong scent of flowers. The eddies seemed to circle faster and faster, until the music wrought itself into a crash, ceased, and the circles were smashed into little separate bits. […] There was a pause, and then the music started again, the eddies whirled, the couples circled round in them, until there was a crash, and the circles were broken up into separate pieces. (Ibid.)

As happens elsewhere in *The Voyage Out*, Woolf describes sound in highly tangible terms; the music is embodied by the movement of the dancers in the analogy to a "swirling pool." Several subsequent waltzes are overheard or experienced in the novels that follow: Jacob, pointedly, cannot dance to the waltz; Jinny is repeatedly associated with it; Sara overhears a waltz outside her bedroom window in *The Years* and one is also played at the party in the "Present Day" chapter; and a waltz is included in the many tunes that come out of the gramophone's trumpet in *Between the Acts*. In this scene, Woolf records a synaesthetic experience for the reader in an effort to represent, and indeed enact, musical sonority – not a description of what it might mean, but a depiction of it in movement. Indeed, as Helen exclaims later in the chapter, "'I *am* enjoying myself […] Movement – isn't it amazing?'" (*VO* 178). Moreover, although the genre of music is described – a waltz – the composer is not named. In her first novel, then, Woolf repeatedly spatializes music, typically considered a time-bound art form, yet commingles this physicality with the rhythmic momentum that music can elicit.[7]

Furthermore, the music continues to be described in tangible form as the scene continues, and the performer's import is also emphasized after the musicians have packed up their things and left. Those who remain ask Rachel to play the piano so they can continue dancing. Rachel complies. Knowing very little popular dance music, however, she proceeds instead to play a Mozart sonata:

> "But that's not a dance," said some one pausing by the piano.
> "It is," she replied, emphatically nodding her head. "Invent the steps." Sure of her melody she marked the rhythm boldly so as to simplify the way. Helen caught the idea; seized Miss Allan by the arm, and whirled round the room, now curtseying, now spinning round, now tripping this way and that like a child skipping through a meadow.
> "This is the dance for people who don't know how to dance!" she cried.
> (*VO* 185)

Helen, who clearly appreciates what music brings to the moment, is the first to experiment with this new dance. Rachel's piano playing inspires a reconfiguration of the traditional and gendered organization of bodies, even if the music itself would connote an amateur drawing-room fete (as when Elsbeth Siddons sings Schubert *lieder* at the Durrants' party in *Jacob's Room*). But Woolf uses the moment to loosen the social "mechanism[s] of behaviour" (*ND* 438) rather than tighten them. Rachel's willingness to play this culturally permeated piece out of traditional performance context (and even encourage others to dance to it) defamiliarizes the sounds of the Mozart sonata. Helen, "like a child skipping through a meadow," leads her partner Miss Allen, instead of being led by a male partner; the gendered hierarchy of traditional dancing – whereby the man leads and the woman follows – is challenged, as are the heterosexist assumptions maintained by these typically imbalanced relations.

The initial model upon which this "new dance" is predicated, however, is still provided by the highly structured music of Mozart; it is simply employed in an atypical manner. But in the description that follows, the "invisible strings" and "unacted part[s]" (*BA* 137), later twitched and stirred in Woolf's final novel, are here enacted in nascent form as Rachel creates a musical medley on the spur of the moment:

> The tune changed to a minuet; St. John hopped with incredible swiftness first on his left leg, then on his right; the tune flowed melodiously; Hewet, swaying his arms and holding out the tails of his coat, swam down the room in imitation of the voluptuous dreamy dance of an Indian maiden

dancing before her Rajah. The tune marched; and Miss Allan advanced with skirts extended and bowed profoundly to the engaged pair. Once their feet fell in with the rhythm they showed a complete lack of self-consciousness. From Mozart Rachel passed without stopping to old English hunting songs, carols, and hymn tunes, for, as she had observed, any good tune, with a little management, became a tune one could dance to. By degrees every person in the room was tripping and turning in pairs or alone. (*VO* 185–6)

Rachel's commingling of unorthodox musical combinations creates efficacious possibilities out of old conventions in the domain of sound, which subsequently enable the performatic. Woolf's emphasis on bodily moment, even though it is articulated in the language of her novel, asks that the reader "also pay attention to milieu and corporeal behaviors such as gestures, attitudes, and tones not reducible to language" (Taylor 28).

Rachel's medley of various pieces – from minuets to hunting songs to hymn tunes – foretells similar moments in *The Years* and *Between the Acts* that question the primacy of the "work" to foreground the moment of performance. Rachel boldly marks out the rhythm and makes choices in terms of the tunes "with a little management," to inspire her listeners to have a sensory experience of sound. The intermingling of folk music with the Western art tradition implies, at least, a destabilization of the "classical" hierarchies among various categories of music. It is Rachel's playing that initiates and maintains these new patterns of interaction and exchange. Unconventional combinations and physical movement have changed the social relations on the dance floor, however briefly.

Yet, Rachel's playing generates a tension between patriarchal order and new conditions of possibility. The performers (player and dancers now) still seem to be searching for an alternative method, much like Woolf at this point in her career. While some hierarchical models between men and women are questioned (Miss Allen parodically bows to the male-male "pair" [*VO* 186], St John Hirst and Terence Hewet), others, determined according to race and class, are reinscribed. The imitation of the Indian princess, for example, suggests not only the group's obliviousness to the privilege they enjoy as English subjects of the British Empire but also the stereotypical eroticization assigned to women of colour, despite Hewet's part in reversing gender roles. Correspondingly, the novel's formal innovations are also limited, producing friction between generic conventions and resistance in terms of female subjectivity.

Mozart stimulates similar tensions in Woolf's subsequent novels *Night and Day* and *Jacob's Room*. But the performance of the female pianist is used to different effect in the novels that follow *The Voyage Out*. As Sutton has argued, "Rachel and Cassandra are antithetical examples of Woolf's reflections on the social and gender politics of female amateur music" (*Virginia Woolf and Classical Music* 55).[8] Indeed, when Cassandra plays in *Night and Day*, although the listeners experience a certain amount of reverie and autonomy, the pianist herself fades into the background as a vessel for the proper execution of the "score." In chapter 30 Cassandra performs for the Hilberys, but "Mr Hilbery alone attended. He was extremely musical, and made Cassandra aware that he listened to every note. She played her best, and won his approval" (*ND* 438). Cassandra is able to be what Rachel is not: a self-conscious automaton for the sake of patriarchal approval. Correspondingly, the melodic content of Mozart's music is emphasized throughout the chapter: "The music went on. Under cover of some exquisite run of melody, [William] leant towards [Katharine] and whispered something" (*ND* 439). Subsequently, the reader is informed, "the music, which had ceased, had now begun again, and the melody of Mozart seemed to express the easy and exquisite love of the two upstairs" (*ND* 446). Characterizations of such music are in stark contrast to moments in *The Voyage Out*, where music is often specified (Beethoven's Opus 111, for example) or the technique involved in playing it is foregrounded. Moreover, neither the performer nor her listeners embody the sounds in the ways that occur in Woolf's first novel.

The reader is apprised in *Jacob's Room* that, similar to Cassandra, Clara plays sonatas, monotonously even: "The flamingo hours fluttered softly through the sky. [...] No wonder that Italian remained a hidden art, and the piano always played the same sonata. [...] Clara Durrant procured the stockings, played the sonata, filled the vases, fetched the pudding" (*JR* 113). But there is no scene of her actually playing the piano in the novel. Her self-effacement is made complete when the reader is informed that one of the guests, Miss Julia Eliot, cannot figure out whether or not Clara is accompanying Elsbeth Siddons in the continuation of her lacklustre performance or simply turns pages for someone else: "'Now Elsbeth is going to sing again. Clara is playing her accompaniment or turning over for Mr Carter, I think. No, Mr Carter is playing by himself – This is *Bach*,' she whispered, as Mr Carter played the first bars" (*JR* 119–20). There are no physicalized renditions of the sound either, nor does anyone dance. The conventions of the female pianist and the importance of this skill for marriageability are palpable in both *Night and Day* and *Jacob's Room*. The performance of music is not an enabler of "freedom" or embodiment for the performer. Instead, Woolf uses it as a marker of gendered confinement, not to perpetuate or condone the practice, of course, but to illuminate its still stultifying effects for women in the second and third decades of the twentieth century. Although Cassandra and William are clearly contrasted to Katharine and Ralph in *Night and Day* to articulate an alternative engagement scenario that nevertheless borders on embarrassment for the family (in chapters 32 and 33 the aunts, uncles, fathers, and mothers reveal what is at stake in Katharine choosing Ralph), a union between Clara and Jacob is thwarted by the end of that novel's party (discussed above), when Clara returns to her duties as hostess instead of having a conversation with Jacob. The exceptionally insipid nature of the party in *Jacob's Room* speaks to Woolf's more critical stance in this formally innovative novel published in 1922.

II. Performing Personal History in *The Years*

In an essay on this novel, I examine the episode in which Sara Pargiter overhears an actual waltz outside her bedroom window (the "1907" chapter) to argue that Woolf integrates aspects from the art forms of music and Greek drama to articulate aesthetic efficacy.[9] In his book *Performance Theory* (1988), Richard Schechner maintains that traditionally, the idea of performance carries with it a dyadic relation (he describes it as a braid) between efficacy/ritual and entertainment/theatre. In this dichotomy, the ritual side of performance is transformative for Schechner. Although not oppositional to entertainment, rituals tend towards functionality, something, I argue, Woolf is concerned to elaborate in this novel. As she mentions in a letter to Stephen Spender, for example, one of her objectives in *The Years* is to "exhibit the effect of ceremonies" (*L6*: 116). This is especially urgent for Woolf in the latter half of the 1930s, as she was well aware of Adolf Hitler's growing power on the continent. The music and noises of the gathering outside Sara's window are insistent, as are the noises that drift into homes throughout the text. I contend such moments suggest the possibility of combining mind and body for Woolf, of making an intellectual state performative in order to create change. In this section I build on that argument to suggest that, in *The Years*, the performatic is also politicized and linked to history as a resistance to tyrannical thought.

Sara is the last example of a female piano player in Woolf's oeuvre. Interestingly, she commingles several aspects of Woolf's musical thinking. She is both a pianist and a singer, so it is not a surprise that she voices the earcon I discuss in chapter 2, but she also embodies sound in her performances. Yet musical performances manifest quite differently in *The Years* from in *The Voyage Out, Night and Day*, and even *Jacob's Room*. A novel that is especially concerned to examine what constitutes history in narrative, *The Years*, as Anna Snaith has summarized in the Cambridge edition, is a "combination of socio-political critique and formal experimentation" (*TY* xli). Indeed, Snaith argues, "faced with a decade inaugurated and characterized by political and economic crisis, [Woolf] responded by making that uncertainty her subject" (*TY* xxxix).[10]

Correspondingly, I argue that musical performances are improvisational and embedded in the everyday. Sara repeatedly combines songs and piano pieces impromptu together with melodies that she overhears from the streets outside her room, an invigorated version of Rachel's medley. The improvisation occurs in the new and atypical combinations of the music. In terms of traditional performance practice, Sara's willingness to conjoin and commingle various musical styles would be counter to the training she would have received as a young Victorian girl being groomed for the marriage market. Often, what Sara hears also instigates movement in her body – her play acting or the movements of dance, for example – representing a different way of knowing. Indeed, Sara's body repeatedly takes over as she sings and acts out or reenacts the events in and around her daily life or creates versions of the people she encounters, as I shall demonstrate. It is significant, therefore, that as an overlooked and ignored woman with a visible disability – when the reader first encounters her she is described as having a "very slight deformity […]. She had been dropped when she was a baby; one shoulder was slightly higher than the other" (*TY* 108) – who, in the marriage market, is supposedly doomed to spinsterhood from an early age, she has an "outsiders'" knowledge. Woolf theorized the "outsider" in *Three Guineas*, the non-fictional work published after *The Years* but initially meant to be interspersed with it. I am suggesting that Woolf values and articulates Sara's divergent way of knowing, the musically performatic, precisely because it questions the presumptions of historical "fact."

Despite the appearance of conventionality in the novel's form, Woolf is nevertheless concerned with generic innovation. As is well known, the initial design for the text was that of a "novel-essay," an attempt to merge another time-honoured pairing: the fictional with the non-fictional. Also of great concern to her during the writing process was to somehow imbue the work with "drama," to use her word, by creating "scenes" and getting the "right" rhythm. The aurality of this performativity is foregrounded when she notes, in the early stages of writing, that she composes out loud: "About a week ago, I began the making up of scenes – unconsciously: saying phrases to myself; and so, for a week, I've sat here, staring at the typewriter and speaking aloud phrases of The Pargiters" (D4: 143). The diary records that she is thinking about Shakespeare's methods as a dramatist in relation to the novel (D4: 145, 172, 207, 219 [when she visits his house in Stratford-on-Avon], and 309). Thus, in July 1933 she ponders how to inject drama into the text:

> I am again in full flood with The P.s after a week of very scanty pages. The trouble is to get the meat pressed in: I mean to keep the rhythm & convey the meaning. It tends more and more, I think – at any rate the E[lvira]. M[aggie]. scenes – to drama. I think the next lap ought to be objective, realistic, in the manner of Jane Austen: carrying the story on all the time. (D4: 168)

Although her thoughts about her writing do not fix her intentions for me, they do provide new and alternative ways to understand and experience the novel. The ideas in this excerpt are intimately tied to her notion of rhythm, which suggests the audible (but non-verbal) pulse of musical movement she hopes to capture by adding drama. Moreover, in addition to referring to the episodes as theatrical "scenes," Woolf renames the segment she is writing about (above) the "1910" chapter, in which Sara (Elvira is a possible name for the character during the initial stages of writing) plays the piano and sings. This chapter is the most musically infused of the *The Years*. As noted in chapter 2, Sara's episodes at the piano in Hyams Place bookend Kitty Lasswade's visit to the opera *Siegfried*. Perhaps, as Jane Marcus suggests, *The Years* is in some ways Woolf's *Götterdämmerung*.[11]

Appositely, then, musical performance in the novel helps Woolf to historicize the present. Once again, the score/archive is not privileged over the performatic in this text. Instead, the idea of the score and its instantiation of the composer is largely absent (genres and various styles are recalled but specific composers undetermined), and visuality is frequently destabilized (Sara cannot see the musicians playing for the party in the "1907" chapter, for example, nor does she see the singer and trombonist outside her window in the "Present Day"), so that aurality is foregrounded. The one specific reference to a composer's work is the opera scene in the "1910" chapter that I note above.[12] Yet, although the name of the opera is obliquely disclosed, the name of the composer, Wagner, is not. In addition, Woolf's usual references – Mozart, Bach, Beethoven – are all absent from *The Years*.

Thus, in place of the earlier female piano players – Rachel, Cassandra, Clara – this novel presents the reader with Sara, who sits "at the piano" and sings in her "reedy" (*TY* 167) voice, largely for herself, but also to interact with her sister, Maggie, as I discuss in chapter 2. Unlike the previous pianists, Sara plays for the sheer joy of it. There is no display of her abilities per se, even if only for an informal gathering such as the engagement party in *The Voyage Out* or the salon of the Durrants. Moreover, her performative mode of being illuminates what Schneider calls the "warp and draw of one time in another – the *theatricality* of time – or what Gertrude Stein, thinking about *Hamlet*, referred to as the nervousness of 'syncopated time'" (Schneider, *Performing Remains* 6). Schneider continues,

> the subject is the trouble between history proper and its many counter-constituents: the resilience of the seemingly forgotten (that nevertheless recurs); the domain of error and unreliability known as flesh memory in the embodied repertoires of live art practices. (Ibid.)

There is a difference between official, historical time and theatrical temporality. Woolf's scene commingles performance and history in a parallel way, all the more apposite given Schneider's reference to Woolf's contemporary Stein. In her lecture entitled "Plays," Stein discusses the different ways of perceiving theatrical productions and in the process questions the notion of linear time (and progressive history); indeed, all of Stein's operas and plays disrupt temporality in language. In her words, "in order to know one must always go back. What was the first play I saw and was I then already bothered bothered about the different tempo there is in a play and in yourself and your emotion in having the play go on in front of you. I think I may say I may say I know that I was already troubled by this in that my first experience at a play. The thing seen and the emotion did not go on together" (94). Also like Woolf, although via very different styles, Stein utilizes language and form to enact the content of her discussion.

Sara (a representative in *The Years* of the "seemingly forgotten") counterbalances official, historical narratives with her performative art practices. Recall, for example, that the "1910" chapter ends with the announcement of King Edward VII's death, just after Sara has remembered the events of her day by imitating the voices and actions of those at the suffrage meeting she attends with Rose – all while accompanying herself on the piano. Indeed, Rishona Zimring argues that "it is especially through Woolf's artistic figure, Sara Pargiter, that the text foregrounds linguistic creativity as a struggle between solitude and intrusive sound" (130). Although I agree that Sara Pargiter is Woolf's artistic character in the novel – akin, I would submit, to Lily's visually ekphrastic significance in *To the Lighthouse* – I read her as having special access to and facility with the performatic as much as to "linguistic creativity" – Sara excels at the non-discursive processes of meaning making.

In the "Present Day" chapter, for instance, Sara incorporates music she hears outside her window and intersperses it with the personal histories of the Pargiter family, as she has done in the earlier chapters. This time she will incorporate ambient and musical sounds into her conversation with her nephew, North, when he visits her at her flat on Milton Street before attending the novel's final party at Delia's. Appositely, his journey to her home is inundated by urban sonics. As Melba Cuddy-Keane has shown, North's experience of the city's sonorities initially suggests his discomfort but, as with Sara, ultimately demonstrates that he "is beginning to relate and compose the different sounds of the city, merging vehicular sounds into the keynote sound of traffic, and perceiving simultaneously, over the background sound, a variety of individual voices" ("Modernist Soundscapes" 392). But his arrival by automobile is also accompanied by musical sounds, a woman doing vocal warm-ups in a nearby house: "He dribbled up to the door. He stopped. A voice pealed out across the street, the voice of a woman singing scales" (*TY* 280). Throughout the visit, North and Sara are repeatedly interrupted by the sound of this vocalise that comes through the window. The music, not that of a composer but the unguarded, unselfconscious practising of (perhaps) a working musician, provides the aural backdrop to what North thinks is a "'low-down street to live in'" (*TY* 280). Covertly suggesting the material conditions of musical practitioners, in addition to Sara's circumstances, the singer's voice is joined by a trombone as the scene continues. This unseen but live (within the confines of a written text) musical accompaniment enables Woolf to underscore the non-discursive elements of music, which are subsequently, as the sonics unfold, embodied by Sara.

Similar to Woolf's description in her first novel of Rachel's practising, musical sound is also realized in the metaphor of a staircase in *The Years*: "From across the road came the voice of the singer deliberately ascending the scale, as if the notes were stairs; and here she stopped indolently, languidly, flinging out the voice that was nothing but pure sound. Then he heard somebody inside, laughing. That's her voice, he said" (*TY* 281). The physical metaphors suggest the practical, corporeal labour involved in honing skills – the day-to-day, time-on-task element needed to make one's living by artistic performance. But the bodiless voice does not suggest the omniscient *acousmêtre* discussed in Part 2; instead, the voice of the singer is local and, as I shall demonstrate, subsequently attached to material conditions. To paraphrase Schneider, the scene represents the *body as archive* that finds itself in repetition.

Indeed, in *The Years* and *Between the Acts*, repetition, especially of musical sounds, functions to foreground reenactment in addition simply to enactment. Repeated sonorities mark both of the final novels, and this is because, I would submit, they are both urgently concerned with troubling the unconscious yet destructive conjoining of history and progress. As Snaith argues in reference to *The Years*, "the novel does not rest easily on notions of gradual progress, or sudden transformation" (*TY* xliii). Accordingly, a character such as Sara, dedicated to repeating phrases from her own and others' memories, enables Woolf to disrupt the forward motion of linear narrative (of both fiction and history). Congruently, the segment with North and Sara in the "Present Day" chapter continually fluctuates between the past and the present, dislodging the notion of untroubled linearity. Both characters are outsiders (North because he has been out of touch with the family, away in Africa working on a farm, and Sara because of her spinsterhood). They attempt, throughout the scene, to reconcile their memories of each other and the past of the family with the present-time situation: "He sat down on the chair she had pushed out for him, and she curled up opposite with her foot under her. He remembered the attitude; she came back in sections; first the voice; then the attitude; but something remained unknown" (*TY* 282). As memories continue to flood in – "he remembered. He had come to her the evening before he left for the war" (*TY* 283) – the vocalist interjects again:

> The voice of the singer interrupted. "Ah – h-h, oh-h-h, ah – h-h, oh – h-h," she sang, languidly climbing up and down the scale on the other side of the street.

"Does she go on like that every night?" he asked. Sara nodded. The notes coming through the humming evening air sounded slow and sensuous. The singer seemed to have endless leisure; she could rest on every stair. (Ibid.)

Using sound and music to add to the drama of the moment, when North asks about the singer's intrusion, Woolf turns ambient, unnoticed or unacknowledged repetitive noises into part of the narrative, using what will become a cinematic technique of making nondiegetic, background sounds or music diegetic, and, therefore, noticeable and integrated into the narrative.

Moreover, as they discuss "society or solitude; which is best" (*TY* 285), a trombone interposes, this time as if in answer: "[Sara] broke off; for now a trombone player had struck up in the street below, and as the voice of the woman practising her scales continued, they sounded like two people trying to express completely different views of the world in general at one and the same time. The voice ascended; the trombone wailed. They laughed" (ibid.). A non-discursive, sonic reflection of the issue under discussion as well as the two people overhearing these sounds, the musical impromptu and atypical duet, much like North and Sara themselves, enact a dialogic moment, as opposed to a summary trajectory with closure. The voices are not oppositional; they are both/and, expressing different views yet simultaneous.

By the end of the scene, Sara is tapping out the rhythm of the melodies she overhears, performing them herself. She integrates the sounds and then enacts them, yet "remains differently" (*Performing Remains* 146), to use Schneider's words, rather than disappearing into ephemerality as the performer. While the trombone intrudes on the conversation, the characters repeat the events in their lives – their personal histories – that they have exchanged over the years in their letters. North's thoughts of loneliness and his possible (but unspoken) tryst with a man at a bar near his farm in Africa are accompanied by the trombonist, who

had moved his station and was wailing lugubriously under the window. The doleful sounds, as if a dog had thrown back its head and were baying the moon, floated up to them. She waved her fork in time to it.[13]

"Our hearts full of tears, our lips full of laughter, we passed on the stairs" – she dragged her words out to fit the wail of the trombone – "we passed on the stair-r-r-s" – but here the trombone changed its measure to a jig.

"He to sorrow, I to bliss," she jigged with it, "he to bliss and I to sorrow, we passed on the stair-r-r-s." (*TY* 289)[14]

Sara incorporates the sounds and rhythms of the howling trombone into her discussion with North, while she recites lyrics that echo their mutual decision, made separately, to stop writing each other years ago. They are in dialogue about their separate pasts. Following the tempo of the trombonist, she stretches out her words, creates melodies out of their sounds, to play along with the music she is hearing. When the music changes to a jig, she changes with it, embodying the sonics with both her conducting and her integration of the words as melodic material. With no score in sight (and not even a visual realization of the player), Sara riffs off the dance rhythm as a jazz musician might. What her performance enacts is their intersubjectivity, switching, as she does, "he" for "I" in the jig portion. Her use of words does not completely suspend their meaning, but her deployment of music adds non-discursive knowledge – a different way of knowing – to the scene, showing how personal histories depend upon performance rather than a reiteration of the discursive domain, for Sara enacts their personal archives (letters) and finds a way in the present to perform the past of their relationship musically. Sara's improvisation, moreover, counteracts the disappearance of the performer, simultaneously turning her into a composer, of sorts, herself.

Sara's performance during the discussion with North precedes one more comment about their letter writing which she then reenacts and repeats: North's memory that she wrote him an "angry letter; a cruel letter" (*TY* 289). It is difficult for the reader to glean why Sara writes, "this is Hell. We are the damned" and calls North a "coward; hypocrite, with your switch in your hand; and your cap on your head," and subsequently utters the word "Poppycock!" (*TY* 290). The reader must do the work to piece together several moments from Sara's past that she mentions and physically demonstrates to North: on the Strand, where people pad along the pavement with wreaths in their hands; her comment that she "went over the bridge" (ibid.) and then "stood and looked down [...] and thought; Running water, flowing water, water that crinkles up the lights; moonlight; starlight – " (ibid.), memories from 1910; and lastly, recollections from 1907, when she sees two upper-class people dressed for the evening, a man and a woman, the latter applying lipstick under the lamplight – "'And she, sitting beside him, in a fur-trimmed cloak, took advantage of the pause under the lamplight to raise her hand' – she raised her hand – 'and polish that spade, her mouth.' She swallowed her mouthful" (ibid.). As that last quotation reveals, interspersed among these recalled scenes is Sara's reenactment of them in the present moment, "like a copy or perhaps more like a ritual" (Schneider, *Performing Remains* 104). Referring to the status of history in Civil War reenactments, Schneider argues,

> To the degree that it remains, but remains differently or *in difference*, the past performed and made explicit as (live) performance can function as the kind of bodily transmission conventional archivists dread, a counter-memory – almost in the sense of an echo … If echoes … resound off of lived experience produced in performance, then we are challenged to think beyond the ways in which performance seems, according to our habituation to the archive, to disappear. We are also and simultaneously encouraged to articulate the ways in which performance, less bound to the ocular, "sounds" (or begins again and again, as Stein would have it), differently, via itself as repetition – like a copy or perhaps more like a ritual – like an echo in the ears of a confidence keeper, an audience member, or a witness. (Ibid.)

Woolf has Sara realize the memory of her letter, the written archive, in performance because it provides the reader (the witness) with a counter-memory, enacted in the live moment of the now. Moreover, her "copy" or repetition of other people's bodily movements and verbal phrases turns her conversational mode into a performance; it "sounds" for the reader in order to remain in the present day, rather than disappear into the void of official history.

III. Historical Reenactments: *Between the Acts*

The character of Sara demonstrates that Woolf's musical performers do not typically vanish into the score/archive. Although Rachel's dilemma in *The Voyage Out* is somewhat different, her musical experiences reveal the start of sonic embodiment in Woolf's oeuvre. Nevertheless, her struggle is to prevent herself from being passed over, to "remain," even if this pessimistic text is, finally, unable to grant her such an existence. In Woolf's first novel, her protagonist's artistic practice does not enable her to live out her life in a fulfilling way whether unmarried or not. Woolf's other female piano players subsequent to Rachel demonstrate the hold that the Victorian mindset has on women musicians. Perhaps this is because, as she states in *A Room of One's Own* when discussing the "enormous body of masculine opinion to the effect that nothing could be expected of women intellectually," the bite of such criticism is still affecting female performers in 1929: "But for painters it must still have some sting in it; and for musicians, I imagine, is even now active and poisonous in the extreme" (*AR* 70). The painter Lily Briscoe, therefore, is Woolf's first exemplary and overtly artist figure who *remains* both in body and self-determination; Woolf is able by 1927, perhaps because of her sister and her own career, to envision a female artist figure in new ways. But Lily is, obviously and admittedly, not a musician (although rhythm is essential to her inspiration in painting, as I shall address in the Coda). Sara, however, created during the early 1930s, experiences the playfulness of having a musical way of being. Much like Lily, she lives her art, even if it will only be heard by herself and her family (akin, I would suggest, to Lily's paintings being stored in the attic). After Sara, Miss La Trobe is Woolf's representative female artist figure. Her primary mode of expression is drama that is richly resonant with a quilt of musical and ambient sounds, but she is no longer tied to the piano – she wields a gramophone, a megaphone, and even sings. Fascinatingly, she creates and then directs a pageant of what would usually be considered a written archive: English history.

In addition to being artists, the characters from these works also have in common a slippage into anonymity – examples include Lily's decidedly unarchived paintings, Sara's unnoticed existence, and Miss La Trobe's refusal to claim ownership or accolades once the performance of her pageant is finished. As Brenda Silver has documented,[15] Woolf was writing her unpublished work tentatively titled "Anon" concurrently with *Between the Acts*. The short piece was most likely meant to be the first chapter of an idea she had been ruminating on since 1938, a "Common History book – to read from one end of literature including biography; and range at will, consecutively" (*D5*: 318). The essay is intimately tied to her final novel because of the focus both on history and on human artistry. As Silver notes,

> The portrayal of Anon in the essay enlarges her portrait of the artist, Miss La Trobe – often referred to as "Miss Whatsername" – in the novel she was then revising, and provides an historical ancestry for the creator of the mid-summer village pageant in *Between the Acts*. Anon, "sometimes man, sometimes woman," emerges from the essay as an outsider whose social isolation gave him or her the freedom to "say out loud what we feel, but

are too proud to admit," and whose ability to tap the reservoir of common belief resulted in tolerance, if not acceptance, from all classes of society. (380)

Clearly, there is overlap between this "Anon" personage and the singers who voice the earcon that I discuss in Part 1, especially the "old woman" from *Mrs. Dalloway*. But Woolf's concern to focus on the community in this novel – "but 'I' rejected: 'We' substituted [...]. 'We' ... composed of many different things ... we all life, all art, all waifs & strays" (*D5*: 135) – changes the singularity of this singer. As I demonstrate in regard to the earcon, *Between the Acts* incorporates several articulations of the cry as well as nonhuman components – bellowing cows and a sudden downpour of rain – so that there is no single or solitary enunciation of it. In what follows, then, even though the concepts in the "Anon" figure overlie those of the earconic singers and choristers, there is more to discuss about this enigmatic voice of "common history." I have chosen to focus on the connections to Woolf's late essay here because of this chapter's concentration on performance and the archive.

Miss La Trobe's inconspicuousness is clearly demarcated in the novel. Filtering and disclosing the community's gossip about her, the narrator wonders, "but where did she spring from? With that name she wasn't presumably pure English. From the Channel Islands perhaps? Only her eyes and something about her always made Mrs. Bingham suspect that she had Russian blood in her" (*BA* 42). As noted previously, it is also implied she is a lesbian: "She bought a four-roomed cottage and shared it with an actress. They had quarreled. Very little was actually known about her" (ibid.). Although this unknowability is couched as a detriment – "outwardly she was swarthy, sturdy and thick set; strode about the fields in a smock frock; sometimes with a cigarette in her mouth; often with a whip in her hand; and used rather strong language – perhaps, then, she wasn't altogether a lady?" (*BA* 42–3) – it becomes a meaningful component of the pageant's effectiveness in making those who see and hear it question the "unacted parts" they themselves play in everyday life.

The significance of nameless obscurity for Woolf becomes quite clear in the late essay: Anon "is the common voice singing out of doors, He has no house. He lives a roaming life crossing the fields, mounting the hills, lying under the hawthorn to listen to the nightingale .... He was a simple singer, lifting a song or a story from other peoples [*sic*] lips, and letting the audience join in the chorus" ("Anon" 382). Anonymity speaks to a time before written, official history is instantiated as the archive, laden as it is with gender imbalance. Moreover, separation between performer and audience is impossible for this figure, as is ownership over what the performer produces: "Sometimes he made a few lines that exactly matched his emotion – but there is no name to that song" ("Anon" 382–3). Thus, "anonymity was a great possession. It gave the early writing an impersonality, a generality. It gave us the ballads; it gave us the songs. It allowed us to know nothing of the writer: and so to concentrate upon his song" ("Anon" 397). Critiquing the masculinism of "the great man" embedded in the written word of condoned history, Woolf attempts instead to find an anonymous, inclusive state of being that questions the social authority bestowed on the writer, and, one could add, the composer and his score.

The essay also provides a connection between this concept of history Woolf is theorizing at the end of her life and a distinction between the performed art of sound and that of the written word. In "Anon" Woolf imagines the birth of human signification as the reenactment of melodic birdsong. Ricocheting with references in *Between the Acts* to the book Lucy Swithin reads, "an Outline of History" (*BA* 6), Woolf opens "Anon" with a quotation from "the historian" about the physical geography of Britain. Subsequently, humanity's first artistic utterance is described:

> On those matted boughs innumerable birds sang; but their song was only heard by a few skin clad hunters in the clearings. Did the desire to sing come to one of those huntsmen because he heard the birds sing, and so rested his axe against the tree for a moment? But the tree had to be felled; and a hut made from its branches before the human voice sang too…. The voice that broke the silence of the forest was the voice of Anon. ("Anon" 382)

Woolf suggests here that the repetition (reenactment) of melodic sound created the first expressions of humanity; significantly, this places music at the origin of language.[16]

Subsequently, the essay equates the loss of this performative iteration as a mode of art with the advent of the printing press: "It was the printing press that finally was to kill Anon" ("Anon" 384). Never one to theorize that reversals are simple, however, she adds, "but it was the press also that preserved him" (ibid.). The issue is not that writing is inherently bad and performance is good, of course, but that with the change to the permanence of publication, the things that music (and drama) still capture in performance are threatened into solidification:

"When in 1477 Caxton printed the twenty one books of the Morte DArthur he fixed the voice of Anon for ever" (ibid.). Enacted repetition of the past, therefore, becomes a way in Woolf's novel, penned just before this essay, to dislodge the fixity of historical documentation. *Between the Acts* resonates with the process of reenactment, perhaps more so than any other of Woolf's novels.

Indeed, the very idea of a pageant about English history is itself the performance of the archive.[17] In Woolf's rendering, the pageant reveals that history is "not limited to the imperial domain of the document" (Schneider, *Performing Remains* 104), especially when it is staged by this assemblage of villagers. Instead, it fundamentally unsettles "the word" through its reenactment. This manifests in several ways: words themselves are imbued with their own performativity, just as the myriad musics and sounds in and around the pageant add to the active nature of performance and foreground other ways of knowing, the non-discursive; the "performers" (in quotations because this includes animals and the weather in addition to audience members, as noted) embody the words and even the sounds they utter – in other words, they do not disappear into the archive/score; and lastly, Woolf's embedded pageant plays with the slippage between what, on the surface, is typically presumed to be oppositional: the present and the past, or theatre and history. The integration of the country pageant enables Woolf to commingle the *now* of this audience with British heritage, interrogating, in the process, what seems inevitable and, on a June day in 1939 (the temporal setting of the novel), terrifyingly destructive: the future. These various ways of dislodging the archive combine to demonstrate that history depends upon performance, rather than the other way around.

Early on in the novel, words paradoxically seem to contain their own force and are expressive of their own subjectivity. The narrator imbues them with action that is outside their semantic meaning. As Lucy Swithin and her brother Bartholomew Oliver show the local gentry Mrs Manresa and William Dodge the grounds and Pointz Hall, they talk about the performance they are about to see and what plays they have shown in the past: "'One year we wrote the play ourselves. The son of our blacksmith – Tony? Tommy? – had the loveliest voice'" (*BA* 43). The focus shifts to the younger generation of Isa and Giles, the latter of whom conspicuously "hated this kind of talk this afternoon. Books open; no conclusion come to; and he sitting in the audience" (*BA* 43–4). Then quoted material, with no assignation, interrupts, or perhaps calls to attention, Giles and the group as a whole:

"We remain seated" – "We are the audience." Words this afternoon ceased to lie flat in the sentence. They rose, became menacing and shook their fists at you. This afternoon he wasn't Giles Oliver come to see the villagers act their annual pageant; manacled to a rock he was, and forced passively to behold indescribable horror. His face showed it; and Isa, not knowing what to say, abruptly, half purposely, knocked over a coffee cup. (*BA* 44)

The fierceness of the words implies gesticulating fascist leaders, or a physical and violent altercation, at the very least, a reflection most likely of Woolf's experience of listening to Adolf Hitler's voice on the wireless. Giles, the man who will step on a snake with a toad in its mouth and then have blood on his shoes, is no stranger to totalitarian methods. That words have their own audible force, however, distinct from their meaning is suggestive of a non-discursive process of meaning making. Somehow, words can shake their fists in this novel, an acknowledgment on Woolf's part that language not only can incite action but can also even contain force itself.

But the dynamism that words comprise is not always violent. When Lucy lets Mrs Manresa and William see "the nursery": "Words raised themselves and became symbolical. 'The cradle of our race,' she seemed to say" (*BA* 52). The words appear to contain their own action apart from who says them, although they do reflect the subjectivity to which they are attached. Yet, in this instance, the narrator only states that Lucy "seemed to say" what was symbolical in the moment. The reader is left to wonder, after the fact, does Lucy enunciate these words, or does the narrator just assume that the words echo in the air for all three people even though no one has spoken them? No answer is supplied, but again, language itself becomes infused with its own force. These strange comments bring up the difference between telling and showing often ascribed to the distinction between narrative and drama or music. Here, the words do not tell a story, they perform actions as though they are capable of such a thing; they are dramatized, suggesting that even language itself contains within it other ways of knowing.

The reader has limited access to the written version, or score, of the pageant, although there are moments when a play within the pageant is signalled in the text with name designations as though it is a dramatic text. Even though Miss La Trobe is also described "with her eye on her script" (*BA* 129), "brand[ishing] her script" (*BA* 130), or "crush[ing] her manuscript" (*BA* 88), the reader encounters the performance, proverbial warts and all. Indeed, the novel records the live events of the afternoon, as if a movie camera has been set up to record the pageant but also the audience watching it and the natural environment well beyond the limits of the makeshift stage (although one would need a sort of bird's-eye view camera to include all this simultaneously). Examining the novel's similarities to John Cage's compositional practice of hearing music in ambient sound in his composition "4'33," Cuddy-Keane has noted similarly that it is "as if a microphone had been set up in a village on a day in June in 1939[.] *Between the Acts* records a multiplicity of disparate, varying, and often contradictory voices, diffused through time and space yet sounding together" ("Virginia Woolf, Sound Technologies, and the New Aurality" 92). The representation of the pageant, therefore, because of its placement within this novel, is more than the words of its script. Indeed, in her medium of the novel, Woolf attempts to do the impossible: to capture a live performance (its physicality, its noises, its optics) in language, rather than the other way around, a written play instigating a drama yet to be. The pageant, being in this narrative, is not live, of course, but Woolf is, nevertheless, interested in attempting to depict the interstice between action and archive. This is why, I would suggest, the pageant is especially improvisatory, a "mellay; a medley; an entrancing spectacle" (*BA* 68).

Similarly, parentheses and dashes used during the scenes from the pageant detail, not the desires of the playwright to control bodily gestures or blocking, but the actual real-time movements of the actors – enabling Woolf to embody the meaning of the words because of the hybrid genre she has created. The actions are in the *now* of the play, rather than being prescriptions for future movements, as a play that contains conventional stage direction would have it. There are many examples, but the first extended speech in the Elizabethan era, by Queen Bess, will suffice to demonstrate the function of these actions to crisscross the performed word with the corporal.

> The Queen of this great land ...
> – those were the first words that could be heard above the roar of laughter and applause.
> Mistress of ships and bearded men (she bawled)
> Hawkins, Frobisher, Drake,
> Tumbling their oranges, ingots of silver
> Cargoes of diamonds, ducats of gold,

Down on the jetty, there in the west land, –
(she pointed her fist at the blazing blue sky)
Mistress of pinnacles, spires and palaces –
(her arm swept towards the house)
For me Shakespeare sang –
(a cow mooed. A bird twittered)
The throstle, the mavis (she continued)
In the green wood, the wild wood,
Carolled and sang, praising England, the Queen,
Then there was heard too
On granite and cobble
From Windsor to Oxford
Loud laughter, low laughter
Of warrior and lover,
The fighter, the singer.
The ashen haired babe
(she stretched out her swarthy, muscular arm)
Stretched his arm in contentment
As home from the Isles came
The sea faring men....
Here the wind gave a tug at her head dress. Loops of pearls made it
top-heavy. She had to steady the ruffle which threatened to blow away.
(BA 61–2)

The brackets and side comments are obviously humorous, poking
fun at the mishaps that can occur in any live event, let alone one that
is outside, as well as the bad acting reduced to mimicry, but they capture the non-discursive realm in ways that would be difficult if the
live performance was not implied. Moreover, these physical details
foreground the present moment in the novel. They incorporate the
lived environment of the now. When the surrounds again threaten
to upend the script in the final section of the play, as I have discussed, the reader learns that, according to La Trobe, "'reality [is] too
strong.'" "'Curse 'em!'" she mutters (BA 129). Yet, when the "shower
fell, sudden, profuse" (ibid.), La Trobe realizes "'that's done it'" (BA
130). Non-discursive knowing, not the script, rescues the experience
of the pageant.

While words are suffused with their own force, apart from their
semantics, and the movements of the body are laid bare to heighten

the non-discursive and the now, music and language are commingled in the idea of song to add to the active capacities of the verbal. At the start of each act of the pageant, music is used to summon the audience to their seats. It is also deployed in various forms – songs sung by the chorus and a multitude of tunes played by the gramophone[18] – throughout each section. In addition, music informs the audience that each act is over, dismissing them for the interval or the end of the program with a refrain that allows them to leave their seats: "The music chanted: Dispersed are we. It moaned: Dispersed are we. It lamented" (*BA* 69–70). But the combination of words and music is foregrounded in what seems to be a sort of shorthand for Woolf of musical notes that then turn into words.

To muster the audience to return to their seats, the first iteration of a melody is overheard by Lucy and William in the greenhouse:

> They had left the greenhouse door open, and now music came through it. A.B.C., A.B.C., A.B.C. – someone was practising scales. C.A.T. C.A.T. C.A.T.... Then the separate letters made one word "Cat." Other words followed. It was a simple tune, like a nursery rhyme –
>
> > The King is in his counting house,
> > Counting out his money,
> > The Queen is in her parlour
> > Eating bread and honey.
>
>   They listened. Another voice, a third voice, was saying something simple. And they sat on in the greenhouse, on the plank with the vine over them, listening to Miss La Trobe or whoever it was, practicing her scales. (*BA* 83–4)

Woolf captures her version of language becoming archive – from a musical scale to the written word – in this short segment, inserting it into her pageant to enliven the words with music. The first three letters, ABC, coincide with the notes of a scale (although they are also the first three letters of the alphabet and its well-known song), but typically, a singer practising scales (like those Woolf incorporates in *The Waves* and *The Years* who vocalize to "Ah") would not speak the letters. However, the text states outright that it is "someone practicing scales." Woolf then describes the letters turning into the word "Cat" to suggest a nursery rhyme topic and then follows it with an actual quote from a different nursery rhyme – there is no cat in "Sing a Song of Sixpence," which, as Mark Hussey explains in his notes (*BA* 213, 247–8), is the song cited by Woolf. Although Woolf does not include it here – she chooses instead to focus on the gender differences between the King (linked with money) and the Queen (linked with food) – the rest of the rhyme refers to the blackbirds singing in the pie into which they have been cooked. The commingling here, almost mutual dependence of music and language, is striking and another instance, I submit, of Woolf's attempt to inject rhythm into language.

The anonymous nature of the singer – is it Miss La Trobe, someone practising scales, or a recording, "and the gramophone began A.B.C., A.B.C." (*BA* 89)? – is not clarified when the alphabet letters are repeated right after the rain completes the dreadfully awkward "ten mins. of present time" (*BA* 129): "Music began – A. B. C. – A. B. C. The tune was as simple as could be. But now that the shower had fallen, it was the other voice speaking, the voice that was no one's voice. And the voice that wept for human pain unending said: The King is in his counting house" (*BA* 130). "No one's voice," referred to earlier as the "third voice," only instantiates the anonymity of the author/composer of this tune, dislodging any certainty as to ownership, despite that Miss La Trobe "brandish[es] her script" (ibid.) for security's sake. Even if, as Cook has argued, in the Western art tradition the body is "disciplined and reconfigured by notation" (*Beyond* 319), there is no clear delineation of a composer behind Woolf's dubious and illusive glyphs.

Indeed, as noted earlier, after all this, La Trobe refuses to take credit for the day's performance, despite having "a passion for getting things up" (*BA* 43). This is not about personality negation or humility but about anonymity and inclusivity, a present-day version of Woolf's Anon, "a simple singer." The ultimate refusal to ascribe compositional authority occurs at the close of the "interpretation" (*BA* 137) by Reverend Streatfield, who has trouble maintaining the thread of his discourse after being overwhelmed by the "distant music?" (*BA* 138) of the "twelve aeroplanes in perfect formation like a flight of wild duck [that] came overhead" (ibid.):

"And now," he resumed, cuddling the pipe lighter in the palm of his hand, "for the pleasantest part of my duty. To propose a vote of thanks to the gifted lady ..." He looked round for an object corresponding to this description. None such was visible. "... who wishes it seems to remain anonymous." He paused. "And so ..." He paused again.

It was an awkward moment. How to make an end? Whom to thank? Every sound in nature was painfully audible; the trees; the gulp of a cow; even the skim of the swallows over the grass could be heard. But no one spoke. Whom could they make responsible? Whom could they thank for their entertainment? Was there no one? (*BA* 139–40)

In place of the usual accolades of authorship, a clear delineation of responsibility, for good or bad, the audience is left with myriad questions, a refusal by Woolf to fix the archive to an owner. Instead, as Bartholomew notes, "'Thank the actors, not the author,' he said. 'Or ourselves, the audience'" (*BA* 146), suggesting that the performers (and "ourselves") do anything but disappear at the behest of the script.

Interestingly, in the midst of all this dislodgement of documentary history, something explicitly noticed by Colonel Mayhew and his wife – "'Why leave out the British Army? What's history without the Army, eh?'" (*BA* 113) – Woolf takes the time to provide an example of the performer enslaved by her or his score. Clearly marked out lines are drawn according to the gender of the bodies that vocalize the chorus. But this particular group is embedded in the midst of the Victorian play within the pageant, as opposed to the nameless chorus that weaves in and around the actors chanting rhythmic phrases that usually closes or opens the acts. As Cuddy-Keane points out, "the nineteenth century act resembles the light comic operas of Gilbert and Sullivan, with their satiric spoofs on Victorian institutions and behavior, and their parodic replications of melodramatic plots" (Introduction and Annotations 199). Thus, the idea of a musical score providing the written component for this section is more resonant. Woolf indirectly comments on the lack of understanding even in Gilbert and Sullivan parodies of how the ramifications for women on the stage differ from those for men. Although both are clearly automaton versions of the performer, the differences in the parts they play are made lucid:

> Here a chorus composed of villagers in Victorian mantles, side whiskers and top hats sang in concert:
> Oh has Mr. Sibthorp a wife? Oh has Mr. Sibthorp a wife? That is the hornet, the bee in the bonnet, the screw in the cork and the drill […].
> MR. HARDCASTLE … (brushing flakes of meat from his whiskers) Now …[.]

Now that we have gratified the inner man, let us gratify the desire of the spirit. I call upon one of the young ladies for a song.

CHORUS OF YOUNG LADIES ... Oh not me ... not me ... I really couldn't ... No, you cruel thing, you know I've lost my voice ... I can't sing without the instrument ... etc., etc.

CHORUS OF YOUNG MEN. Oh bosh! Let's have "The Last Rose of Summer." Let's have "I never loved a Dear Gazelle."

MRS. H. (authoritatively) Eleanor and Mildred will now sing "I'd be a Butterfly."

(Eleanor and Mildred rise obediently and sing a duet: "I'd be a Butterfly.")

MRS. H. Thank you very much, my dears. And now gentlemen, Our Country!

(Arthur and Edgar sing "Rule Britannia.") (*BA* 121–2)

Enlisting the familiar songs that markedly speak to the very different expectations for Victorian women and men (and those in the early twentieth century), these singers "obediently" perform their roles in ways that disclose, as Cook would argue, the "performing body as a site of meaning production in Western art music" (*Beyond* 308).

Lastly, the generic hybrid that is *Between the Acts* reveals Woolf's keen perception that both theatre and history are forms of discourse about temporality. As Schneider observes, "the connection ... can be simple if we keep in mind one thing – time ... theatre, like history, is an art of time. Even, we could say, *the* art of time" (*Theatre and History* 7). Woolf blends the two in yet another type of writing, the novel, in order to focus on the disjunction/conjunction of the present moment with the past and the future. The ticking gramophone, for example, functions much like Big Ben in *Mrs. Dalloway*: to mark what Woolf describes in *Orlando* as the "extraordinary discrepancy between time on the clock and time in the mind" (*OR* 95). Yet, there is also a difference between the tick, tick, tick of the machine and the giant timepiece because the sound reproduction device is not, of course, on Greenwich Mean Time; it is part of the performance's sequence of events, suggesting multiple temporalities at the very least. (Interestingly, the illumination of Big Ben's clock was stopped to conform to blackout rules between 1939 and 1945; its seeming inexorableness was therefore undoubtedly threatened by Hitler's Blitzkrieg.)

The passage of time and its menacing advancement are linked also to the pressures of the stage, dealing with the steamroller, so to speak,

of temporality with which a performer is forced to contend when she
sings or acts for an audience. Miss La Trobe's directorial anxieties suggest that another aspect of the performer-as-automaton issue is the
impingement of clock time:

> Chuff, chuff, chuff went the machine in the bushes, accurately, insistently.
>   Clouds were passing across the sky. The weather looked a little
> unsettled. [...]
>   Ducking up and down [La Trobe] cast her quick bird's eye over the
> bushes at the audience. The audience was on the move. The audience was
> strolling up and down. They kept their distance from the dressing-room;
> they respected the conventions. But if they wandered too far, if they began
> exploring the grounds, going over the house, then.... Chuff, chuff, chuff
> went the machine. Time was passing. How long would time hold them
> together? It was a gamble; a risk.... And she laid about her energetically,
> flinging clothes on the grass. [...]
>   Tick, tick, tick, the machine continued. Time was passing. The audience
> was wandering, dispersing. Only the tick tick of the gramophone held
> them together. There, sauntering solitary far away by the flower beds was
> Mrs. Giles escaping.
>   "The tune!" Miss La Trobe commanded. "Hurry up! The tune! The next
> tune! Number Ten!" (*BA* 108–9, 111)

The audience still appreciates the social contracts of theatrical time and
space, even though La Trobe's worry to maintain such codes is painfully, but humorously, apparent in the passage. Correspondingly, the
gramophone suggests that the past weighs on the present, imperial history almost enlisting the machine to do its "insistent[]" bidding. Thus,
the anxiety of time passing means doubly, reflecting both the temporality of the pageant's drama and that of official history unfolding, as it is
in the now of the novel, towards war. Still, as noted earlier, La Trobe's
angsts are ultimately buffeted by the cows and the rain, among many
other heterogeneous sounds and sights, so that she too learns to let go
of, even reorient, her understanding of a theatrical "failure" (*BA* 150).
Stirred by the starlings that pelt the tree behind which she has hidden
when summoned to take credit for the performance – "birds syllabling
discordantly life, life, life" (ibid.) – she has the inspiration for her next
creation: "'I should group them here,' she murmured, 'here.' It would
be midnight; there would be two figures, half concealed by a rock. The
curtain would rise. What would the first words be? The words escaped

her" (*BA* 151). Language has not yet congealed for her at this point, but she has envisioned the performatic domain of her next act.

Isa, Lucy, and William provide a fitting precis of this conjoining of theatrical and historical time in a scene that directly broaches the topic. Lucy, who has lived during the reign of Queen Victoria, questions the idea of progress embedded in time and nineteenth-century imperialism explicitly in the interval after the Gilbert and Sullivan parody mentioned above:

> "Were they like that?" Isa asked abruptly. She looked at Mrs. Swithin as if she had been a dinosaur or a very diminutive mammoth. Extinct she must be, since she had lived in the reign of Queen Victoria.
>
> Tick, tick, tick, went the machine in the bushes
>
> "The Victorians," Mrs. Swithin mused. "I don't believe" she said with her odd little smile, "that there ever were such people. Only you and me and William dressed differently."
>
> "You don't believe in history," said William.
>
> The stage remained empty. The cows moved in the field. The shadows were deeper under the trees. (*BA* 125)

Suggesting that they are the same people outfitted in different garments brings to the fore several issues about the linkage of theatre and history in the book, all marked by the tick, tick, tick of the gramophone. Isa's prompt is directed at Lucy because she wants to know about the "real" history of the period, as opposed to the, perhaps unconvincing, version she has just witnessed in the pageant. The gramophone subtly supports her understanding of history as fact. Lucy's response is quite remarkable: we, in the present, were there, in the past, we just wore different clothes. Questioning linear time while marking the theatricality of everyday life, Woolf finishes the moment with William's poignant, yet fundamentally paradoxical, words, which capture all these intertwined issues in one phrase: "You don't believe in history." To this, pointedly not a question but a statement, Lucy does not respond directly. As the stage remains empty, the time of the natural world is shown to continue, but subsequently, the reader is given access to Lucy's thoughts about the "gigantic ear attached to a gigantic head [...] [by which] we reach the conclusion that *all* is harmony, could we hear it" (*BA* 125). But if she did reply, she might possibly have quipped that history depends on performance.

Woolf's materialist aesthetics work to question then-contemporary notions of temporality, history, art, and everyday life. Her willingness to think across artistic borders, to reach transmedially towards other art forms, such as music, and other sensory domains, such as sound, enables her to imagine and reenact in her novels new possibilities for the future. Her exploration of the interstices of the arts breaks open fissures in conventions, those held so dear by the audience members in the novel. This may have been an especially, and understandably, pessimistic moment in history for her to do so, and the satire of *Between the Acts* is not shy with its critical edge, but art, where Woolf is concerned, living it, performing it, hearing it, still seems to hold the possibility for some sort of renewal.

Chapter Six

The Performativity of Language:
The Waves Musicalized

Hamlet or a Beethoven quartet is the truth about this vast mass that we call the world. But there is no Shakespeare, there is no Beethoven; certainly and emphatically there is no God; we are the words; we are the music; we are the thing itself.

Woolf, "A Sketch of the Past" (1939), MB 72

In chapter 5 I concentrated on the performer and the sounds that reverberate in the novels in scenes that explore music. In chapter 6 I modify this focus to examine the performativity of language on the level of the sentence, but also as embedded in the thematics and structure of Woolf's most formally innovative book, *The Waves*. It is in this novel that her ideas about music become integral to her method. If the first chapter of Part 3 focuses on the concept of enactment as negotiating a space between the body and the archive, then the second chapter shows how language and structure can be infused with performance to produce new fictional methods. Hence, in what follows, I investigate what Woolf might have meant when she said that she writes "to a rhythm and not to a plot" (*L4*: 204), for in this novel musical pulse is not only thematized but also performed in language through what the intermedial theorist Werner Wolf would call *word music*. In addition, a specific piece of music, I argue, enables Woolf to transform novelistic character and structure in new ways. Thus, this chapter employs theories about the musicalization of fiction to scrutinize the performative nature of Woolf's prose – both its rhythmic qualities and its structural elaboration – illuminating one possible clarification of Woolf's comment, late in her life, that a play "or a Beethoven quartet is the truth about this vast mass that we call the world" (*MB* 72).

I. Word Music: "(The rhythm is the main thing in writing)"

Most readers of Woolf criticism are familiar with the references to rhythm by Woolf herself in her letters to Vita Sackville-West (written during the time she was composing *To the Lighthouse*, a subject to which I shall return in the Coda) and Dame Ethel Smyth (penned as she was drafting and redrafting *The Waves* in 1930 and 1931). Yet, Woolf's seemingly straightforward summations of her compositional methods in her comments to the composer, for example – the aforementioned writing "to a rhythm and not to a plot" (*L4*: 204) on 28 August 1930, but also the declaration that "all writing is nothing but putting words on the backs of rhythm" (*L4*: 303) on 7 April 1931 – are anything but simplistic. Earlier, in the letter to Sackville-West (16 March 1926), she boldly asserts that style "is all rhythm" (*L3*: 247), explaining further that it "goes far deeper than words. A sight, an emotion, creates this wave in the mind, long before it makes words to fit it; and in writing […] one has to recapture this" (ibid.). Woolf's notion of rhythm is similarly formulated in her early essay "Street Music" (1906). Suggesting that language has lost some of its revitalizing capabilities, Woolf declares, "when the sense of rhythm was thoroughly alive in every mind we should if I mistake not, notice a great improvement not only in the ordering of all the affairs of daily life, but also in the art of writing, which is nearly allied to the art of music, and is chiefly degenerate because it has forgotten its allegiance" (*E1*: 31). As Emma Sutton rightly notes in her illuminating essay on *The Voyage Out*, Woolf "characterizes rhythm as animated, purposeful and autonomous" ("'Putting Words'" 177) in her first novel. I contend, then, that as Woolf's thinking on the concept develops, the performative nature of rhythm grows as she finds ways to integrate it on the level of the sentence, most strikingly represented in her highly experimental novel.

Woolf's query in her diary, "Could one not get the waves to be *heard* all through? Or farmyard noises?" (*D3*: 236; my emphasis), is simultaneously highly suggestive and cleverly elusive. Nevertheless, it is provocative in terms of what it suggests for intermedial study. Indeed, she transforms the possibilities of prose with such determinations, attempting, no less, to revolutionize narrative and its forms. To do so, I argue, she takes advantage of several types of *intermedial reference* – when the gesture to another art form remains within "a single semiotic system" (Wolf, "Intermediality Revisited" 28), such as a novel that is indebted to a musical form or a verbal description of a visual work (or ekphrasis). Within *intermedial reference*, interart links are typically made either *thematically* (through representations of music, for example) and/or *mimetically* (through analogous imitations of musical properties). For a novel to be considered musicalized, it should incorporate both of these subforms, a combination Wolf argues is apparent in Woolf's short story "The String Quartet." In *The Waves*, I argue, Woolf integrates thematization (the "characters" each engage with music in some way), musical attributes in terms of language (with *word music*), and structural analogy (a late string quartet of Beethoven's, in particular).

Undoubtedly, then, *The Waves* is also a musicalized fiction in these terms – on both representational and imitative levels, as I shall discuss in the final sections of this chapter. But to explore, more specifically, the attributes of Woolf's notion of rhythm, I shall focus first on its performative exposition through something called *word music*: "a musicalizing technique which exploits the basic similarity between verbal and musical signifiers" (Wolf, *Musicalization* 58). Aiming "'at poetic imitation of musical sound' (Scher 152) [it] gives the impression of a presence of music by foregrounding the ... acoustic dimensions of the verbal signifiers" (Wolf, *Musicalization* 58). Wolf explains further, "in ... these cases, literary language must be 'heard' rather than merely read, and this requires ... a special effort in fiction, which is not normally read aloud" (ibid.). Woolf's desire to make language "heard," then, can be gleaned in her word music, which also elaborates the performativity of language.

In what follows, I shall target my study by analysing Woolf's prose in a particular section of *The Waves* that thematizes the word "rhythm" to see if discernible imitative patterns in the language emerge. This doubling does, indeed, occur in the third soliloquy section of the text. Much of the content of this episode explores issues of language explicitly, and more particularly, the differences between the rhythms of prose and poetry. The comparison is provided for the reader by the characters Bernard and Neville, as the segment features an exchange between the two, not, of course, in a typical conversational format in a text, but in a structure that juxtaposes their soliloquies to provide a back-and-forth weaving effect. By this point in the novel, the reader has learned to expect that, although Bernard visits Neville in his room and Neville shows Bernard his poetry, the action and exchange still only come to the reader/listener through the individual thoughts of the "characters."

In addition, Louis contemplates the "pulsation of life" and his lack of access to it in the third portion of soliloquies as well. Noting the "rhythm of the eating-house. [...] The average men, including her [the waitress's] rhythm in their rhythm" (*TW* 73), he states: "Here is the central rhythm; here the common mainspring. I watch it expand, contract; and then expand again. Yet I am not included" (ibid.). Thus, all three male "characters" employ the word "rhythm" specifically in the third episode of the novel.

Conversely, the three female characters engage with rhythm by enacting their particular sonic or musical associations with it, but they do not use the word itself. Susan and Jinny describe their individual rhythmic associations – farmyard noises and the waltz at a dance – while Rhoda, fittingly and like Louis, is outside the social rhythms depicted. The pattern of the episode, therefore, emulates the novel as a whole, which tends to situate, before Bernard's final "summing up," the intellect and the verbal in the male figures, while the body and the natural world find expression in the female ones. Indeed, I agree with Pamela Transue, who argues that the female characters are "locked into sex-determined roles" (137). But Transue also makes the important point that "they are nonetheless complete in themselves, so that their identities are evolved for us completely without reference to their associations with men. Very few novels in the history of literature so completely disavow the centrality of relations with the opposite sex in exploring female character and experience" (ibid.).

In terms of subject matter in episode 3, Bernard and Neville are at university, Louis is in a coffee-house, Susan is settled in the country, and Jinny and Rhoda are at parties. All of them contemplate their environments and the new experiences they are encountering in their early twenties, a time when their social world is expanding. Bernard, the writer, is composing a letter to "the woman who made me Byron" (*TW* 200). The poet Byron surfaces frequently in the text, most poignantly in this segment about letter writing and again in the final episode that brings the six subjectivities together. In the third episode Bernard contemplates both prose – with the epistolary form – and poetry – by the poet who, Woolf asserts in her essay "Poetry, Fiction, and the Future" (1927),[1] "pointed the way; [Byron] showed how flexible an instrument poetry might become, but none has followed his example to put his tool to further use. We remain without a poetic play" (*E4*: 434). Thus, Bernard considers this generic crossover in *The*

Waves, as does Woolf in her writing of this novel that might encapsulate "poetic drama" (*E4*: 430).

In addition, Bernard's soliloquies – he has three of them interspersed with two from Neville and the third followed by Louis – foreground in language "the acoustic dimensions of the verbal signifiers" (Wolf, *Musicalization* 58), of word music, by exploring variations in rhythmic patterns. Generally speaking, Bernard's phrases in the first few paragraphs of the episode hover around five, six, and seven syllables; this can be contrasted to Neville's phrases, which, at least in his first soliloquy in the episode that comes on the heels of Bernard's, accentuate shorter phrases of two, three, and four beats. After stating, "Nothing should be named lest by so doing we change it," Neville proclaims:

> [4] Let it exist, [2] this bank, [3] this beauty, [2] and I, [4] for one instant, [4] steeped in pleasure. [4] The sun is hot. [5] I see the river. [12] I see trees specked and burnt in the autumn sunlight.[3] Boats float past, [3] through the red, [3] through the green. [6] Far away a bell tolls, [4] but not for death. (*TW* 63; syllable count in square brackets)

The pattern of short phrases composed according to syllable and given rhythmic pulse by punctuation is demonstrable. I am taking my cue for reading the syntax in *The Waves* in this manner from Merete Alfsen, who has written a highly informative essay about her experience translating *The Waves* into Norwegian. She deduces, "in Virginia Woolf, the *sine qua non* is, without a doubt, the *rhythm*. Any sensitive reader will perceive that. What the translator-reader has to pay particular attention to is how these rhythms come about by use of syllables, commas, semicolons" (32). Rather than a strict metre composed according to feet, as in the poetry alluded to in the episode (Byron's *Don Juan*), Woolf writes according to the phrase, which I am taking to mean, as it does generally in English grammar, "(gen.) any syntactic unit larger than a word and smaller than a clause" (*OED* online). Woolf pays special attention to syllables, commas, and semicolons, but also, I would add, to anaphora, dashes, and parentheses. Elsewhere in her oeuvre, as critics have shown, chiefly Patricia Laurence, ellipses become very important as well; but in *The Waves* they are less frequent, because, most likely, she is creating the smooth flow and effect of undulation in the language, a claim made by both Mark Hussey and Julie Vandivere with which I certainly agree.[2]

For the sake of comparison with a poetic metre, one could examine the syllable count in the *ottava rima* from Byron's *Don Juan*, which follows iambic pentameter quite strictly. This is the last stanza from Canto 1:

[10] "Go, little book, from this my solitude!
[10] I cast thee on the waters – go thy ways!
[10] And if, as I believe, thy vein be good,
[10] The world will find thee after many days."
[10] When Southey's read, and Wordsworth understood,
[10] I can't help putting in my claim to praise –
[10] The four first rhymes are Southey's every line:
[10] For God's sake, reader! take them not for mine.
[80] *Total syllables*

One can see the telltale even line length, with variations in the iambic feet for emphasis but strict adherence to ten syllables per line. Visually and aurally the poetry reveals its exacting metre. I have chosen the last stanza because in it Byron makes a thought-provoking, intertextual gesture to reading (the quotation is from the final stanza of Robert Southey's "Epilogue to the Lay of the Laureate," Byron's gibe, of course, at the poet with the most prestigious title in England), writing (distinguishing himself from Wordsworth and Southey), and books.

Compare Byron's stanza to what amounts to one sentence from the third paragraph of Bernard's soliloquy in the third episode. Again, I am counting the phrases by syllables (not feet):

[7] I shall pass from the service
[6] for the man who was drowned
[6] (I have a phrase for that)
[9] to Mrs. Moffat and her sayings
[6] (I have a note of them),
[7] and so to some reflections
[7] apparently casual
[7] but full of profundity
[6] (profound criticism
[9] is often written casually)
[9] about some book I have been reading,
[6] some out-of-the-way book. (*TW* 61)
[78] *Total syllables*

This section is near the end of the paragraph and it leads to Bernard's comment in parentheses that "(the rhythm is the main thing in writing)" (ibid.), which occurs in the penultimate sentence of the paragraph. The entire soliloquy is littered with parenthetical comments about Bernard's abilities and anxieties concerning authorship. What I have cited is only one long sentence. I have taken the phrases set in parentheses as my basic, syllabic guide (the first two contain six syllables) because they set up a rhythmic counterpoint to the rest of the phrases in the sentence. I have also broken the line when a pause in speech would most likely occur because of the way Woolf has written it, at the beginning of prepositional phrases, for example, or the clause following a conjunction. Another instance of the structure of six and nine syllables occurs with the passive sentence construction in the third parenthesis "(profound criticism is often written casually)." This phrase creates a syllabic rhythm that emulates the first parenthesis and its subsequent phrase, also six and nine syllables, "(I have a phrase for that) to Mrs. Moffat and her sayings." Indeed, organized according to phrase, the whole sentence, which is almost the length of a paragraph (a striking contrast to what comes after with Neville), is syntactically ordered according to this paired construction of six and nine, which tends towards an antecedent/consequent rhythm: a wavelike rhythm, I would suggest. The parentheses accentuate the different intonations one would hear in one's inner audition of the reading experience, and almost beseech the reader to enunciate aloud to get the effect of the rhythm. Lastly, the sentence creates a unit; it is almost a verse paragraph or stanza that is close in total syllable count to *ottava rima* (eighty in comparison to Woolf's sentence, which is seventy-eight).

But subsequently, Woolf also vividly changes this rhythm set up in the long sentence cited above. With Woolf there is no strict metronome, keeping the same periodic tempo. The rhythm changes according to the larger pattern of the segment and the subject matter to engage the style performatively with the content. After a comment about the woman's admiration of his letter-writing style, Bernard reflects, "it is the speed, the hot, molten effect, the laval flow of sentence into sentence that I need. Who am I thinking of? Byron of course. I am, in some ways, like Byron. Perhaps a sip of Byron will help to put me in the vein. Let me read a page" (*TW* 61):

[1] No;
[3] this is dull;

[4] this is scrappy.
[7] This is rather too formal.
[9] Now I am getting the hang of it.
[11] Now I am getting his beat into my brain
[10] (the rhythm is the main thing in writing).
[9] Now, without pausing I will begin,
[8] on the very lilt of the stroke –
    [8] Yet it falls flat. It peters out. (Ibid.)

Woolf emphasizes the growing urgency of Bernard's insecurities by using semicolons, commas, and periods to produce a sort of galloping rhythm that gains momentum because of the placement of the pauses. Indeed, the language enacts a disjunctive, "dull" and "scrappy" line with phrases that build in length. Caesuras accentuate Bernard's failure to find the right rhythm, to match his own rhythm to the poet Byron's. Woolf notes a similar disjunction of her own when she writes to Smyth a month before creating the third typescript of the novel that "the loud-speaker is pouring forth Wagner from Paris. His rhythm destroys my rhythm" (*L4*: 303). Notably, and in her own mischievous and Byronic way, Woolf puts the ten-syllable phrase about rhythm – what she herself declares elsewhere is her method – in parenthesis, doubling the irony. The paragraph culminates with the striking, suspended tension of a dash: "Now, without pausing I will begin, on the very lilt of the stroke –" which is effectively deflated with the four-syllable lines that begin a new paragraph, "Yet it falls flat. It peters out." These sentences demonstrate that Woolf infuses poetic phrases into her writing when the characters speak about rhythm, producing, I suggest, word music in the process. Perhaps this illuminates another facet of her comment to Smyth that "though the rhythmical is more natural to me than the narrative, it is completely opposed to the tradition of fiction and I am casting about all the time for some rope to throw to the reader" (*L4*: 204).

But what is musical about this technique? It is rhythmic, certainly, and lyrical. Indeed, Woolf is using, yet transforming, the conventions of poetry in her own sort of free verse, in a similar fashion to T.S. Eliot (also a model, most critics agree, for Louis). The section is a performance of Woolf's own emulation of Byron as well, as I have shown. Michael Herbert and Susan Sellers's annotations in the Cambridge edition of the novel make evident that the free play of her language is also richly intertextual.[3] This particular passage, therefore, works doubly on the levels of both thematization and mimesis. But these phrasal methods are not unique to this section on rhythm; she deploys them throughout to perform in language the subject matter under discussion (Neville's contrasting rhythms provide a case in point).

A phrasal compositional technique, however, is not just linguistic, but also exceptionally prevalent in the classical tradition of music, particularly in the composers to which Woolf often refers, such as Bach and Mozart, and especially, Beethoven, a composer who functions historically, in many ways, as the musical equivalent to his Romantic contemporary Byron. Phrases are the basic building blocks of melody. Defined by the *OED* under the subject *Music* as "a short *sequence* of notes forming a more or less distinct *unit* or *pattern* within a passage, movement, or piece" (*OED* online), a musical phrase characterizes what happens in Woolf's sentences perhaps even more than the usual grammatical definition of a phrase as "a syntactic unit larger than a word or smaller than a clause." In addition, the antecedent/consequent pattern is a pervasive phrasal structure in the common practice period (the Baroque, Classical, and Romantic eras) of traditional Western music, especially ubiquitous and important in the procedures of counterpoint, something that becomes integral to Beethoven's style in his late period.

II. The Case of Ludwig van Beethoven

The idea of music, more generally, also figures in *The Waves* as an important intermedial signifier, perhaps because the combination of the sonorous art and her own was on Woolf's mind, given that she shared a platform with Smyth titled "Music and Literature" at the London and National Society for Women's Service on 21 January 1931.[4] Correspondingly, the significance of a particular composer, in addition to concerns about authorship in writing, surfaces in Bernard's final soliloquy. He reports buying a picture of Beethoven, a visual version of a person who creates symphonies and string quartets, among many other musical forms. Strangely, Bernard seems to choose this picture over that of other *writers*. A composer who was notoriously Romantic in his conception of himself as an autonomous artist, Beethoven signifies the ideological underpinnings and gendered stereotypes of the "great" male artist alongside which Bernard is attempting to place himself:

'I rose and walked away – I, I, I; not Byron, Shelley, Dostoevsky, but I, Bernard. I even repeated my own name once or twice. I went, swinging my stick, into a shop, and bought – not that I love music – a picture of

Beethoven in a silver frame. Not that I love music, but because the whole of life, its masters, its adventurers, then appeared in long ranks of magnificent human beings behind me; and I was the inheritor; I, the continuer: I, the person miraculously appointed to carry it on. So, swinging my stick, with my eyes filmed, not with pride, but with humility rather, I walked down the street. (*TW* 203)

One soon finds, however, that even this supposed "humility" is a delusion, for after Bernard describes the potential regimen of an "inheritor," the "long ranks" behind him are shown to be illusory: "But it is a mistake, this extreme precision, this orderly and military progress; a convenience, a lie" (*TW* 205). This particular "whole of life" is evoked by a static thought/vision of Beethoven; consequently, it turns out to be a "false start" to Bernard's conception of himself as "the continuer," another example of Woolf's dislodgement of the primacy of the composer/score, as I argued in chapter 5.

In addition, on 26 March 1927 the *Nation and Athenaeum* published a short review article by Leonard Woolf about the various biographies that had been written concerning "The Man Beethoven" (the subtitle of the essay). The appraisal reveals how the various versions of the "great man" conflict with each other because they are invested in the process of myth making, much like Woolf's exposé in *The Waves*. Leonard characterizes the situation in the following manner: "About the art of Beethoven there is a beautiful unanimity. But about his life and character, about the relation of Beethoven, the Man, to Beethoven, the Artist, there is a pained and painful controversy" ("The World of Books" 894). Leonard is presciently aware of the role that biography can play in what critical musicologists and historians such as K.M. Knittel now understand as the "construction of Beethoven."[5] Although both Woolfs would agree on the unfixed nature of a recounted life, Virginia Woolf also associates biographical instantiation with gendered imbalance in her novels, as Bernard's thoughts of Beethoven imply.

As is well known, Beethoven was a pivotal figure between the eighteenth and nineteenth centuries who is often credited with ushering in a new musical era. Woolf is sceptical of this homage to the "great man," as she discloses in the novel itself, yet her suspicion does not lead her to dismiss Beethoven's music, only the limited conception of him as an elite or elevated artist. Instead, she would excise the artist's role in favour of the art itself, as the epigraph from "A Sketch of the Past" suggests: "There is no Beethoven; certainly and emphatically there is no

God" (*MB* 72). As discussed previously in relation to *Between the Acts*, the notion of artistic anonymity will become even more important in her later work, encapsulated in the unpublished essay "Anon," written in 1941.

Moreover, in *The Waves*, her most structurally innovative text, the connections among Beethoven's music, her innovations in form, and "character" are substantial. More specifically, Woolf utilizes a particular piece of music, I argue, to which she was listening while creating the novel, to reconfigure her compositional methods: Beethoven's late String Quartet in B-flat Major, Opus 130, including the piece's original finale, the *Grosse Fuge*, Opus 133. Beethoven's chamber work provides Woolf with a structural analogy to reconceive not just the "form" of her novel but also the concept of character, as form and content become inextricably linked in *The Waves*.[6]

In what follows I return to the process of the novel's composition, correlating Woolf's rhetorical and narratological experiments with her musical listening practices – the actual sounds that filled her ears. Consistently, Woolf takes her cue from the functional and structural possibilities of intermediality. But one of Woolf's significant contributions to modernist aesthetics is that her focus on "formal" properties does not privilege structure over her political and/or social concerns. Music facilitates this intermingling of "form," subjectivity, and cultural critique, which are inseparable in her experimental novels. In *The Waves* the thoughts of the characters become the structure of the nine episodes; outside commentary by a narratorial voice is almost entirely evacuated by the pervasiveness of the first-person interior monologues. The shape of the work follows the patterns of life development that many bildungsromans feature, but Woolf does this with six interspersed lives simultaneously and also largely excises the material world, which the reader accesses only through the six consciousnesses. The exceptions to this pattern in the episodes are the italicized interlude passages, which simultaneously record a day and the seasons of a year in the natural world – significantly, this tangible domain in the novel does not contain the perspective of a human subjectivity.

As detailed in the Introduction, Woolf attended the Beethoven festival week at Æolian Hall in 1921 to listen to the London String Quartet play all seventeen Beethoven string quartets in chronological order. In addition, the Woolfs obtained an Algraphone in 1925; they listened to music in the evenings on a regular basis. Leonard wrote record reviews for the *Nation and Athenaeum* between 1926 and 1929 but also kept a

Diary of music listened to, 1939–69 in which he recorded their listening practices. There are also forty-one loose card catalogues, most likely written before 1939, but they do not have dates as the *Diary* does. The reviews and the *Diary* reveal that the Woolfs had an extensive collection of traditional Western art music ranging from the orchestral and small ensemble works of well-known composers such as Bach, Mozart, Haydn, Brahms, Schubert, Schumann, and Beethoven to the lesser-known Baroque composers Scarlatti, Corelli, and Rameau and the moderns Bartók and Stravinsky. They were also well versed in the operas of Mozart, Verdi (the first entry in the *Diary* is *La Traviata*), and Wagner, as well as the vocal music of Richard Strauss and Schubert. Suffice it to say, they had an extensive knowledge of standard Western repertoire.

But what we know of Woolf's objectives concerning the novel is notoriously scant. As Nigel Nicolson has claimed in reference to Woolf's letters, "we will never know why Virginia Woolf recast *The Waves* so many times, nor why she made her detailed changes … [Her] letters tell us next to nothing about her methods of composition … It was a private labour, the printed book the only public declaration of her intent" (*Letters* 4: xxi). The novel's metanarrative material, however, speaks so frequently about the art form of music that the connection is viable regardless of any explicit comments about her writing process or apparent intentions. But her observations can only point, at best, towards a certain direction; they cannot lead in any way to the "truth" of the novel's methods. Therefore, I understand her remarks about Beethoven and her listening experiences while composing the novel as signifying not an influence but an intermedial reference, as noted above. By this I also want to imply a kinship with the concept of intermediality as framed by Julia Kristeva in her study of Mikhail Bakhtin. As Irina Rajewsky suggests, "intertextuality in its various narrow or broad conceptions has been a starting point for many attempts to theorize the intermedial" (47). The idea that any and all texts always already refer to other texts, then, can be applied to the interrelations among media as well. Thus, rather than mapping one art form onto another – an endeavour the novel itself thwarts – my discussion of the associations between Opus 130 and *The Waves* will focus on the effect of that intersection, what comes out of the integration of and the incongruities between literature and music. Woolf's observations about her own methods provide a fruitful backdrop to her fiction, but I do not understand them as a confirmation that places fixed limits on the "meaning" of her work, or forever attaches Beethoven's late quartet to the novel. Moreover, I am mindful of what

Rajewsky calls the "as if" dilemma: "an intermedial reference can only generate an *illusion* of another medium's specific practices" (55). My objective is not, therefore, to prove that Woolf's novel *is* music, but to explore the possibilities that emerge when she develops her medium of language by thoroughly engaging with another art form.

Correspondences between Beethoven's work and *The Waves* are numerous, however. The composer is mentioned in Woolf's diary in the early phase of the novel's conception, on 18 June 1927, the second time she "suddenly [...] rhapsodized" and envisioned the work as a whole: "I do a little work on it in the evening when the gramophone is playing late Beethoven sonatas" (*D*3:139). The latter are comparable to the late quartets in terms of style and innovation, as mentioned in chapter 5 in reference to Rachel's practising of Opus 111 in *The Voyage Out*. Not only do the piano sonatas utilize similar contrapuntal textures and techniques, but they also emulate the almost chaotic play between light-hearted abandon and concentrated severity found, for example, in Beethoven's "Hammerklavier" Sonata, Opus 106 (1818). This diary entry comes three months after Leonard Woolf wrote his article about "The Man Beethoven," in which he suggests that it is not a surprise that "the man who wrote the Hammerklavier sonata in 1818 was a trying companion to people who could neither write nor understand the Hammerklavier sonata" (894). By the time Woolf writes *The Waves*, she is very familiar with the late music of the sonatas and the quartets.

The diary entry that makes the explicit connection between her method in *The Waves* and the composer's quartets occurs during the second redrafting of the novel, when she alters the structure. On Monday, 22 December 1930, she writes,

> It occurred to me last night while listening to a Beethoven quartet that I would merge all the interjected passages into Bernard's final speech, & end with the words O solitude: thus making him absorb all those scenes, & having no further break. This is also to show that the theme effort, effort, dominates: not the waves: & personality: & defiance: but I am not sure of the effect artistically; because the proportions may need the intervention of the waves finally so as to make a conclusion. (*D*3: 339)

Although it starts in 1939, Leonard's *Diary of music listened to, 1939–69* contains references to both the late sonatas and quartets, including Opus 130 on 28 October 1939 and 9 March 1940, and the *Grosse Fuge*, Opus 133, on 2 March 1941, the month in which Virginia died.

(Incidentally, the entry on 27 March, the day before her suicide, also belongs to Beethoven, the *Appassionata* Piano Sonata No. 23 in F minor, Opus 57.) Her appreciation of his music is considerable, therefore, and that Opus 130 and its well-known finale were part of the record collection documented later suggests a sustained familiarity.

But so do Leonard's earlier record reviews. On 13 April 1929, Leonard comments on the recording history of Beethoven's late quartets. He laments the fact that Columbia Records has yet to produce a complete set: "It is to be hoped that the gramophone companies will complete the recording of the Beethoven quartets. There remain now unrecorded only Opus 18, No. 5; the magnificent Quartet in C-sharp minor which Beethoven himself and many other people have held to be the finest of them all, and the 'Grosse Fugue,' Opus 133. We hope that it will not be long before Columbia gives us records of Opus 131 and Opus 133" ("New Gramophone Records [I]" 56). In May 1929 Leonard notes that Opus 131 has been issued and that Columbia are "therefore, to be congratulated on at last producing it." He again requests that "Columbia will follow this up with a recording of the 'Grosse Fugue'" ("New Gramophone Records [II]" 252). Unfortunately, Leonard does not return to this issue again before his last review on 31 August 1929.

Woolf's mention of her inspiration for ending the novel in tandem with hearing Beethoven's music suggests her own sense of listening as a practice, which changes historically because of the accessibility and repeatability of recorded music; it allows, perhaps, for less focused concentration, but at the same time a sort of intimate "half-listening" (*TY* 215) that Woolf frequently details in the novels (recall Mrs Ramsay's aural reveries, the "half-heard melody" (*TL* 192) in "Time Passes," or Martin's conversation with Sara in *The Years*, for just a few examples). Woolf's experience reported in her diary is even foretold (to a certain extent, albeit in a "live" performance situation) in one of her own novels – *Night and Day*, when Cassandra plays the piano for the Hilberys: "At the sound of the first notes Katharine and Rodney both felt an enormous sense of relief at the licence which the music gave them to loosen their hold upon the mechanism of behaviour. They lapsed into the depths of thought. Mrs Hilbery was soon spirited away into a perfectly congenial mood, that was half reverie and half slumber, half delicious melancholy and half pure bliss" (*ND* 438). Similarly, Mary Datchet walks on the Strand, musing to herself "much as the mind shapes all kinds of forms, solutions, images when listening inattentively to music" (*ND* 271). Mary's experience is, nevertheless, thought-provoking: "from an acute consciousness of herself as an individual, Mary passed to a conception of the scheme of things in which, as a human being, she must have her share. She half held a vision; the vision shaped and dwindled. [...] Her vision seemed to lay out the lines of her life until death in a way which satisfied her sense of harmony" (ibid.).

The various levels of listening documented by the small but captive audience in *Night and Day* or made by analogy with one of the novel's characters, Mary, suggest that Woolf was acutely tuned to the mind's reception of music, which lends credence to the specificity of the connection she establishes between Beethoven and *The Waves* in her diary. Although Woolf's principal familiarity with Beethoven's late music is facilitated by a gramophone recording, which provides a fixed performance without the physical presence of its performers, with its mechanical sounding body it delivers other advantages that potentially enable a more thorough engagement with the sonorous art for her compositional process. In other words, I would suggest that, without the introduction of the gramophone into her home, the ability for repeated playings, potential volume control, as well as an intimate proximity to its sounds, the experience of listening to music that subsequently inspires her own novel's finale might not have occurred.

So the sounds of Beethoven's late music, especially, are in Woolf's ears at the time she is writing and redrafting *The Waves*. Significantly, the music Beethoven wrote later in life is highly innovative: thematically, harmonically, rhythmically, and formally. Indeed, Igor Stravinsky hailed the *Grosse Fuge* as quintessentially modern, gushing about "this absolutely contemporary piece of music that will be contemporary forever ... this fugue, I love it beyond any other" (*Dialogues and a Diary* 24). As Richard Taruskin chronicles in the *Oxford History of Western Music*, musicologists typically divide Beethoven's oeuvre into three periods – early (characterized as formative or "classical"), middle ("heroic"), and late (introspective or the "inwardness" period). Although, as Michael Spitzer illuminates, debates continue as to what constitutes his "late style," Opus 130 and 133 fall within the latter category not only chronologically in terms of biography but also in terms of experimentation.[7] The "fingerprints" of these late works are Beethoven's deployment of fugue and variation: "the great fugal finales of the 'Hammerklavier', the Quartet Opus 130 and the Credo of the Mass ... constitute some of the late style's most emblematic moments ... Variation – the essentially decorative genre in which a melody is varied ever more elaborately – militates against sonata because it is tonally static (no modulation) and formally repetitive (the phrase rhythm never changes). All five of the late quartets are dominated by central slow movements in variation form" (Spitzer, "Notes on Beethoven's Late Style" 194).

While Opus 130 and 133 remain within the confines of tonality, Beethoven's late output often jarred and appalled the ears of contemporaries. On a first listening to the *Grosse Fuge*, I would submit, the melodic disjunction, chromaticism, and polyphonic textures test the limits of the apperceptive ear even now. The musicologist William Kinderman confirms: "the last quartets in particular seem to push beyond established traditions to discover whole new seas of thought and feeling" (Introduction 1). And Leonard concurs. He admits in "Beethoven the Man," "again and again the last five quartets, the Great Fugue, the Mass in D, the last five pianoforte sonatas, and the Ninth Symphony are referred to as something *sui generis* in music, something above and beyond the reach of other composers" ("The World of Books" 894). Clearly, the Woolfs were intimately familiar with the experimental nature of Beethoven's late work. The compositions referred to by Leonard comprise Beethoven's late period (those written after circa 1817 till his death on 26 March 1827).

This phase in Beethoven's oeuvre repeatedly features expansions of melodic material that extend the traditional subject statements made in both sonata-form and counterpoint, and these experiments do not always occur, as they more typically would, in the development sections. The *Grosse Fuge*, which begins by exploiting several different versions of the same melodic material, is a case in point. Withholding narrative termination on the level of the musical sentence, the start of Opus 133 plays with its listeners: suggesting a melody then retracting it, boldly starting again only to rescind it once more before it comes to completion. Joseph Kerman describes the opening *Overatura* as follows: "This section hurls all the thematic versions at the listener's head like a handful of rocks ... In a shattering four-octave *unisono*, the lumbering version of the A♭ Fugue accelerates into its violent trill; then comes the simple dancelike version in 6/8 time; then the self-abnegating version that will provide the G♭ *fugato* with its *cantus firmus*" (277). Woolf makes similar thematic studies, commenting during the early stages of crafting *The Waves*, "I write variations of every sentence; compromises; bad shots; possibilities. [...] I incline now to try violent shots – at London – at talk – shouldering my way ruthlessly – & then, if nothing comes of it – anyhow I have examined the possibilities" (*D3*: 275).

Beethoven's late works also increasingly utilize contrapuntal textures. Stephen Rumph has argued, "it is no exaggeration to say that
counterpoint becomes a way of thought in Beethoven's late style, as
pervasive as sonata-form in his earlier works" (99). Beethoven made
a study of both J.S. Bach and G.F. Handel as a way to find inspiration
(Solomon 230); consequently, the fugue has a resurgence in the music
of his late period. Again his methods resemble Woolf's fully realized
work; her thematic and structural materials emulate simultaneous
separation and correlation, as does musical counterpoint. Melodic
themes – the subject – hold a fugue together through repetition and
variation. Similarly, according to Bernard, "we exist not only separately but in undifferentiated blobs of matter. [...] And I am so made
that, while I hear one or two distinct melodies, such as Louis sings, or
Neville, I am also drawn irresistibly to the sound of the chorus chanting its old, chanting its almost wordless, almost senseless song that
comes across courts at night" (*TW* 197). As Cuddy-Keane suggests,
the chorus of the natural world, the modern city, and the six voices
of the narrative convey an "apprehension of ongoing, interrelational
life" ("Virginia Woolf, Sound Technologies, and the New Aurality"
88). For Cuddy-Keane, music in *Between the Acts* is representative of a
new model for social organization, one that dislodges "conventional
meaning, because it attempts to impose unity" and instead depicts
music's lack of "definite articulation [which] is fully inclusive and
therefore truly unifying" ("Politics" 282). But this description in *The
Waves*, I am suggesting, imagines interconnected lives, not just as
music in general, but as the technique of counterpoint.

To elaborate more specifically, and correspondingly, in the *Grosse
Fuge*, once the introductory material finishes, the subject is first played
independently, as a solo line, as is standard for fugues. This is followed
by another entrance of the same melody but at a relational interval to
the first one, in chordal harmony. When the second melody comes in, it
is foregrounded. The first subject continues after its initial pronouncement but it is de-emphasized so as to stress the independence of the
second iteration of the subject. This pattern continues on as there are
four voices to the fugue; each time the subject is highlighted upon its
first entrance. Yet, all four voices work in harmony together, in terms of
the Western tonal system. By the time all four voices have entered – two
violins, a viola, and a cello – each line has simultaneously maintained a
melody and also been put into harmonic relation with the other voices.

Thus, a fugue enacts concurrent independence and unity, something at issue throughout Woolf's novel in its very method, as well as its content. Woolf reveals separate character traits and thematics, but then also interweaves the characters' thoughts in the episodes, and finally commingles them in Bernard's last soliloquy that ends the novel.

Beethoven also experiments with new sonorities through chromaticism, making further demands on his listeners by increasing melodic and harmonic tension. The difficult melodic leaps and chromatic harmonies in the *Grosse Fuge* tax both the musicians who play them and the audience who hears them. Likewise, as Kinderman documents, Beethoven's friend Karl Holz, a violinist for the quartet that first performed Opus 130 in 1826 (with the original finale of the *Grosse Fuge*), told the composer when preparing to practise for the concert, "everything will go easily, except for the fugue."[8] This movement demands physical engagement on the part of the performer to contend with "the bowing, clarity, and ensemble of the sections in swift tempo involving triplets and leaps in register" (Kinderman, "Beethoven's Last Quartets" 301). The community of string players must work to sound their parts not only together but also in distinction from each other with highly independent melodic lines, a situation generated by the difficult (dissonant and disjunctive) nature of this late work. As I shall demonstrate below, this tension between independence and interconnection, harmony and dissonance, is both a thematic and structural component to the novel, a paradox that is never resolved and is reflected in the final italicized words – "*The waves broke on the shore*" (*TW* 238) – which resist closure by implying the cyclical and never-ending undulation of the ocean.

Moreover, Opus 130 and 133 have very interesting compositional histories in light of Woolf's novel. Not only do the works showcase all of the features mentioned above, but Beethoven adds movements to the string quartet form: six instead of the traditional four. Other quartets from Beethoven's late period, such as Opus 131 (seven movements) and Opus 132 (five) also feature additional movements. Kinderman suggests that Opus 130 and, indeed, the middle three of the late quartets "expand the cycle of movements beyond the conventional framework that had, with few exceptions, served Beethoven adequately throughout his career. Formal expansion beyond the four-movement framework is a remarkably consistent feature of this group of works" ("Beethoven's Late Quartets" 301). In Opus 130 (and 133) each piece performs a unique yet interconnected part of the whole, strikingly similar to the interrelated soliloquies of the six "characters" (Neville, Louis, Susan, Jinny, Rhoda, and Bernard) in Woolf's novel. In addition to the overall and unique structure of a six-movement string quartet, there is even a "silent" yet significant and conventional seventh movement – coinciding with Percival – in Beethoven's rewritten and more traditional finale.

Not a typical fugue by any means as I have explained, Beethoven's first version of the quartet ends with the *Grosse Fuge*; it threatens convention not only formally but also in terms of performative skill and tonality. Then-contemporary audience reaction to the initial finale was subdued, especially by comparison to the other movements (they demanded encores of the *Alla danza tedesca* and the *Cavatina*). Beethoven's response (he waited in a nearby tavern for reports of the reaction) was one of disparagement: "'Yes, these delicacies, but why not the fugue?' ... 'Cattle! Asses!'" (Solomon 323).[9] Yet, he was persuaded (as was rarely the case) to write a new, non-controversial finale shortly before his death in 1827. Thus, this particular quartet and its two finales represent and perform not only Beethoven's radical experimentation but also his own conflict with critical reception of his work's innovations – marking convention, yet simultaneously resisting it. According to Michael Steinberg, by the 1920s (when Woolf was listening to the quartets), concert performance practice favoured playing Opus 130 with its original finale, Opus 133, restored (239). Thus, a parallel pattern of a "silent" seventh movement can be found in Woolf's deployment of the conventional "character," Percival, who dies a senseless death in India by falling off a horse (conspicuously, he is not in battle). Woolf's novel answers tradition by never giving this conventionally heroic figure[10] a "voice" (he has no soliloquy), suggesting the subversion of the British colonial enterprise. Thus, in parallel fashion to Beethoven, Woolf's silencing of Percival marks convention yet resists it. As I shall demonstrate below, the "characters" in the novel can be linked to the overall thematics enacted in the different movements of the quartet as well. The fact that the seventh, more conventional, movement did not typically get played during the performances that Woolf most likely attended and that the *Grosse Fuge* was familiar to both Virginia and Leonard Woolf as a significant work in Beethoven's late oeuvre suggest a similar pattern in terms of the novel's allotment of "characters."

Moreover, similar to *The Waves*, this string quartet modifies and reconfigures the form and content of its generic tradition. The first finale produces a particular version of the quartet that leads to the fugue, reminiscent of the overall structure of Woolf's novel that crescendos with Bernard's final soliloquy. Steinberg argues that the fugue changes the focus of the quartet's overall structure. The more conventional finale puts the weight of intensity on the fifth movement, the *Cavatina*. Barbara R. Barry concurs: "the inordinate length and density of the *Grosse Fuge* provides a powerful end-weighting and directional focus to the quartet, whereas with the alternative finale, which complements the lighter character and proportion of the first movement, the *Cavatina* is felt to be the expressive center of the work" (357). Importantly, however, the quartet and the novel both interlink the structures that constitute the whole. As Barry reveals, "the *Grosse Fuge* is conceptually related to the third, fourth and fifth movements, and even more, the fugue subject is demonstrably related to the opening *Adagio, ma non troppo* of the first movement" (356). Thus, the movements in Beethoven's quartet speak to, reflect, and invert each other; Woolf's "contested subjectivit[ies]" (Goldman 186) interact similarly. Indeed, as Jane Goldman has argued, "to talk of 'separate people' in *The Waves* is perhaps to miss the point" (ibid.). Although these figures have names and particular attributes that seem to distinguish one from the other, they are also inseparable from each other, signifying that there is no "Absolute Subject" (ibid.). They have individual soliloquies, but they also recall each other's phrases, comment on one another's social behaviours, and celebrate or lament the effect of each other's company. As is often the case for Woolf, subjectivity can be, perhaps even must be, simultaneously capable of maintaining connection yet allowing for difference.

Similarly, the structural patterns of the first and last movements in the quartet speak to each other. The *Adagio non troppo* previews almost all of the musical ideas that will follow in the *Allegro*, as the *Overtura* that begins the *Grosse Fuge* also foretells the subsequent *Fuga*. In *The Waves*, the chirping birds at dawn mentioned by the children in the first pages of the novel preview the themes of solitude and community that will follow, and then return in the last pages filtered through Bernard's mind.

Woolf's structure, however, is not exactly the same as Beethoven's six movements: there are nine episodes and ten interludes, if one includes the final italicized sentence. But in this book that reconfigures traditional novelistic form by reinventing the concept of "character" and splintering it into six interconnected consciousnesses, the very concept of separate "movements" is undermined (like Beethoven's quartet, albeit on a smaller scale – he questions the separation among the movements with so much melodic interconnection, for example). In Woolf's reworking of the structural patterning for the novel, the thoughts of the six interconnected subjectivities become her method; "character" and form, therefore, are indivisible, as noted earlier. Only the "characters'" contemplations, rather than plot points or events, are the content of the episodes, so these meditations are what structure the novel. Thus, although the novel's overall design is not analogous to the arrangement of six characters' reflections in succession, the model of six intertwined subjectivities is. Indeed, the movements in the quartet are typically described by critics as "character pieces" (Steinberg 232), suggesting Beethoven's own intermedial gesture towards narrativity. Each movement is distinct in its tempo and melodic material, yet they are simultaneously interconnected. Ultimately, I am suggesting that Woolf develops this musical, experimental form and expands it even further by intermingling the themes and voices of her "characters" rather than keeping them separate, a possibility she did indeed contemplate in August 1930 but then abandoned: "The Waves is I think resolving itself (I am at page 100) into a series of dramatic soliloquies. The thing is to keep them running homogeneously in & out, in the rhythm of the waves. Can they be read consecutively? I know nothing about that" (*D*3: 312). Accordingly, life and time organize the novel, both in the interludes (one day) and the inter-chapters (six interwoven lifelong journeys), but the overall structure of the novel is not divisible into the same form of six (and one silent seventh) interconnected movements as in Beethoven's quartet. Nevertheless, the fact that there are six subjectivities (plus one) is a striking similarity. Plausibly, Woolf transforms even Beethoven's radical innovations in her tour de force written more than a century later.

III. Transforming Beethoven's Opus 130 and 133 into Words

The exchange between the B-flat Major Quartet and *The Waves* can be elaborated further by exploring what Werner Wolf observes are the two primary strategies of intermedial reference in literature: thematization and mimesis. In general, as I have shown throughout this book, Woolf's novels explore the *thematization* of music on a consistent and noteworthy level, as a signified or a referent – a mode of "telling" (Wolf, *Musicalization* 44). But *The Waves* functions on the level of *imitation* as well, whereby the second medium (music in this case) gives the impression of being represented by enacting or performing its qualities through language (the word music I analysed earlier) and/or structure – a mode of "showing" (Wolf 45). Each "character" experiences a moment in the text that thematizes music. In addition, each exhibits attributes similar to a corresponding movement in Opus 130. The thematizations interact with the subject matter, while the mimetic characteristics create the overall structure of the episodes. Through Woolf's utilization of these two levels of intermedial reference, her insistence on the inseparability of form and content is disclosed, and, in turn, so too is her particular rendering of modernist fiction.

The following musical analysis will necessarily be general because I am interested in focusing on what Woolf might have heard as a non-musician (yet highly perceptive listener). She did not study the score, as far as I know, nor was she well versed in music theory and harmony. She did take music lessons as a child, however, and, as her letters often document, was capable of hearing different melodies, instrumental textures and ranges, tempo changes, or rhythmic alterations (see the Introduction). The fact that Leonard wrote about the very pieces I am considering in his reviews within the time frame leading up to the novel's composition also supports the possibility that the Woolfs might have conversed about the music to which they were listening together in the evenings, suggesting more, at the very least, than a cursory knowledge on her part.

In addition, in what follows, I incorporate examples from the musical score, not to instantiate Beethoven's status or authority as a composer or to privilege the written archive as a vehicle of supposed composer intentions – indeed, I do not even want to suggest that Woolf looked at the score, as I mention above – but to enable the reader to "hear" (in her or his inner audition) the patterns of melodic movement and harmonization to which I refer. But I am using the written score in lieu of sound files. Ideally, the reader would hear an actual recording, as Woolf did. At the very least, even if the reader does not understand musical notation, she or he can see the configurations I point out in the arrangements of the notes on the page. Intriguingly, this very fact illuminates a clash between art forms, as literature, the dominant medium in this case, is traditionally silent. Remarkable to me, as I hope the book as a whole demonstrates, are the steps Woolf takes to have her language heard.

The six movements in Beethoven's quartet, as mentioned, can be associated with the six subjectivities that inhabit *The Waves*. Each

Example 1. The beginning of Opus 130

"character" is also linked in some way with music thematically. Neville can be connected to the first movement of Opus 130, for example. This *Adagio ma non troppo* (a slow section with legato and chromatic, melodic material) is in sonata-form, yet it toys with that structure by playing with conventions, which, as in Woolf's novel, set up expectations only to upend them. Although the movement maintains a traditional formal arrangement, it subtly and quickly begins to subvert the notion of musical "order." To begin with, Beethoven de-emphasizes the entry of the second, lower fugal subject (see example 1, mm. 15–16 Violin II). Violin II plays the five-note melody of the second subject, which unsettles a more typical pronouncement: the phrase enters on a "weak" beat (the second one), yet paradoxically contains the dynamic marking of *forte*, while the higher note to which the melody leads, which lands on the characteristically "strong" first beat of the bar, is destabilized with a *piano* marking. Conventionally, the high note of the melody (E-flat) would beckon for a crescendo, not the opposite. The effect is to disturb expectations about rhythm, melodic phrasing, and accent, in addition to counterpoint, upon the entry of the second subject.

Furthermore, featuring an exposition, development, recapitulation, and coda (the typical format of sonata-form), the movement alternates between the *Adagio ma non troppo* and an *Allegro* (a fast-paced fanfare with running sixteenth notes), confronting the audience with extremes – unisons are followed by dense, contrapuntal segments, calmness usurped by intense flourish. This begins right from the start, as one can see in example 1: the *forte non legato* sixteenth-note runs that begin at the end of bar 14 contrast the opening quarter- and eighth-note melody marked *piano*. Even an inattentive listener could hear the distinction between the two main themes of this first movement as a sedate and peaceful beginning is suddenly interrupted by a burst of sound announcing the divergent second theme.

Neville, with his focus on precision and order, is portrayed in much the same way as the first movement of the quartet. He follows the conventional models of privileged social organization in that he has a typical male education in the British school system, and eventually becomes a poet. In so many respects, he seems quite content to comply with the traditional structures of the day. Indeed, early on when he arrives at school, he is invested in them: "'I come, like a lord to his halls appointed. That is our founder; our illustrious founder, standing in the courtyard with one foot raised. I salute our founder. A noble Roman air hangs over these austere quadrangles'" (*TW* 23). Similarly, he comments in the third episode when meeting Bernard at college, "'here we are masters of tranquillity and order; inheritors of proud tradition'" (*TW* 67). Moreover, his perceptions of Bernard solicit an interesting comment on his fellow writer's methods: "'We are all phrases in Bernard's story, things he writes down in his notebook under A or under B. He tells our story with extraordinary understanding, except of what we most feel. For he does not need us'" (*TW* 54). Sonata-form, as I have noted, depends upon alternating theme groups typically categorized as A and B. The two contrasting melodic units I described above would serve as A and B in Beethoven's first movement. Sonata-form is much more complicated than this, but for a non-musician, picking out the A and B themes, as I have suggested, would be simple, especially given their contrast from one another, not only in thematic material but also in tempo. Even though Bernard will also describe several phrases or scenes under other letters later on in the novel, it is Neville who understands and illuminates the A-B structure of Bernard's methods.

At the same time, Neville's conformity to social codes of behaviour is subverted by his same-sex desire for Percival. His passion for another man represents sedition against the prevailing heterosexist and socially condoned model for human relations. Analogous to the opening movement of the quartet, Neville has two overarching themes that are contrary although indissolubly linked; he is, as he describes, simultaneously inside and outside. As he comments when approaching London, "'the centre, and my heart draws out too, in fear, in exultation'" (*TW* 55). His themes and desires at once maintain "order" yet question its limitations, thwarting both conservative social expectations and the reader's assumptions.

A rushing *Presto* follows the more expansive first movement of Opus 130. Aptly, descriptions of the movement by music critics strikingly connote another character in Woolf's novel: Louis. Beethoven's "fierce, touch-me-not theme" (Imeson 164), which is nonetheless performed in a "mad whisper" (Steinberg 232), is interrupted only by the "stomping interlude for the first violin" (ibid.) with a short trio. Throughout the piece, a three-note pattern (*L'istesso tempo*; see example 2) that sounds like tramping feet unifies both the melodies and the accompaniment in this dance-form work, set to a tempo that is impossibly too fast for dancing.

In the first section, the three-note pattern (m. 18) arrives at the end of the main melody, finishing each phrase with its stomping effect. The opening consists of a descending melody, as though rolling down a hill, but it is repeated four times so that one hears this downward movement begin over and over again. In the next section (the *forte* trio) the melodic material repeats an upward-moving pattern. Underneath the upper voice, which also plays the same rhythm of the three-note stomp, the lower voices repeat the intense figure in each bar as accompaniment, rather than at the end of the melodic phrase as in the first theme. This trio section becomes extreme, creating the effect of a hurried, but brooding, back-and-forth leap from one foot to another. Woolf has integrated this notion of leaping from one foot to the other to describe several of her characters – in particular, Sara Pargiter from *The Years*. All of the voices in the quartet alternate in succession between *forte* and *piano*, loud and soft. The effect is that of a see-saw romp characterized by extremes of severity and muted concentration.

Example 2 Second movement, the beginning of the *Presto*

Louis's menacing and constant refrain from his *aural* memory is that he "'hear[s] something stamping. [...] A great beast's foot is chained. It stamps, and stamps, and stamps'" (*TW* 5). Although threes are prevalent throughout the novel, Louis's three-patterned stamp,

stamp, stamp marks out a surprisingly similar rhythm to the one that dominates the *Presto* and trio, not to mention that it is another conspicuous instance of the rhythm of threes. Louis's stamping beast characterizes his angry dissatisfaction with life, but also his suffering – he too feels perpetually outside English society because of his Australian accent, the marker of his difference. He resolves to defeat this sorrow, "'afraid of much, I of my accent, Rhoda of figures; yet resolute to conquer'" (*TW* 18).

Suitably, as in Beethoven's romp, Louis's musical moment connotes the fast-paced rhythm of the city: the "'dive and plunge like guillemots whose feathers are slippery with oil'" (*TW* 73). At the eating-house, he understands the world in quite rhythmic terms, as noted earlier; the description connotes the see-saw motion of the *Presto* and trio frolic:

> "Meanwhile the hats bob up and down; the door perpetually shuts and opens. I am conscious of flux, of disorder; of annihilation and despair. If this is all, this is worthless. Yet I feel, too, the rhythm of the eating-house. It is like a waltz tune, eddying in and out, round and round. The waitresses, balancing trays, swing in and out, round and round. [...] The circle is unbroken; the harmony complete. (Ibid.)

The waltz surfaces again with Jinny (and in Beethoven's fourth movement), as well as in *The Years*, as I have discussed. In Louis's narrative, it provides a model for interaction in the city.[11] Yet as in Beethoven's version, the dance of the metropolis is too fast for Louis, so he is not integrated into its "central rhythm." He experiences his exclusion from this hurried pace.

The third movement of Opus 130 begins with pathos but quickly shifts to playful fun (see example 3 m. 3). The heading *Andante con moto ma non troppo*, which means a walking pace with motion but not too fast, seems to "hedge its own bets," so to speak (Steinberg 233). Encapsulating topsy-turvy contrast, the movement begins slowly in B-flat minor, yet is designated a *Poco scherzoso* (a little jokingly). At the end of the second bar the passage quickly turns to a cheerfully paced D-flat major segment until measure 10, at which point the *pizzicato* (plucked) strings provide the transition to the next theme.

Just the start of the movement demonstrates that Beethoven encourages the listener's expectations but then suddenly dashes them. As Steinberg suggests, "the score reader who has seen the word *scherzoso* knows that something is up; the innocent listener could well take this pathos at face value, as Beethoven probably hoped he or she would"

Example 3. Third movement, *Andante con moto ma non troppo – Poco scherzoso*

(233). The lighthearted melody is accompanied, according to Sylvia Imeson, by a "jolly little sewing-machine sort of figure in the bass, in a conjunction that teasingly comments upon the self-conscious theatricality of the opening" (167). Incidentally, in a coincidence with Imeson's description of the sewing-machine pattern of Beethoven's *scherzoso*, Susan notes her mother's knitting and sewing capabilities: "'Though my mother still knits white socks for me and hems pinafores and I am a child, I love and I hate'" (*TW* 10). Subsequently, Susan will sew for her own child. The third movement is also in sonata-form. Its two major themes are interrupted by *staccato* melodies that function as delaying tactics, subverting the usual drive towards cadential closure. Thus, the playful movement that begins with an exceptionally deceptive contrast (evoking one mood but then quickly overturning it) utilizes various articulations to communicate its melodic material.

Similarly, at the start of Woolf's novel, Susan utters words of contrast: "'I love,' said Susan, 'and I hate'" (*TW* 10). As Gillian Beer suggests, "this is Susan's recurrent refrain" (Introduction and Notes 249). Like the beginning of the *scherzoso*, Susan's declaration articulates prominent dissimilarity, while her actions correspond to the playful walking pace of Beethoven's movement. As Bernard describes, "'Susan has passed us. [...] She was not crying. [...] Now she walks across the field with a swing, nonchalantly, to deceive us'" (*TW* 9). Emulating the beginning of the *Andante*, Susan wishes to dupe her playmates; her cheerful, undulating walk performs actions similar to Beethoven's opening few bars that mislead listener expectations.

Susan's musical moment also recalls the changing climate and various articulations of the third movement. Her experience of music encompasses the natural world, the diverse utterances of animals, and farm noises: "'Sleep I sing – I, who am unmelodious and hear no music save rustic music when a dog barks, a bell tinkles, or wheels crunch upon the gravel. I sing my song by the fire like an old shell murmuring on the beach'" (*TW* 136). Like the assorted articulations from the *Andante* that include *legato*, *pizzicato*, and *staccato*, the various farm sounds of barks, tinkles, and crunches imitate Beethoven's music while they thematize an "unmelodious" yet natural version of vocality. Susan's "music" demonstrates a very material manifestation of sound and seems to describe her comfort with domestic life. It also provides a crucial figurative contrast to Louis's alienating urban soundscape.

The fourth movement of Opus 130 is another dance, *Alla danza tedesca* (in the manner of a German dance). It is played at a quick pace but not

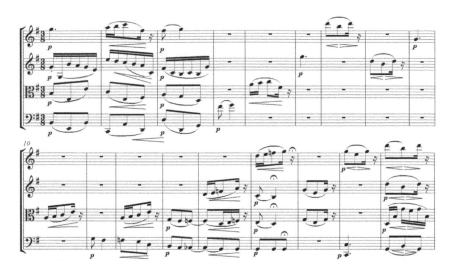

Example 4. Fourth movement, the end of the *Alla danza tedesca – Allegro assai*

in the furious tempo of the *Presto*. Indeed, people could actually dance to this movement. One of its most salient attributes is the continuous stream of circular motion, performed by the repetition of triplet figures in the melodies that travel across the four different voices. Melodies are passed among the voices throughout, but just before the conclusion, the main melody is divided up among the four voices so that the instruments continue or finish each other's melodic phrases, adding a merry-go-round effect (see example 4, mm. 4–15).

From the beginning of the novel, Jinny is associated with dance and movement. Her character does not just see the whirling actions of others (like Louis) but actually engages in them. Jinny, similar to Eugénie in *The Years*, is the performer of the waltz. Even at Elvedon, Susan notices that Jinny "'danced in flecked with diamonds light as dust'" (*TW* 9). Similarly, Susan describes her actions: "'Jinny spins her fingers on the table-cloth, as if they were dancing in the sunshine, pirouetting'" (*TW* 18). Later Susan will remember "'Jinny's pirouetting, all of a piece, limbs and body'" (*TW* 77). Analysing the musico-literary links of Woolf's novel reveals just how inextricable her concepts of form and subjectivity are; in addition to employing music (in an albeit transformed analogy) to radicalize her narrative structure, she also describes music's capacity to reconfigure human interaction. Through-out her canon, as discussed earlier, Woolf produces this crucial connection between sound and the social through physical movement, during which the body becomes the medium of performance and articulation for structured sounds. In *The Waves*, Jinny's existence is also highly corporal; her partnered and unpartnered dances enable the narrative to probe the possibilities of human interaction with her sonically infused movement.

Jinny's musical moment, perhaps not surprisingly, is the waltz segment after the six all leave school in the third episode. It begins when "'the fiddlers have lifted their bows'" (*TW* 79). Woolf again connects social relations between people with the process of music. As Jinny describes just before the instrumentalists begin to play, "'I am arrayed, I am prepared. This is the momentary pause; the dark moment'" (ibid.). Evoking the melody that is passed among the melodic voices in Beethoven's *Alla danza tedesca* at the conclusion of the movement, Jinny agrees to dance with one of the many "'black-and-white figures of unknown men'" who look at her. Suggesting the merry-go-round effect of Beethoven's fourth movement, she soliloquizes, "'I say to this one, 'Come.' Rippling black, I say to that one, 'No.' One breaks off from his station under the glass cabinet'" (*TW* 80). The music takes over:

> "We yield to this slow flood. We go in and out of this hesitating music. Rocks break the current of the dance; it jars, it shivers. In and out, we are swept now into this large figure; it holds us together; we cannot step outside its sinuous, its hesitating, its abrupt, its perfectly encircling walls. Our bodies, his hard, mine flowing, are pressed together within its body; it holds us together; and then lengthening out, in smooth, in sinuous folds, rolls us between it, on and on. Suddenly the music breaks. My blood runs on but my body stands still. (*TW* 80–1)

In contrast to Louis but similar to Susan, Jinny does not feel excluded from this music or from the circumstances it creates. The music represents a similar mechanism to the others' experiences in that it "'holds us together'" as the dancers are swept "'in and out'" by "'this hesitating music'" as though they are Beethoven's melodic phrases.

One of the most prominent features of the fifth movement of Opus 130, the *Cavatina*, is its lyrical or songlike quality. Emphasizing the solo voice, a *Cavatina* is defined as a short aria without *da capo* (meaning it does not return to its opening again to create ternary structure). Thus,

Beethoven imports a vocal, even operatic, genre and manner into the string quartet. This integration of vocalic writing is also emblematic of Beethoven's late period of composition, a device which can be found as well in the *Adagio* of the String Quartet in E-flat Major, Opus 127 or the lyrical first movement of the C-sharp minor Quartet, Opus 131 (one of Leonard Woolf's favourites, according to his record reviews). Yet the texture of the *Cavatina* tends to avoid the typical scenario for an over-riding solo voice by shifting constantly from the top voice to the other voices and vice versa. The effect, aurally, is that a solo voice is gestured towards yet destabilized at the same moment, establishing an ethereal, "disembodied mood" (*TW* 183). But there is also (famously) a con-trasting middle section entitled *Beklemmt*, which means that which is constricted, oppressed, weighed upon, suffocated, straitened, anxious (Steinberg 237). This section mimics a sobbing – yet unsentimental – singular, human voice (see example 5; the *Beklemmt* begins at m. 6). At measure 12 the solo melody begins to merge again with the others. It passes to the second violin and the viola, then back to the first vio-lin, and again to the second violin before being folded back into the cohesive harmonies that preceded the *Beklemmt*. Sometimes it is diffi-cult to distinguish one voice from another, as the instruments are set in the same register to accentuate the continuity of the vocalic utterances. Although the segment is only eight measures (mm. 6–13), it enacts a remarkably candid recitative through its defeated and fragmented mel-ody. It is another example of Beethoven's own imitative intermediality in that the section emulates vocal utterances found in opera (and life).

The links between the heartrending *Cavatina* and Rhoda (who dies as a result of suicide) are straightforward. She is the quintessence of *beklemmt*: "'I am afraid of you all. I am afraid of the shock of sensation that leaps upon me, because I cannot deal with it as you do – I cannot make one moment merge in the next. To me they are all violent, all separate; and if I fall under the shock of the leap of the moment you will be on me, tearing me to pieces'" (*TW* 102). Rhoda is so separated from others, so outside inclusive social interaction, that she becomes insubstantial as the novel progresses. Repeatedly, she is also associated with singing, a solo and solitary voice; like the *Cavatina*, however, she has difficulty distinguishing her own voice from others, as when she methodically follows Jinny and Susan, and imitates them by pulling on her stockings as they do, or speaking only after they speak (*TW* 103). Moreover, from the beginning Rhoda's perspective is aural, as noted in chapter 4; she hears "'a sound [...] cheep, chirp; cheep, chirp'" (*TW* 5). Yet quickly, one

Example 5. Fifth movement, the *Beklemmt* section

bird is alienated from the others: "'the birds sang in chorus first,' said Rhoda. 'Now the scullery door is unbarred. Off they fly. Off they fly like a fling of seed. But one sings by the bedroom window alone'" (*TW* 6).

Rhoda has two musical experiences in addition to the birdsong: one describes a singer in a concert hall and the other a quartet of string players. Appositely, then, as previously discussed, it is Rhoda who encounters the "'sea-green woman [who] comes to our rescue'" (*TW* 128). This vocal performance (recalling the *Cavatina*, which is an operatic form) is decidedly non-verbal. Like Beethoven's intermedial mimesis – instrumental music that imitates vocality – Woolf attempts to replicate the weeping voice, also excising from this utterance any linguistic, propositional content. Both represent and perform a heightened but non-verbal emotional moment. Indeed, the segment repeats the word "'Ah!'" five times and describes it as a "cry" rather than a word that addresses a particular person (for more on this section, see chapter 2). Both Beethoven and Woolf perform mimetic vocality in these intermedial works to produce an intense sense of mood, yet resist the notion of transparent signification. While Beethoven moves closer to the realm of speech, Woolf slides nearer to music, fashioning her own version of a *Beklemmt* section.

As mentioned, the *Grosse Fuge* (Opus 133) finale represents a trend in Beethoven's late works towards contrapuntal textures. According to Imeson, the *Grosse Fuge* exemplifies Beethoven's "reshaping of the overall aesthetic sequence of movements. The structural paradigm shifts from the Classical emphasis on the first movement, accompanied by a shift in weight to the finale … Fugues in particular served Beethoven well as summations" (175). (Notably, another example of this trend in Beethoven's works appears in the late "Hammerklavier" piano sonata in B-flat, Opus 106, to which Woolf was also listening during the writing of *The Waves*.) In the *Grosse Fuge*'s highly academic fugal finale, the *Overtura* sounds improvisational, and it is strikingly dissonant because of its combination of large leaps and chromatic intervals (see example 5). Indeed, the opening of the final movement begins five times, in a sense, as each start, like the *Alla danza tedesca* and the *Cavatina Beklemmt*, casts melodic material about among the instruments, performs different rhythmic variations of the pending ideas, or sounds snippets and half-finished phrases.

Testing the limits of the instrumentalists' technical abilities, the opening octave leaps are not only played *fortissimo* and *sforzando*, but also in unison, necessitating especially skilful tuning to create the bold yet dense tapestry of all the voices sounding together. The demands placed on each player throughout the piece are immense, especially since, after the opening passage that almost dares the musicians to attempt unity, the double fugue bursts out of this early constraint, taking virtuosic advantage of the notion of counterpoint. Each voice illustrates its own line, sometimes excelling and sometimes supporting the others. Ultimately, the fugal finale is a model of incorporating yet enabling heterogeneous voices. Although it self-referentially looks back to earlier movements, bringing together previous ideas and key associations, transforming them into new and radical material, it also concludes the quartet by testing the limits of tonality, performance practice, and genre.

The final episode in *The Waves* also enacts the intermingling and reconfiguring of content and structure. The following diary entry of 7

Example 6. The opening of the *Grosse Fuge*, Opus 133

January 1931 lends credence to the particular association between the *Grosse Fuge* and Bernard, who soliloquizes the entire section, as a "character." Woolf notes that she will listen to the fugue (and Smyth, the composer, will also probably drop by for a visit) on the heels of declaring she is writing Bernard's soliloquy:

> Few books have interested me more to write than The Waves. Why even now, at the end, I'm turning up a stone or two: no glibness, no assurance; you see, I could perhaps do B[ernard]'s soliloquy in such a way as to break up, dig deep, make prose move – yes I swear – as prose has never moved before: from the chuckle and babble to the rhapsody. [...] We shall play the Grosse Fugue tonight – Ethel, I daresay, will ring up. (*D4*: 4–5)

Conspicuously, then, Bernard is the one character who not only embodies similar actions to one of Beethoven's movements but also emulates its function and position. Put another way, Bernard's intermediality is imitative on two levels: he performs actions in the novel analogous to Beethoven's finale, and his final soliloquy is also positioned in a similar manner in terms of the novel's structure. Hence Woolf's comment that "while listening to a Beethoven quartet" she decides to "merge all the interjected passages into Bernard's final speech" (*D3*: 339).

Bernard's "character" emulates the music of Opus 133 throughout the novel. At Elvedon, like Beethoven's finale, "'everything is strange. Things are huge and very small. The stalks of flowers are thick as oak trees. Leaves are high as the domes of vast cathedrals. We are giants, lying here, who can make forests quiver'" (*TW* 16). Moreover, Bernard's "character," the maker of phrases who does "'not believe in separation'" (*TW* 52), brings people and things together – "'we are not single'" (ibid.) – yet he paradoxically declares, "'a good phrase, however, seems to me to have an independent existence'" (*TW* 53). The section cited above from the Elvedon episode also commingles, even in this first chapter, Bernard's thoughts and Rhoda's impending musical experience with both the singer and the quartet (the quivering note that splits the apple and the reference to Wren's cathedral). From the very beginning, Bernard is characterized as bringing the others together, similar to the methods of the *Grosse Fuge*. With his repetitions of other characters' phrases – this occurs throughout the novel for each of the other subjectivities, but especially in his last soliloquy – he also performs this function. In this way, Bernard, especially, foretells both Sara's and Miss La Trobe's musical way of being, discussed in chapter 5.

One of the most conspicuous features of the *Grosse Fuge* is not only its radical use of fugal form but also its dissonant melodic content. Correspondingly, Bernard's musical moment incorporates "concord" and "discord" into a "symphony," widening from the quartet to encompass not just the six from the novel but "a thousand others" (*TW* 206) and implying multifarious instrumental sounds. Thus Bernard finds a way to maintain inclusion and exclusion simultaneously, unlike the others, who each function as only one part of the whole either inside or outside their social circumstances. Bernard is able to include both the concord and discord of each subjectivity and give the *effect* of completion; the performative analogy Woolf utilizes to communicate such an ability is, not coincidentally, music.

> "Faces recur, faces and faces – they press their beauty to the walls of my bubble – Neville, Susan, Louis, Jinny, Rhoda and a thousand others. How impossible to order them rightly; to detach one separately, or to give the effect of the whole – again like music. What a symphony with its concord and its discord, and its tunes on top and its complicated bass beneath, then grew up! Each played his own tune, fiddle, flute, trumpet, drum or whatever the instrument might be. (*TW* 205–6)

Thus, Bernard finds a way to maintain inclusion and exclusion simultaneously, unlike the others, who function as only parts of the whole either inside or outside their social circumstance. Yet, as the final italicized sentence of the novel will record, "*The waves broke on the shore*" (*TW* 238), resisting closure by indicating that the cycles of concord and discord will continue.

The interchange between musical sounds and linguistic narrative enables Woolf to reconceptualize the notions of both subjectivity and "form" in *The Waves*. I have moved from scenes that explore performatic characters in chapter 5 to language permeated with performativity in chapter 6. Rhythm, for example, becomes an active element of her language in the word music of episode three. Thus her most formally experimental text is infused with musicalization on the levels of both thematization and mimesis – the latter manifesting in the sentences of her prose, but also in the structure of the novel, which is, ultimately, not a simple imitation but an intermedial transformation that develops even Beethoven's radical experimentation. Language is doubly imbued, therefore, with the performative nature of music. The novel splinters the idea of six separate "characters" (analogous to Beethoven's six "character pieces") into nine episodes that interweave the voices, producing a new method in the process. What could have been individual subjectivities become the interlaced text, "a rhythm and not [...] a plot" (*L4*: 204). For Woolf, music – even Beethoven's – does not transcend life, nor does the figure of the artist. Instead, "we are the words; we are the music; we are the thing itself" (*MB* 72).

Coda

A Meditation on Rhythm

Then, as if some juice necessary for the lubrication of [Lily Briscoe's] faculties were spontaneously squirted, she began precariously dipping among the blues and umbers, moving her brush hither and thither, but it was now heavier and went slower, as if it had fallen in with some rhythm which was dictated to her (she kept looking at the hedge, at the canvas) by what she saw, so that while her hand quivered with life, this rhythm was strong enough to bear her along with it on its current.

TL 215

You have found out exactly what I was trying to do when you compare [*Roger Fry*] to a piece of music.

Virginia Woolf to Elizabeth Trevelyan, *L*6: 425–6

I am ending where I began: with Woolf's statement that she "always thinks of [her] books as music before she writes them" (*L*6: 426). Although the quotation is frequently cited, the book to which Woolf refers, her biography of Roger Fry, is rarely discussed in musical terms.[1] But a Coda that engages with the biography of Woolf's friend, the painter and art critic, must also return to the concept of rhythm as a meditative node. Indeed, Trevelyan herself makes the connection between the two in her comments to Woolf about the book's musically infused ideas and structure: "I was always conscious of a beautiful rhythm in the book – perhaps in the sense that Roger used the word? – but also more closely in the musical sense, and in a way which I have felt before in your books." Woolf's riposte, "and especially with the life of Roger" (ibid.), suggests that there are links among Fry's theories, Woolf's version of them in the biography, and the importance of rhythm as a concept that is significant across art forms, including music, literature, and painting; indeed, as the artist Lily Briscoe in *To the Lighthouse* observes, "this rhythm was strong enough to bear her along with it on its current" (*TL* 215). Hence, in these last few pages I shall put forward some final thoughts on Woolf as an intermedial thinker, "bringing back the first theme in the last chapter" (*L6*: 426) – to echo her musical method.

As Woolf's friend and contemporary E.M. Forster admits in his final lecture from *Aspects of the Novel* on "Pattern and Rhythm," these words are notoriously difficult to define lucidly: "Unfortunately both these words are vague – when people apply rhythm or pattern to literature they are apt not to say what they mean and not to finish their sentences: it is, 'Oh, but surely the rhythm …' or 'Oh, but if you call that pattern …'" (151). Indeed, his own characterization of rhythm and its significance to the novel is rather nebulous, with two types – an "easy" sense (defined as repetition plus variation), and a rhythmic wholeness analogous to "when the orchestra stops, we hear something that has never actually been played" (169) – that are more suggestive than precise. For T.S. Eliot, poetry is also enabled by rhythm and structure, but it is the former, in an embryonic yet protean form, that inspires the setting down of the words. As he explains in his essay "The Music of Poetry" (1942), written while he was composing *Four Quartets*, "but I know that a poem, or a passage of a poem, may tend to realize itself first as a particular rhythm before it reaches expression in words, and that this rhythm may bring to birth the idea and the image" (114). Earlier in his career, he attached the designation "auditory imagination" to this generative, poetic experience. In "Matthew Arnold" (1933), Eliot asserts,

> What I call "auditory imagination" is the feeling for syllable and rhythm, penetrating far below the conscious levels of thought and feeling, invigorating every word; sinking to the most primitive and forgotten, returning to the origin and bringing something back, seeking the beginning and the end. It works through meanings, certainly, or not without meanings in the ordinary sense, and fuses the old and obliterated and the trite, the current, and the new and surprising, the most ancient and the most civilized mentality. (111)

Thus, both the novelist (Forster) and the poet (Eliot) agree that rhythm is essential and fundamental to their writing. Forster determines that it is multilayered, being part of a novel's method but also somehow able to encapsulate its "wholeness"; Eliot envisions it as a sort of primordial, sensory experience that fuses both past and present. But their understanding of how it functions differs considerably. Indeed, rhythm is one of modernism's "keywords," according to Melba Cuddy-Keane, Adam Hammond, and Alexandra Peat, because of the "term's very elusiveness ... [which] was central to its appeal to modernist writers looking for a way of capturing that which escaped final description, representation, or categorization" (203).[2]

Woolf, who was not only familiar with the work of the writers noted above but also engaged in debates and conversations about art and artistic processes with them, is also particularly captivated with the concept and its applicable properties to her own medium of language, as I have already explored in relation to the word music of *The Waves*. But rhythm functions in another way for Woolf also, by means, I suggest, that current intermedial theorists would call transmedial. In fact, the word's ability to traverse various art forms is a crucial part of its significance for Woolf. A transmedial concept, according to Werner Wolf, can

> appear in more than one medium and can therefore form points of contact or bridges between different media ... Transmediality as a quality of cultural signification appears, for instance, on the level of ahistorical formal devices that occur in more than one medium, such as motivic repetition, thematic variation, or to a certain extent even narrativity. ("Intermediality Revisited" 18–19)

I am proposing, therefore, that rhythm crosses the borders of media in a manner similar to narrativity, as a larger idea that can be found in different art forms; it *travels* in thorough and significant ways across music, literature, and painting.[2]

In addition, for Woolf, although the word navigates various media, its special import for language and the novel is musically infused, as I have argued particularly in chapter 6. In this way, her understanding of rhythm is akin to the active nature of Walter Pater's employment of "the great *Anders-streben* of all art" (106) in "The School of Giorgione" essay, the chapter from *The Renaissance* in which the dictum that *"all art constantly aspires towards the condition of music"* (ibid.) is stated.[3] Pater's understanding of *"Anders-streben,"* translated as "other-striving," is fundamentally relational: "although each art has thus its own specific order of impressions, and an untranslatable charm ... each art may be observed to pass into the condition of some other art ... a partial alienation from its own limitations, through which the arts are able, not indeed to supply the place of each other, but reciprocally to lend each other new forces" (105). Difference is not abolished, but "new forces" are imparted in the act of movement towards another art form. Even as early as 1906 in her essay "Street Music," Woolf's rather Paterian understanding of the relations among the arts is in nascent form: "in spite of all that we have done to repress music it has a power over us still whenever we give ourselves up to its sway that no picture, however fair, or words however stately, can approach" (*E1*: 30). Even though Woolf echoes Pater's notion about all arts constantly aspiring towards the condition of music in this early iteration, her interest is not so much in the merging of form and content that excites Pater's imagination but in the active and invigorating component of which the conjoining is made – what she calls in the essay music's "soul" (ibid.) – in a word, rhythm. Woolf, however, develops the idea in a distinct direction from Pater. Particularly informed by the transmedial capacity of rhythm, her rendering invigorates the notion of actively striving after other art forms in ways that foretell our current intermedial age.

For her friend and colleague Roger Fry, rhythm is also a fundamental concept, even if it is difficult to glean precisely how it functions within his artistic principles. Indeed, echoing Pater, Fry places rhythm at the heart of the "imaginative life" in his lecture delivered at the close of the first Post-Impressionist Exhibition at the Grafton Gallery in 1911: "Rhythm is the fundamental and vital quality of painting, as of all the arts – representation is secondary to that, and must never encroach on the more ultimate and fundamental demands of rhythm" ("Post Impressionism" 105–6). In his move away from the representational in art to validate the Post-Impressionists, Fry beckons to rhythm as a quality that enables "significant form," the phrase later coined by Clive Bell in his book *Art* (1913). Fry's understanding is first and foremost image-bound, however, and perhaps more closely allied with Paul Cézanne's concept of sensation, as Anthony Uhlmann has recently indicated. Although Fry gestures towards the arts generally, and, according to Woolf, was an enthusiast of music,[4] understandably, the rhythm of line on the canvas is what he foregrounds in "An Essay in Aesthetics" (1909). Similarly, rhythm is again in service of the visual for Fry in the posthumously published, unfinished essay "Principles of Design" (c. 1920). Fry contends in this essay fragment that there are two impulses in the action of painting pictures: the first is the "externalization" of the image, and the second is the "decoration impulse," which is a result of the "psychic and quasi-intellectual pleasure in rhythm" (218, 219).

Woolf herself recognizes how important the word is to Fry in her biography. Citing as a gift Fry's "power to suggest," she notes that even his "hottest sayings like 'There is great danger in a strong personal rhythm … unless [the artist] constantly strains it by the effort to make it take in new and refractory material it becomes stereo-typed' [...] – break off heavy with meaning. They go behind the picture; they bring into being a rich background which we explore half-consciously while we read" (*RF* 228). Her admiration for Fry's criticism is palpable in the biography, not because Fry delineates concise or touchstone aesthetic principles, but because his writing and his praxis evoke a lack of fixity. Correspondingly, Fry's understanding of social relations is rhythmical. As she notes, "the heard on the one side, the individual on the other – hatred of one, belief in the other – that is the rhythm, to use his favourite word, that vibrates beneath the surface" (*RF* 232). Woolf, at one and the same time, suggests that rhythm, Fry's privileged term, resonates behind outward appearance, yet she distils what seems to be somewhat oppositional thinking on Fry's part between the community and the individual.

Fry, although well practised in making interartistic gestures in his writing, is more attached to medial specificity. According to Elizabeth Prettejohn, he developed a "fascination for the sensuous traces of the work's making" (39). Moreover, "it is not merely the pattern of forms and colours, but also the sensuous particularity of the materials from which the work is made that constitutes what he calls its 'quality'. His descriptions of works dwell on the special characteristics of their materials" (ibid.). Woolf agrees. In her introduction to the Memorial Exhibit in Fry's honour in 1935, Woolf confirms, "I want to say that his understanding of art owed much to his understanding of life, and yet I know that he disliked the mingling and mixing of different things. He wanted art to be art; literature to be literature; and life to be life," even though she admits "he was a man of many interests and many sympathies" (*E6*: 61). When it comes to his materials or even the concepts of art and life (as he illuminates in the lead essay from *Vision and Design*), according to Woolf, he prefers not to commingle the arts for fear of "sloppiness," "vagueness," or "sentimentality" (ibid.). Woolf clarifies further in the biography: "It is perhaps, in the first place, that Roger Fry makes painting different from the other arts. It is not literature; it is not biography; it is not music. It is the art of painting that he is writing about"

(*RF* 227). Thus, Woolf explicitly recognizes that Fry's theories about painting are particularly invested in the differences among the arts as opposed to their relationality. Put another way, according to Woolf, Fry is not interested in rhythm because of its transmedial capacity.

Another area of distinctness for Fry, as Woolf describes it, is that between "art and life." In an essay of the same name, he is at pains to distinguish between "the work of art" and "the life of the time which produced it" (Fry, *Vision and Design* 1). Distrusting the initial and presumed link between art and history, Fry argues that the correspondence "requires much correction" (ibid.). Woolf's disagreement with Fry in this regard becomes clear in the biography when she suggests again that, almost despite himself, Fry's many interests and variegated lifestyle contradict some of his artistic tenets:

> Art and life are two rhythms, he says – the word "rhythm" was henceforth to occur frequently in his writing – "and in the main the two rhythms are distinct, and as often as not play against each other." [...]
>
> This suggests [...] that there were two rhythms in his own life. There was the hurried and distracted life; but there was also the still life. [...] If he survived the war, it was perhaps that he kept the two rhythms in being simultaneously. (*RF* 214)

If Fry maintains the dissimilarity between the age in which an artwork is created and the value of the work itself, it is perhaps because of the difficulties he faced keeping the Omega Workshop active during the First World War: its disbandment is often attributed to the military conflict. But Woolf reveals that the "two rhythms" are side by side in Fry's own life not to undermine her friend's integrity but to show the relational nature of the aesthetic and material worlds, a focus in the novels written before and after *Roger Fry* (1940): *The Years* (1937) and *Between the Acts* (1941). The interconnection of art and life is also animate in the commingling she initially envisioned in language and structure for *The Years*, although she abandons it, with her conception of the novel-essay method meant to explore the family saga of *The Pargiters* – it attempts to combine "fiction and fact" in a new generic hybrid.

Furthermore, I have demonstrated throughout this book that art and life are inseparable for Woolf with my materialist line of argument, and that her multilayered and consistent crossover with music (and sound more generally) helps her to elaborate this political stance and to ground the often transcendentally identified art form of music in the everyday.

In the biography, her subtle teasing out of Fry's ideas about rhythm (later in life, after she had investigated the visual art connection herself in *To the Lighthouse*) brings to the fore some of her differences in terms of her own intermedial aesthetics. As this monograph has revealed, Woolf is not only drawn to medial relations but also adept at incorporating other arts into her writing. Indeed, her comment that she writes "to a rhythm and not to a plot" (*L4*: 204) suggests such transmediality. Unlike many of her contemporaries, who, according to Klemens Gruber and others (as noted in the Introduction) gravitate towards medial specificity (Fry included), Woolf reaches outward from her own medium and thoroughly engages with other art forms to delight in their perceived similarities, as well as to experiment in the intermedial gaps created by their divergences.

This book has focused on the particular intermedial combination of literature and music as elaborated in Woolf's novels. Throughout, I endeavour to demonstrate a sense of the kind of critical work that can be done when one combines these two art forms. As I hope has become clear, Woolf's particular deployment of music and sound is multilayered and various. The depth of her intermediality is borne out by the burgeoning field of scholars interested in this crossover, but also, I have maintained, by the diversity of integration one finds in her fiction: music is explored as a concept, for its thematic importance, for its linguistic experimentation, and for its structural analogy, revealing, in the process, what a thorough engagement with the sense and medium of sound brings to this writer's art form. In addition, she is a prescient thinker in terms of understanding music as an art laden with social and political import; as elaborated throughout the book, music and patterns of sound are part of her materialist critique. Accordingly, Woolf theorizes an interart aesthetic that is intimately tied to human relations – distinct from Fry, further developed from Pater, and certainly inspired by her sister's methods, as critics have also disclosed – but ultimately, a rhythm of her own, "strong enough to bear her along with it on its current" (*TL* 131).

Notes

Introduction

1 I do not mean to suggest by starting with (and subsequently referring to) Woolf's biographical reflections on music that her letters, diaries, or even essays provide answers to the ideas that flow in and around her fiction. I include her thoughts on sound and music to provide context, not to prove my points by demonstrating supposed author intention. Following Woolf's lead in the Introduction to the second American edition of *Mrs. Dalloway*, "once a book is printed and published it ceases to be the property of the author" (*MD*, "Appendix: Introduction (1928)," 356). Thus, I consider her paratextual comments as other elements, not primary ones, in the circulation of perspectives that surround the novels and essays.

2 Dame Ethel Smyth, the British composer, feminist, and suffragette, became one of Woolf's closest friends in the last eleven years of her life. For more on the relationship between Woolf and Smyth and its echoes in *Between the Acts*, see my article "Virginia Woolf, Ethel Smyth, and Music: Listening as a Productive Mode of Social Interaction." For what I consider to be Smyth's response to Woolf's *A Room of One's Own*, see my "'As Springy as a Racehorse': Ethel Smyth's *Female Pipings in Eden* as Rejoinder to Virginia Woolf's *A Room of One's Own*."

3 Of course, Woolf's texts do not make actual sound, but they do actively engage with the aurality of language in particularly sonorous ways. This project is concerned primarily with the sound and music that filled her ears, but, ultimately, as novels are effectively silent artifacts, the sonorities I shall discuss will not be heard in the same sense that sound is. Garrett Stewart has theorized the importance of "inner audition," as he calls it, in the practice of reading. For more on how "reading voices" internally, see Stewart's book of the same name.

4 Phyllis Weliver's publications that focus on the nineteenth century are excellent in this regard also. See *The Musical Crowd in English Fiction, 1840–1910*, but also *Women Musicians in Victorian Fiction, 1860–1900*; Emma Sutton's book on Woolf, *Virginia Woolf and Classical Music*, especially chapter 5, "What It Really Means to be English," is also illuminating.

5 See also Sutton's contribution to Bryony Randall and Jane Goldman, eds., *Virginia Woolf in Context*.

6 See Michelle Pridmore-Brown, Rishona Zimring, Angela Frattarola, and Kate Flint, in addition to Melba Cuddy-Keane's articles. Also, at the Nineteenth Annual Conference on Virginia Woolf (2009), coincidentally, both Anna Snaith and I explored the connection between space and sound. My paper, which investigates aural architecture in *Jacob's Room* and *The Years*, is included in the conference proceedings, as is her abstract for her plenary that explored acoustic space in *The Years*; she also plans to publish on modernism and noise in interwar Britain.

7 For a concise summary of the literary and visual art interchange in Woolf's work, see Diane Gillespie, "Virginia Woolf, Vanessa Bell and Painting."

8 Throughout this book I use square brackets around ellipses within quotations from Woolf's writing to indicate that they are my excisions. Woolf herself employs ellipses so often, especially in the later novels, that it is necessary to distinguish between hers and mine.

9 In Woolf, *A Passionate Apprentice, The Early Journals 1897–1909*, Mitchell A. Leaska documents that Woolf kept lists of books she was reading at the end of her 1904–5 journal. "Paters [sic] Renaissance" is included in a list from January 1905 (274). "Street Music" was published in March of the same year; the review of *The Oxford History of Music* was published in June 1905 and referred to in her diary on Christmas Day 1904, as well as in May 1905. All three of these musical texts are read and contemplated in close proximity with each other, suggesting that 1905 was a particularly musical year for the emerging writer.

10 This was the first time she would encounter the music of Ethel Smyth, long before they met in 1930. Woolf also enjoyed reading Smyth's first memoir, *Impressions That Remained*, published in 1919, although she denigrated the prose. She did, however, admire Smyth's candour: "I think she shows up triumphantly, through sheer force of honesty," she writes to Lytton Strachey (*L2*: 405). She also reviewed *Streaks of Life* favourably in 1921, another memoir by Smyth.

11 For a thought-provoking discussion of the history of this movement in Britain, consult BBC Radio 3, The Essay, "The Music Appreciation Movement," by Richard Witts. Both Leonard and Virginia were dedicated,

if sceptical, listeners to the BBC, as Todd Avery has discussed in relation to Bloomsbury more generally (*Radio Modernism*). They penned and performed a radio "conversation" for the network in 1927, the first of three broadcasts for Virginia (the other two were "Beau Brummell," 20 November 1929, and "Craftsmanship," 29 April 1937). For a transcription and commentary on their talk called "Are Too Many Books Written and Published," see Cuddy-Keane's essay of the same name in *PMLA*, the "Little-Known Documents" section.

12 Woolf's letter to which de Sélincourt refers is not in the Hogarth Press archive at Reading University or in *The Letters of Virginia Woolf*. The one I have transcribed from his handwriting is dated 26 October (with no year specified). Given his submission of the final essay to Leonard in August 1928 (documented by another letter), I surmise that the year of the first letter to "Mrs Wolfe" is 1927.

13 Leonard corresponds with other writers on music. A letter dated 13 July 1927 from Hull, who was a music journalist best known for his early support of the English composer Arnold Bax, suggests that he and Leonard have discussed a longer version of a previously read essay; he encloses the revised pamphlet with the letter. White, a musicologist who specialized in English opera and went on to publish books elsewhere on Benjamin Britten and Michael Tippett, in addition to a revised version of his book on Stravinsky, appears to have sent his manuscript on film unsolicited. The archives do not contain his initial contact, only the first letter back from Leonard, who responds, "We have read the draft of your essay. The subject interests us and we think it might be worked up into a suitable essay for our series. It is, however, a little difficult to come to an opinion on it in its present form, as it reads somewhat thin. We should be glad to see it again in its final form" (letter to Eric White from Leonard Woolf, 30 November 1927). Although I can find no other account of Leonard's interaction with either of these authors in his autobiography or Glendinning's biography, I suspect that his knowledge of them might have come from his time as a record reviewer (1926–9).

14 Their mutual admiration takes a few more turns in the 1930s. She was aware of de Sélincourt's occupation as a reviewer, which lends credence to her knowledge of him as someone she might have approached for the press. He appraises *The Years* very favourably – she notes this happily in her diary, exclaiming that he "sees it" (*D*5: 68). But he gives the overtly feminist tract *Three Guineas* a poorer review, which Woolf calls "a terrible indictment" (*D*5: 148). For de Sélincourt's reviews see *Virginia Woolf: The Critical Heritage*.

15 For a lucid discussion of the ideological in music, see Derek Scott's
    Introduction to *From the Erotic to the Demonic*.
16 For a thorough and instructive summary of critical musicology,
    particularly as it pertains to musico-literary scholarship of the Victorian
    period, see Phyllis Weliver's "A Score of Change," as well as Scott (noted
    above).
17 As Cuddy-Keane has discussed in her essay on *Between the Acts*, even
    Leonard clarified his statement by suggesting that "she was highly
    sensitive to the atmosphere around her, whether it was personal, social, or
    historical. She was therefore the last person who could ignore the political
    menaces under which we all lived" (*Downhill* 27). Moreover, Cuddy-Keane
    rightly points out that Leonard's understanding here would have involved
    the idea of politics in conventional terms.
18 See Harries' astute discussion of Samuel Beckett and film, "Theater and
    Media before 'New' Media."
19 Most recently, Sutton has argued for the significance of the fugue in *Mrs.
    Dalloway*, for example. See chapter 4 of her book on Woolf and music.
    Earlier attempts to connect the fugue to Woolf's novels include Patricia
    Laurence's "The Facts and Fugue of War." Several Woolf critics have
    also associated *The Waves* and *Between the Acts* with Arnold Schoenberg's
    atonal, pantonal, and twelve-tone structures. See essays by Robin Gail
    Schulze, who explores *The Waves*, and Sonita Sarker, who analyses
    Between the Acts, as well as Sanja Bahun, who discusses the modern
    music of Schoenberg and Igor Stravinsky in relation to Woolf's final
    novel.
20 From the start of the twenty-first century, argues Marjorie Levinson in
    "What Is New Formalism," there has been a resurgence of interventions
    that attempt, on the one hand, to make a continuum between formalist
    and historicist readings, and, on the other, to produce a backlash against
    such approaches in favour of a return to the sharp separation of history
    and art (559). For more on the former, see Caroline Levine's "Strategic
    Formalism," and follow-up responses by Herbert F. Tucker and Carolyn
    Dever. For debates specific to modernism, see Douglas Mao and Rebecca
    L. Walkowitz's Introduction to *Bad Modernisms*, as well as their essay,
    "The New Modernist Studies." For rejoinders consult Max Brzezinski
    and Martin Puchner. More recently, the essay collection *New Formalisms
    and Literary Theory* edited by Verena Theile and Linda Tredennick
    and a special issue of *New Literary History*, "Style, Form, Formalism,"
    tackle the subject. Musicology has also undergone a rethinking of the
    problems with formalist readings, and, by necessity, must engage with

the issues differently, given another historical trajectory of the field and diverse objects with which to contend. Two particularly fruitful areas of investigation include the re-evaluation of the concept of the composer's "work," instigated by Lydia Goehr's groundbreaking study, *The Imaginary Museum of Musical Works*, and the critique of structural listening that has followed Rose Subotnik's *Deconstructive Variations*. Fittingly, Subotnik provides the Afterword for the collection of essays, *Beyond Structural Listening*, edited by Andrew Dell-Antonio.

21 The dilemma of musical narrativity experienced a resurrection in new terms in the 1990s with publications by Jean-Jacques Nattiez and Katharine Ellis, "Can One Speak of Narrativity in Music?" and Carolyn Abbate, whose book *Unsung Voices*, and responses to it, particularly by the musicologist Lawrence Kramer, sparked debates. Nattiez was also the first to attempt a comprehensive semiotics of music in *Music and Discourse*. Anthony Newcomb, Eero Tarasti, and even Roland Barthes could also be included in this type of musical analysis.

22 For more on this long-standing connection, see the collection of essays edited by Férdia J. Stone-Davis, *Music and Transcendence*. But even some Woolf scholars have suggested the link. Emily Crapoulet iterates a version of Woolf and her "musicality" that, I would suggest, depoliticizes both Woolf's understanding of art and the concept of musicality itself. To conclude her essay, Crapoulet asserts, "Precisely because the material of [a musician's] art, cannot 'argue a cause,' as such, it becomes for Virginia Woolf, the model for the ideal art form, one which is both impersonal and apolitical" (85). I shall argue contrariwise, that music is an embodied and social art for Woolf, and therefore, one that is imbricated in the material world.

1. Finding a Voice

1 See Thompson's *The Soundscape of Modernity* and Picker's *Victorian Soundscapes*; also Steven Connor's "The Modern Auditory I." See Jonathan Sterne's seminal *The Audible Past* for a history of sound technology and its social currency, as well as *The Sound Studies Reader*, edited by Sterne, for an introduction and anthology of materials from the field. Another useful, and earlier, collection, edited by Mark Smith, is *Hearing History*.

2 Born has also produced a substantial amount of scholarship on music as a mediated art form. See especially "On Musical Mediation." Her introduction to the collection is indebted to this valuable work, as is the structure of the book. The collection is understandably focused primarily on

actual music, as opposed to how music is represented, but Nicholas Cook's contribution is helpful for thinking about the effect of musical sound on the practices of everyday life, to use Michel de Certeau's phrasing.

3 Tracey Seeley's "Virginia Woolf's Poetics of Space" and Anna Snaith's *Virginia Woolf* are two early treatments of this pairing. See Snaith and Whitworth's essay collection, *Locating Woolf*, for more on the subject. As mentioned in my notes to the Introduction, Snaith has also brought sound into her purview.

4 See my Introduction for a clarification of how I understand these spheres, which I do not read as simply antithetical to each other. Woolf, I shall show, troubles such an easy divide.

5 For more on the ineffable as a concept in Woolf and others, see Dora Zhang's "Naming the Indescribable."

6 *The Village in the Jungle* is also the title of Leonard Woolf's first novel (1913).

7 As an example of a daughter of an educated man, Woolf cites Mary Henrietta Kingsley, a nineteenth-century English traveller who wrote two books about her explorations in West Africa. When she returned from her voyages to uncharted territory in West Africa, she was critical of missionaries from the Church of England for trying to change the African people. Woolf explains that Kingsley's education was sacrificed, as was Woolf's, for the benefit of her brother's.

8 For a list of works displayed at the famous exhibit, see Anna Greutzner Robins's "'Manet and the Post-Impressionists': A Checklist of Exhibits," *Burlington Magazine* 152 (2010): 782–93.

9 Jacob's surname is a poignant reminder of the western part of Belgium, where significant and bloody battles took place during the First World War. Cemeteries for the Allies' soldiers punctuate the countryside. Additionally, his first name connotes ancient stories of patrilineage, inheritance, and struggle against an overwhelming opponent.

10 For more on the history of the suburb, see the website, which is quite comprehensive: http://www.hgs.org.uk/index.html. Also, Alison Creedon's article on Henrietta Barnett provides an excellent revisionist, historical reading of this social reformer; see "A Benevolent Tyrant?"

11 Woolf knew Thomas Hardy's work well, as he was a friend of her father's, she wrote a favourable review of his novels, and she also visited him in 1926. See his "The Darkling Thrush" (1900) in which the bird "fling[s] his soul / Upon the growing gloom" (ll. 23–4) of the new century. The association suggests the bird's song is another sound of lament.

12 Anne Olivier Bell and Andrew McNeillie note a connection between a diary episode (*D2*: 47) and the homeless woman in *Jacob's Room*. Brad

Bucknell also discusses her appearance and sonority in his essay "The Sound of Silence," which compares the novel to an opera loosely based on Woolf's book by the contemporary electronic music composer Morton Subotnick. Bucknell suggests that the old woman is part of a "backdrop, the sonic canvas of many of the actions of the book" (769). Intriguingly, in terms of my argument, Subotnick's opera also foregrounds the episode of the drunk woman who cries "Let me in!" outside Jacob's door.

13 The Union of London Bank amalgamated with the private Smith, Payne & Smiths (established 1758) to form the Union of London & Smith's Bank in 1902. It was an exemplar of capitalist expansion, with twenty-four branches in London and its suburbs, and a prestigious head office in Princes Street, City of London. In the aftermath of the First World War, it became the National Provincial Bank, one of the "Big Five" that would dominate the British banking scene for the next half-century.

14 The *Oxford English Dictionary* defines a vocalise as a singing exercise using individual syllables or vowel sounds, or a vocal passage consisting of a melody without words. Both are appropriate to describe the "ee um fah um so" of the old woman.

15 Brenda Silver has meticulously compiled and edited Woolf's last two essays, "Anon" and "The Reader," with an introduction and extensive notes.

16 For more on the significance of this character in *Mrs. Dalloway*, see Leena Kore Schröder and Raymond Peitrequin. According to Schröder, there is an incident upon which the segment might be based, but it does not contain any reference to the female vagrant singing. The episode is recorded in Leonard Woolf's autobiography, *Downhill All the Way* (122–3). David Bradshaw also documents, in the notes to the Oxford University Press edition (2000) of the novel, that Woolf mentions an "old beggar woman" singing aloud in a London street in her diary (see *D*2: 47). As noted above, however, Anne Olivier Bell and Andrew McNeillie connect this diary entry to the homeless woman in *Jacob's Room*.

17 Tadanobu Sakamoto concurs with Clarke that the setting of the song is probably from Eduard Lassen, not only because the words seem closer than Strauss's to what Woolf uses in the novel but also because the tune itself does not require the same sort of virtuosity for the singer. I agree with her in terms of the musical ability required.

18 Woolf makes similar inquiries in the diary entry that recalls the episode she experienced in June 1920 when she saw "An old beggar woman, blind [who] sang aloud." She ponders: "How many Junes has she sat there, in the heart of London? How she came to be there, what scenes she can go through, I can't imagine" (*D*2: 47).

19 Although it is a brief musical event, Woolf details that Elsbeth Siddons sings "Who Is Silvia" (*JR* 118), another well-known art song, this time by Franz Schubert (1797–1828). The text is from Shakespeare's *Two Gentlemen of Verona*. Woolf quotes the verse directly and ends the scene with Clara and Jacob both clapping in appreciation, revealing that the drawing-room performance is still an integral qualification for the marriage market for women in this section set sometime before the First World War. For an excellent examination of how music making played a significant role in the courtship rituals of late Victorian domestication, see Phyllis Weliver's *Women Musicians in Victorian Fiction, 1869–1900*. Other noteworthy considerations in this vein include Paula Gillett's *Musical Women in England, 1870–1914*, Ruth Solie's *Music in Other Words*, especially chapters 3 and 4 for this topic, and Sophie Fuller and Nicky Losseff's valuable collection, *The Idea of Music in Victorian Fiction*.

20 The connection between space and the song, "Allerseelen" ("All Souls' Day" in English), is also strengthened by the fact that All Souls Church, Langham Place, which was consecrated in 1824, was designed by John Nash, who developed Regent's Park and Regent Street. Moreover, the circular columned portico of the church is situated at the north end of Regent Street. It was built to soften the awkward corner that joined to the existing Portland Place, a street that Rezia and Septimus walk down when they leave the park, so theoretically they pass the church.

21 Molly Hoff links the music-hall artiste Marie Lloyd (1870–1922), a "simple singer," to Mrs McNab, who refers here, presumably, to the music-hall stage twenty years earlier. Hoff also argues that "there is something of Marie Lloyd, pocketing her shilling, in the battered singer at Regents Park" (6). The connection made by Hoff strengthens my argument about Woolf's singers. Also, Woolf's close friend T.S. Eliot admired Marie Lloyd, and wrote a tribute to her in the *The Dial* when she died. See "London Letter," *The Dial* 73.6 (December 1922): 659–63.

22 For discussions about the problematical nature of Woolf's working-class representations, see Michael Tratner and Mary Lou Emery.

2. The Earcon Reproduces

1 In her notes to the Oxford World Classics edition of the novel, Gillian Beer specifies that Wigmore Hall is the place in which Rhoda listens to the singer (see notes to pages 132–3). Intriguingly, this recital space is precisely the venue in which one would hear either Strauss's or Lassen's "Allerseelen," under discussion in chapter 1.

2 In the Cambridge edition of the novel, Michael Herbert and Susan Sellers make a number of suggestions given the reference to Venice, but since the piece is not specified in the text these are only possibilities. See explanatory note 128:17–24, p. 343.

3 See Berman's *Modernist Fiction*. Her work is in line with several critics who interpret Woolf's novel of interiority and subjectivity as a text that critiques empire. Jane Marcus was one of the first to suggest that the text is highly critical of imperialism, particularly through the ironic portrayal of Percival, who plays the conventionally colonialist and heroic part yet dies a rather pusillanimous, accidental death in India. See "Britannia Rules *The Waves*"; see also Patrick McGee's response to Marcus in "The Politics of Modernist Form," as well as Gillian Beer's "The Body of the People" in *Virginia Woolf: The Common Ground*.

4 On 17 August 1935, Woolf considered other names for the novel she had tentatively titled *Here and Now*, when she envisioned the ending: "I think I see the end of *Here & Now* (or *Music*, or *Dawn* or whatever I shall call it)" (*D4*: 237). Although, in addition to the other two possibilities mentioned above, she considered *Music* among seven others, including *The Pargiters*, *Sons and Daughters*, *Daughters and Sons*, *Ordinary People*, *The Caravan*, *Other People's Houses*, and finally *The Years*, her inclusion of *Music* as a title speaks not only to her comment to Elizabeth Trevelyan five years later that she always thinks of her books as music before she writes them, but also to the significance of music in the novel, its pervasiveness as a thematic and conceptual device.

5 The year 1910 is a significant one for Woolf; it is the year in which "human character changed" (*E3*: 421), as she declares in her essay "Character in Fiction" (1924). The date implies a significant cultural event: the 1910 Post-Impressionist art exhibit organized by her friend and Bloomsbury colleague, Roger Fry. The show is also a historical node for Woolf that presages the opening of new artistic, ontological, and epistemological possibilities that one could read, with hindsight, as being particularly interdisciplinary. Appositely, the chapter titled "1910" in the novel explores the effect of sight and sound on human consciousness. In addition, it is the year in which King Edward VII dies unexpectedly, thus bringing the Edwardian age to a close. And finally, as Michael Tratner documents, "Woolf's choice of December 1910 also alludes to a specific event in political history: that was the date of the last election won by the Liberal Party, the last election in which the Labour Party was only a minor third" (54). Correspondingly, gender, class, and art are issues that pervade the 1910 chapter in *The Years*, and it ends with the King's passing, as I shall discuss.

6 Maren Linett argues otherwise: that Woolf is more critical of some characters than others. According to Linett, Woolf's portrayal of Sara's Jewish neighbour, Abrahamson, is anti-Semitic, "sustained alongside and even within the fervent antifascist commitments that animate *The Years*" ("The Jew in the Bath," 357).

7 See Snaith's explanatory note, 169:20, p. 472 in the Cambridge edition.

8 Snaith documents, most recently, that no direct source, if one exists, has been identified. See explanatory note 386:24–387:11.

9 For more on this topic, see Brenda Silver, "Virginia Woolf and the Concept of Community."

10 For connections to other pageant writers, especially Mary Kelly, see Sei Kosugi's "Representing Nation and Nature: Woolf, Kelly, White," in Snaith and Whitworth, eds. *Locating Woolf*, 81–96.

11 See Cuddy-Keane's "Virginia Woolf, Sound Technologies, and the New Aurality."

12 Gillian Beer argues that Woolf's first and last novels engage most directly with the idea of the primeval in "Virginia Woolf and Prehistory" (*Virginia Woolf: The Common Ground*). Others have also noted the significance of the prehistoric world for Woolf; see Alex Zwerdling and Mark Hussey.

13 During the First World War, military leaders preferred the euphemism "wastage" to delineate the number of men lost, on a daily, weekly, and monthly basis, to death and wounds. See Paul Fussel, *The Great War and Modern Memory* (New York: Oxford University Press, 1975).

3. Initial Apperceptions

1 This chapter is an expansion of theoretical ideas I have published previously and discussed in relation to *Between the Acts* in "Virginia Woolf, Ethel Smyth, and Music."

2 In her essay "The Rhetoric of Feminist Conversation," Melba Cuddy-Keane argues that Woolf's rhetorical strategies are typically conversational, or dialogic in a Bakhtinian sense. Cuddy-Keane notes, however, the "astonishing disparity between Bakhtin's secure place in the contemporary critical canon and the lack of recognition and, indeed, understanding accorded to Woolf's equally provocative approach" (138).

3 As noted in the Introduction, see Garrett Stewart's *Reading Voices* for further explanation of this term.

4 Several critics have investigated the sonics of Woolf's novels. In addition to Cuddy-Keane, who explores the matrix of New Music, technology, and

sound, Steven Connor notes Woolf's use of the "diffusive but assimilatory ear" in *Mrs. Dalloway*; Kate Flint, Michelle Pridmore-Brown, and Rishona Zimring have each explored the significant and discerning application of noise in a variety of Woolf's later fictions, especially; and Angela Frattarola's examination of "found sound" also considers this layer of sonority.

5 The combination of such technologies and the acousmatic circumstances (although not discussed in such terms) is noted by Bonnie Kime Scott, for example, in her article on *Between the Acts*: "Thomas Edison's early phonograph (patented 1877) not only reproduced sounds, but could record them – giving rise to the advertising slogan, 'His Master's Voice,' applied to the widely circulated image of an endearing dog, gazing loyally at the antique horn that served as the speaker for masculine authority" (97). Kime Scott also documents that when Woolf was still in the process of writing her first novel, "records became a mass medium" (ibid.).

6 For a discussion of Woolf's understanding of and interest in the language, see Rebecca Nagel's essay, "Virginia Woolf on Reading Greek."

7 Clare Davison gave an informative and insightful talk on some of the musical connections to the masque in her paper about opera and *The Voyage Out* at the Twenty-Sixth Annual International Conference on Virginia Woolf in Leeds, UK (2016).

8 For a timetable, see "UK Telephone History" taken from the British Telecom Archives website: http://www.britishtelephones.com/histuk.htm, accessed 23 February 2017.

9 As is well known, Katherine Mansfield was critical of Woolf for omitting the First World War from *Night and Day*, published just after the end of the conflict. Woolf would answer this criticism with the pointedly anti-war text *Jacob's Room*.

10 For more on this incident and its connection to the "cry" of chapter 1, see my article "A Different Hearing."

11 It is worth noting that James Joyce also elaborates on the liveliness of sound when the eyes are closed when Stephen Dedalus experiences the "ineluctable modality of the visible" and, later in the episode, the audible, on Sandymount Strand. See episode 3, "Proteus," in *Ulysses*.

12 The Greek connection also suggests a homosexual bond between Septimus and Evans. See Catherine Lord, "The Frames of Septimus Smith."

13 I am using a translation of the French text, *Traité des objets musicaux*, by Daniel W. Smith included in Cox and Warner, eds., *Audio Culture*.

14 Thessaly was an important Greek city in antiquity known particularly for its cavalry.
15 The nightingale and the swallow invoke the ancient Greek myth of Philomela and Procne, sisters who are transformed into birds. Procne, married to King Tereus of Thrace, has a son by him, named Itys. But Tereus has designs on Philomela, which he eventually carries out by raping her. To keep her from disclosing the violence, he then cuts out her tongue and imprisons her. Silenced, Philomela weaves a tapestry to reveal the facts of her situation to her sister. To avenge the crime, Procne kills Itys, cooks him, and serves him to Tereus, who eats his own son for dinner. When Tereus discovers the trick, he tries to kill both women, but all three are turned into birds before he can catch them – Tereus becomes a hoopoe, Procne a swallow, and Philomela a nightingale. As one can see, the tale is littered with violence, betrayal, and sexual oppression, but it also implicitly evokes issues of language, art, and aural signification. Woolf employs it purposefully to show the links between private conflicts in marriage and international ones in the First World War.

4. Bodies and Voices

1 As in *Mrs. Dalloway*, the birdsong, in this case the nightingale's, suggests another allusion to T.S. Eliot and his iconic modernist poem, *The Waste Land*. First published in *The Dial* and *The Criterion* in autumn 1922, it was also produced in pamphlet form by the Hogarth Press in 1923. Notably, the link is not only mythological but also aural, as "'Jug Jug' to dirty ears" (l. 103) is an onomatopoeic representation of birdsong.
2 Ironically, given Hitler's use of Wagner's music and agreement with his anti-Semitism, she learned the language to attempt to understand his operas when she heard them in Bayreuth with her brother and Saxon Sydney-Turner in 1909. By the late 1930s, however, her ability to translate orally was quite rusty.
3 See Snaith's explanatory notes to the Cambridge Edition of the novel, 206:6, p. 487.
4 Sara's learned anti-Semitism is also made plain in the episode in which she comments on the Jewish man with whom she shares a bathroom. Gloria Glendinning describes the scene as Woolf's disclosure of the "spiritual concentration camp" alive and well in 1930s England: "'the Jew ... the Jew ...' Sara reiterates the word until the individual, 'Abrahamson, in the tallow trade,' engaged to a pretty girl in a tailor's shop, is reduced to an

emblem of pollution" (Glendinning 288). For a more critical view of the episode, see Maren Linett's "The Jew in the Bath."

5 Although she does not discuss this scene specifically, Cuddy-Keane does explore Martin's experience at Kitty Lasswade's party at the end of the "1914" chapter. Her analysis examines the the mind's auditory perception as it manifests in Woolf's texts in her article on "Modernist Soundscapes." Other critics who discuss the novel's sonics include Rishona Zimring, Kate Flint, and Angela Fratarolla. Pamela L. Caughie's "Virginia Woolf: Radio, Gramophone, Broadcasting" provides an overview of technology in some of Woolf's novels but does not explore *The Years*.

6 Although coincidental with my terminology, Woolf's description of "profound silence" suggests the significance of the act of listening for her.

7 Most notably, Michelle Pridmore-Brown, Cuddy-Keane, and Angela Fratarolla. Bonnie Kime Scott's discussion of the gramophone in *Between the Acts* also explores the intersection of sonority and social structures.

5. Performing Women

1 For a condensed explication of the issues, context, and debates about music and/as performance, see Cook, "Between Process and Product." For a more comprehensive and varied study see his book, *Beyond the Score*. See also Derek Scott's survey of the major trends in musicology since the 1990s in his Introduction to *From the Erotic to the Demonic*.

2 See Goehr's *The Imaginary Museum of Musical Works*. For a critical stance on Goehr, see Georgina Born's "On Musical Mediation."

3 Carolyn Abbate also discusses the performer as automaton. See *In Search of Opera*.

4 Lucy Honeychurch is a character in *A Room with a View*. Sutton illustrates that Opus 112, the work referred to in *The Voyage Out* in chapter 2 when Rachel is first introduced, is printed incorrectly in the first edition of the novel and thereafter. Citing a letter Woolf wrote to Saxon Sydney-Turner clarifying the opus number (*L2*: 418), Sutton reveals that Woolf confirms that Opus 111 is the sonata Rachel plays in the later passage (chapter 22) as well as ponders in chapter 2. See Sutton, *Virginia Woolf and Classical Music* 60.

5 I am grateful to Claire Davison for mentioning that Opus 111 is notable in music history for its "staircase" segment in her paper "Background Music: *The Voyage Out* and Operatic Tradition" at the Twenty-Sixth Annual International Conference on Virginia Woolf in Leeds, UK (2016).

6 For a short precis of some of the sonata's interesting specifics, with sound files, see Tania Halban (19 March 2014), "Beethoven Piano Sonata op. 111, John Lill," *notesonnotes*, retrieved 23 June 2016.

7 Jim Stewart reads this scene and Rachel herself in this chapter as Dionysian. See "The Birth of Rachel Vinrace from the Spirit of Music."

8 For more on the musical scenes in Woolf's second novel, as well as "The String Quartet," Woolf's early experimental story from *Monday or Tuesday* (1921), see Vanessa Manhire's "'The Worst of Music.'"

9 See Clements, "The Efficacy of Performance."

10 See Snaith's informative Introduction to the new Cambridge edition in which she suggests that Woolf's depiction of history prefigures Walter Benjamin's discussion of historical materialism in *Theses on the Philosophy of History*. See also Elizabeth F. Evans, "Air War, Propaganda, and Woolf's Anti-Tyranny Aesthetic" and Stephen M. Barber, "States of Emergency, States of Freedom."

11 See Marcus, *Virginia Woolf and the Languages of Patriarchy*.

12 As mentioned in chapter 2, for a discussion of the opera's significance to the novel, see Sutton, *Virginia Woolf and Classical Music*, 126–33.

13 Sara and her fork conducting echo an infamous story about Dame Ethel Smyth conducting her suffragette song "March of the Women" with a toothbrush from behind the bars of Holloway Prison.

14 This song is still unidentified, according to Snaith (see Explanatory Notes, 289: 6–7, 511).

15 For a transcription of "Anon" and "The Reader," as well as an excellent contextual introduction, see Silver's "'Anon' and 'The Reader.'"

16 Jean-Jacques Rousseau also suggests that language was most likely born out of music. See his "Essay on the Origin of Languages."

17 Debates still continue as to the pageant's function in the novel – whether or not, together with its creator, Miss La Trobe, it instantiates authoritarianism or disrupts it through democratic principles. In addition to Michelle Pridmore Brown's essay, "1939–40," and Melba Cuddy-Keane's "The Politics of Comic Modes in Virginia Woolf's *Between the Acts*," see Jed Esty's *A Shrinking Island*, especially chapter 2, for an alternative reading of the conservatism invested in the early twentieth-century pageant revival and Woolf's critical, yet sometimes ambivalent, embedding of this genre in her final work. See also Ben Harker's "'On Different Levels Ourselves Went Forward.'"

18 Emma Sutton persuasively argues that the folk music Woolf deploys in the book is her critique of the nationalism entrenched in the English Musical

Renaissance. See chapter 5 of *Virginia Woolf and Classical Music*. For another perceptive reading of the varied musics and rhythms in the novel, see Trina Thompson's "Sounding the Past." Sanja Bahun's "Broken Music, Broken History," in the same collection, makes connections between musical rhythms and patterns in the novel and then-contemporary composers Igor Stravinsky and Arnold Schoenberg.

6. The Performativity of Language: *The Waves* Musicalized

1 The essay is later reprinted with small revisions as "The Narrow Bridge of Art" in the collection *Granite and Rainbow: Essays by Virginia Woolf* (1958).
2 Laurence makes the claim about ellipses in her book *The Reading of Silence*. See also Hussey's *Singing of the Real World* and Vandivere's article "Waves and Fragments."
3 See notes to the novel's pages 60 to 62 on 300–2 in the Explanatory Notes section of the Cambridge edition.
4 This section is based on a previously published article in *Narrative*, "Transforming Musical Sounds into Words: Narrative Method in Virginia Woolf's *The Waves*." I have taken the opportunity to add musical examples to emphasize the sonic component of the comparison.
5 See Knittel's essay, "The Construction of Beethoven," in *The Cambridge History of Nineteenth-Century Music*.
6 Several critics have noted the connections between *The Waves* and Beethoven's compositions. See Gerald Levin, Peter Jacobs, and most recently, Emma Sutton, who addresses his music in relation to Rachel's piano pieces in *The Voyage Out*, as I discuss in chapter 5.
7 See Spitzer's essay "Notes on Beethoven's Late Style" in the thought-provoking collection *Late Style and its Discontents*, as well as his larger study, *Music as Philosophy*.
8 I am using Kinderman's translation of Holz's correspondence in Beethoven's conversation books, *Ludwig van Beethovens Konversationshefte*, which Beethoven used to communicate with friends and colleagues because of his deafness. The quotation is on page 301.
9 A humorous link can be made to another of Woolf's characters: Miss La Trobe, who goes to a nearby tavern after the performance of her pageant in *Between the Acts*. Similar to Beethoven, she swears about the inadequacy of her audience's responses, which seem strikingly comparable to those in this story of Beethoven and the *Grosse Fuge*. At the very least, the

connection supports my suggestion that perhaps Woolf knew about Beethoven's response and his allegiance to his own formal innovations.

10 Like her friend T.S. Eliot, who quotes lyrics from Wagner's operas in *The Waste Land*, Woolf was familiar with the German composer's approach to this Arthurian knight. See Gyllian Phillips for an examination of the opera in relation to *The Waves*. Also, see Sutton's last chapter, "Only Suggest," in *Virginia Woolf and Classical Music* for links to Wagner's *Ring Cycle*.

11 For a discussion of Woolf's pluralistic thinking and its connection to music in the novels, see Cuddy-Keane's "The Politics of Comic Modes" and "Virginia Woolf, Sound Technologies, and the New Aurality."

Coda: A Meditation on Rhythm

1 Peter Jacobs is a notable exception.

2 My definition, taken from Wolf, differs from some other intermedial theorists such as Chiel Kattenbelt, who defines transmediality as the "transfer from one medium to another medium (media change)" (20). See his "Intermediality in Theatre and Performance."

3 As noted in the Introduction, Woolf knew Pater's work quite extensively and had read *The Renaissance*. She studied Greek with Clara Pater, his sister, and later in life, in her biography of Fry, she refers to Pater's writing as significant to his art criticism (see pages 74, 106). For more on music in Pater, see my "Pater's Musical Imagination."

4 In her Introduction to "The Roger Fry Memorial Exhibition," Woolf mentions that "he was a great lover of music" (*E6*: 61).

Works Cited

Abbate, Carolyn. *In Search of Opera*. Princeton: Princeton University Press, 2001.
– *Unsung Voices: Opera and Musical Narrative in the Nineteenth Century*. Princeton: Princeton University Press, 1996.
Albright, Daniel, ed. and commentary. *Modernism and Music: An Anthology of Sources*. Chicago: University of Chicago Press, 2004.
Alfsen, Merete. "'Putting Words on the Backs of Rhythm': Translating Woolf." *Virginia Woolf Bulletin* 2 (1999): 32–6.
Avery, Todd. *Radio Modernism: Literature, Ethics, and the BBC, 1922–1938*. Aldershot: Ashgate, 2006.
Bahun, Sanja. "Broken Music, Broken History: Sounds and Silence in Virginia Woolf's *Between the Acts*." In *Virginia Woolf and Music*, ed. Adriana Varga, 229–58. Bloomington and Indianapolis: Indiana University Press, 2014.
Bailey, Peter. *Popular Culture and Performance in the Victorian City*. Cambridge: Cambridge University Press, 1998.
Bakhtin, M.M. *The Dialogic Imagination: Four Essays*. Trans. Caryl Emerson and Michael Holquist, ed. Michael Holquist. Austin: University of Texas Press, 1996.
Barad, Karen. "Posthumanist Performativity: Toward an Understanding of How Matter Comes to Matter." *Signs* 28.3 (2003): 801–31.
Barber, Stephen M. "States of Emergency, States of Freedom: Woolf, History, and the Novel." *Novel: A Forum on Fiction* 42.2 (2009): 196–206.
Barnett, Henrietta Octavia. *Canon Barnett, His Life, Work, and Friend, by His Wife*. Vol. 2. Boston: Houghton Mifflin, 1919.
Barry, Barbara R. "Recycling the End of the 'Leibquartett': Models, Meaning and Propriety in Beethoven's Quartet in B-Flat Major, Opus 130." *Journal of Musicology* 13.3 (1995): 355–76.

Barthes, Roland. *The Responsibility of Forms: Critical Essays on Music, Art, and Representation*. Trans. Richard Howard. Berkeley: University of California Press, 1985.

Beer, Gillian, ed. Introduction and Notes. *The Waves*. By Virginia Woolf. 1931. Oxford: Oxford University Press, 1992.

– *Virginia Woolf: The Common Ground: Essays by Gillian Beer*. Ann Arbor: University of Michigan Press, 1996.

Beethoven, Ludwig van. *Complete String Quartets and Grosse Fuge from the Breitkopf & Hartel Complete Works Edition*. New York: Dover Publications, 1970.

– *The Late Beethoven Quartets Vol. 2*. CD Recording. Lindsay String Quartet. Academy Sound and Vision, 1987.

– *Ludwig van Beethovens Konversationshefte*. Vol. 8. Ed. Karl-Heinz Köhler and Grita Herre. Leipzig: Deutscher Verlag für Musik, 1981.

Bell, Vanessa. *Notes on Virginia's Childhood: A Memoir*. New York: F. Hallman, 1974.

Benhabib, Seyla. *Situating the Self: Gender, Community and Postmodernism in Contemporary Ethics*. New York: Routledge, 1992.

Berman, Jessica. *Modernist Fiction, Cosmopolitanism and the Politics of Community*. New York: Cambridge University Press, 2001.

Bishop, Edward L. "Mind the Gap: The Spaces in *Jacob's Room*." *Woolf Studies Annual* 10 (2004): 31–49.

Blesser, Barry, and Linda-Ruth Salter. *Spaces Speak, Are You Listening? Experiencing Aural Architecture*. Cambridge, MA: MIT Press, 2007.

Born, Georgina, ed. *Music, Sound and Space: Transformations of Public and Private Experience*. Cambridge and New York: Cambridge University Press, 2013.

– "On Musical Mediation: Ontology, Technology and Creativity." *Twentieth-Century Music* 2.1 (2005): 7–36.

Bradshaw, David, ed. Introduction and Notes. *Mrs Dalloway*. By Virginia Woolf. 1925. Oxford: Oxford University Press, 2000.

Brzezinski, Max. "The New Modernist Studies: What's Left of Political Formalism?" *Minnesota Review* 76 (2011): 109–25.

Bucknell, Brad. *Literary Modernism and Musical Aesthetics: Pater, Pound, Joyce, and Stein*. Cambridge: Cambridge University Press, 2001.

– "The Sound of Silence in Two of *Jacob's Rooms*." *Modernism/Modernity* 15.4 (2008): 761–81.

Byron, Lord. *Don Juan*. Project Gutenberg. Web. 15 December 2016. https://www.gutenberg.org/files/21700/21700-h/21700-h.htm#2H_4_0002.

The Cambridge History of Nineteenth-Century Music. Ed. Jim Samson. Cambridge: Cambridge University Press, 2001.

Caughie, Pamela L. Introduction. In *Virginia Woolf in the Age of Mechanical Reproduction*, ed. Pamela L. Caughie, xix–xxxvi. New York: Garland Publishing, 2000.

– "Virginia Woolf: Radio, Gramophone, Broadcasting." In *The Edinburgh Companion to Virginia Woolf and the Arts*, ed. Maggie Humm, 332–47. Edinburgh: Edinburgh University Press, 2010.

Chion, Michel. *Audio-Vision: Sound on Screen*. Ed. and trans. Claudia Gorbman. New York: Columbia University Press, 1994.

– *Sound: An Acoulogical Treatise*. Trans. and intro. James A. Steintrager. 2nd ed. Durham, NC, and London: Duke University Press, 2010. Kindle ed. Originally published as *Le son: traité d'acoulogie*. 2nd ed. Paris: Armand Colin, 2010.

– *The Voice in Cinema*. Ed. and trans. Claudia Gorbman. New York: Columbia University Press, 1999.

Clarke, Stuart N. "The Old Woman's Song in *Mrs. Dalloway*." *Virginia Woolf Bulletin* 17 (2004): 50–2.

Clements, Elicia. "'As Springy as a Racehorse': Ethel Smyth's *Female Pipings in Eden* as Rejoinder to Virginia Woolf's *A Room of One's Own*." In *Rock Blaster, Bridge Builder, Road Paver: The Composer Ethel Smyth*, ed. Cornelia Bartsch, Rebecca Grotjahn, and Melanie Unseld, 55–69. Munich: Allitera Verlag, 2010.

– "A Different Hearing: Voicing *Night and Day*." *Virginia Woolf Bulletin* 11 (2002): 32–9.

– "The Efficacy of Performance: Musical Events in *The Years*." In *Virginia Woolf and Music*, ed. Adriana Varga, 180–203. Bloomington and Indiana: Indiana University Press, 2014.

– "Pater's Musical Imagination: The Aural Architecture of 'The School of Giorgione' and *Marius the Epicurean*." In *Victorian Aesthetic Conditions: Pater across the Arts*, ed. Elicia Clements and Lesley J. Higgins. Basingstoke: Palgrave Macmillan, 2010.

– "Reconfigured Terrain: Aural Architecture in Woolf's Novels." In *Woolf and the City: Selected Papers from the Nineteenth Annual Conference on Virginia Woolf*, ed. Elizabeth F. Evans and Sarah E. Cornish, 71–6. Clemson: Clemson University Digital Press, September 2010.

– "Transforming Musical Sounds into Words: Narrative Method in Virginia Woolf's *The Waves*." *Narrative* 13.2 (2005): 160–81.

– "Virginia Woolf, Ethel Smyth, and Music: Listening as a Productive Mode of Social Interaction." *College Literature* 32.3 (2005): 51–71.

Comstock, Margaret: "The Loudspeaker and the Human Voice: Politics and the Form of *The Years.*" *Bulletin of the New York Public Library* 80 (1977): 252–75.

Connor, Steven. "The Modern Auditory I." In *Rewriting the Self: Histories from the Renaissance to the Present,* ed. Roy Porter, 203–23. London: Routledge, 1997.

Cook, Nicholas. "Between Process and Product: Music and/as Performance." *Music Theory Online* 7.2 (April 2001). Retrieved 1 October 2007. http://www.societymusictheory.org/mto/issues/mto.01.7.2/mto.01.7.2.cook.html.

– *Beyond the Score: Music as Performance.* New York: Oxford University Press, 2013.

Cox, Christoph, and Daniel Warner, eds. *Audio Culture: Readings in Modern Music.* New York: Continuum, 2006.

Crapoulet, Emily. "Voicing the Music in Literature." *European Journal of English Studies* 13.1 (2009): 79–91.

Creedon, Alison. "A Benevolent Tyrant? The Principles and Practices of Henrietta Barnett (1851–1936), Social Reformer and Founder of Hampstead Garden Suburb." *Women's History Review* 11.2 (2002): 231–52.

Cuddy-Keane, Melba. "'Are Too Many Books Written and Published?' By Leonard Woolf and Virginia Woolf." *PMLA* 121.1 (2006): 382–98.

– "Modernist Soundscapes and the Intelligent Ear: An Approach to Narrative through Auditory Perception." In *A Companion to Narrative Theory,* ed. James Phelan and Peter J. Rabinowitz, 382–98. Oxford: Blackwell Publishing, 2005.

– "The Politics of Comic Modes in Virginia Woolf's *Between the Acts.*" *PMLA* 105.2 (1990): 273–85.

– "The Rhetoric of Feminist Conversation: Virginia Woolf and the Trope of the Twist." In *Ambiguous Discourse,* ed. Kathy Mezei, 137–61. Chapel Hill: University of North Carolina Press, 1996.

– "Virginia Woolf, Sound Technologies, and the New Aurality." In *Virginia Woolf in the Age of Mechanical Reproduction,* ed. Pamela L. Caughie, 69–96. New York: Garland Publishing, 2000.

Cuddy-Keane, Melba, ed. Introduction and Annotations. *Between the Acts.* By Virginia Woolf. New York: Harcourt, 2008.

Cuddy-Keane, Melba, Adam Hammond, and Alexandra Peat. *Modernism: Keywords.* Oxford: Wiley Blackwell, 2014.

de Certeau, Michel. *The Practice of Everyday Life.* Trans. Steven Rendall. Berkeley: University of California Press, 1984.

Dell-Antonio, Andrew. *Beyond Structural Listening: Postmodern Modes of Hearing.* Oakland: University of California, 2004.

DeSalvo, Louise, ed. and intro. *Melymbrosia: A Novel by Virginia Woolf.* San Francisco: Cleis Press, 2002.

Deutsch, David. *British Literature and Classical Music: Cultural Contexts 1870–1945.* London: Bloomsbury Academic, 2015.

Dever, Carolyn. "Strategic Aestheticism: A Response to Caroline Levine." *Victorian Studies* 49.1 (Autumn 2006): 94–9.

Dolar, Mladen. *A Voice and Nothing More.* Cambridge, MA: MIT Press, 2006.

Donne, John. "Mediation 17." Project Gutenberg. Web. 15 December 2016. 107–10. http://www.gutenberg.org/files/23772/23772-h/23772-h.htm.

Eisenberg, Nora. "Virginia Woolf's Last Words on Words: *Between the Acts* and 'Anon.'" In *New Feminist Essays on Virginia Woolf,* ed. Jane Marcus, 253–66. London: Macmillan, 1981.

Eliot, T.S. *The Complete Poems and Plays.* London: Faber, 1969.

– "Matthew Arnold." In *The Use of Poetry and the Use of Criticism,* 103–20. Cambridge, MA: Harvard University Press, 1961.

– "The Music of Poetry." In *Selected Prose of T.S. Eliot,* ed. Frank Kermode, 107–14. London: Faber and Faber, 1975.

– *The Waste Land. The Norton Anthology of Modern Poetry.* 2nd ed. Ed. Richard Ellmann and Robert O'Clair, 491–504. New York: W.W. Norton and Company, 1988.

Emery, Mary Lou. "'Robbed of Meaning': The Work at the Center of *To the Lighthouse.*" *Modern Fiction Studies* 38.1 (1992): 217–34.

Esty, Jed. *A Shrinking Island: Modernism and National Culture in England.* Princeton: Princeton University Press, 2003.

Evans, Elizabeth F. "Air War, Propaganda, and Woolf's Anti-Tyranny Aesthetic." *MFS* 59.1 (2013): 55–82.

Flint, Kate. "Sounds of the City: Virginia Woolf and Modern Noise." In *Literature, Science, Psychoanalysis, 1830–1970,* ed. and intro. Helen Small and ed. Trudi Tate, 181–94. Oxford: Oxford University Press, 2003.

Forster, E.M. *Aspects of the Novel.* Harmondsworth: Penguin Books, 1964.

Frattarola, Angela: "Listening for 'Found Sound' Samples in the Novels of Virginia Woolf." *Woolf Studies Annual* 11 (2005): 133–59.

– "The Phonograph and the Modernist Novel." *Mosaic* 43.1 (2010): 143–59.

Friedman, Susan Stanford. *Mappings: Feminism and the Cultural Geographies of Encounter.* Princeton: Princeton University Press, 1998.

Froula, Christine. *Virginia Woolf and the Bloomsbury Avant-Garde: War, Civilization, Modernity.* New York: Columbia University Press, 2005.

Fry, Roger. "Post Impressionism." In *A Roger Fry Reader,* ed. Christopher Reed, 99–110. Chicago: University of Chicago Press, 1996.

– "Principles of Design." C. 1920. In *Art Made Modern: Roger Fry's Vision of Art*, ed. Christopher Green, 213–21. London: Merrell Holberton Publishers, 1999.

– *Vision and Design*. Ed. J.B. Bullen. London: Oxford University Press, 1981.

Fuller, Sophie, and Nicky Losseff, eds. *The Idea of Music in Victorian Fiction*. Aldershot: Ashgate, 2004.

Gillespie, Diane F. "Introduction: 'The Loves of the Arts.'" In *The Multiple Muses of Virginia Woolf*, ed. Diane F. Gillespie, 1–8. Columbia: University of Missouri Press, 1993.

– *The Sisters' Arts: The Writing and Painting of Virginia Woolf and Vanessa Bell*. Syracuse: Syracuse University Press, 1988.

– "Virginia Woolf, Vanessa Bell and Painting." In *The Edinburgh Companion to Virginia Woolf and the Arts*, ed. Maggie Humm, 121–39. Edinburgh: Edinburgh University Press, 2010.

Gillett, Paula. *Musical Women in England, 1870–1914: Encroaching on All Man's Privileges*. New York: St Martin's Press, 2000.

Glendinning, Victoria. *Leonard Woolf: A Biography*. Toronto: McClelland and Stewart, 2006.

Goehr, Lydia. *The Imaginary Museum of Musical Works: An Essay in the Philosophy of Music*. Oxford: Clarendon Press, 1992.

Goldman, Jane. *The Feminist Aesthetics of Virginia Woolf: Modernism, Post-Impressionism and the Politics of the Visual*. Cambridge: Cambridge University Press, 1998.

Gruber, Klemens. "Early Intermediality: Archaeological Glimpses." In *Mapping Intermediality in Performance*, ed. Sarah Bay-Cheng, Chiel Kattenbelt, Andy Lavender, and Robin Nelson, 247–57. Amsterdam: Amsterdam University Press, 2010.

Halban, Tania. "Beethoven Piano Sonata op. 111, John Lill." *notesonnotes*. 19 March 2014. Retrieved 23 June 2016. http://notesonnotes.org/2014/03/19/beethoven-piano-sonata-op-111-john-lill/.

Halliday, Sam. *Sonic Modernity: Representing Sound in Literature, Culture and the Arts*. Edinburgh: Edinburgh University Press, 2013.

Harker, Ben. "'On Different Levels Ourselves Went Forward': Pageantry, Class Politics and Narrative Form in Virginia Woolf's Late Writing." *ELH* 78.2 (2011): 433–56.

Harries, Martin. "Theater and Media before 'New' Media: Beckett's Film and Play." *Performance Research* 19.3 (2014): 7–25.

Hite, Molly. "The Public Woman and the Modernist Turn: Virginia Woolf's *The Voyage Out* and Elizabeth Robins's *My Little Sister*." *Modernism/Modernity* 17.3 (2010): 523–48.

Hoff, Molly. "The Music Hall in *Mrs. Dalloway*." *Virginia Woolf Miscellany* 41 (1993): 6–7.

Humm, Maggie, ed. and intro. *The Edinburgh Companion to Virginia Woolf and the Arts*. Edinburgh: Edinburgh University Press, 2010.

Hussey, Mark. *The Singing of the Real World: The Philosophy of Virginia Woolf's Fiction*. Columbus: Ohio State University Press, 1986.

Imeson, Sylvia. *"The time give it proofe": Paradox in the Late Music of Beethoven*. New York: Peter Lang, 1996.

Jacobs, Peter. "'The Second Violin Tuning in the Ante Room': Virginia Woolf and Music." In *The Multiple Muses of Virginia Woolf*, ed. Diane F. Gillespie, 227–60. Columbia: University of Missouri Press, 1993.

Kattenbelt, Chiel. "Intermediality in Theatre and Performance: Definitions, Perceptions and Medial Relationships." *Culture, Language and Representation* 6 (2008): 19–29.

Keats, John. "Ode on a Grecian Urn." In *The Norton Anthology of Poetry*. 3rd ed. Ed. Alexander W. Allison, Herbert Barrows, Caesar R. Blake, Arthur J. Carr, Arthur M. Eastman, and Hubert M. English, Jr, 372–3. New York: W.W. Norton and Company, 1983.

– "Ode to a Nightingale." In *The Norton Anthology of Poetry*. 3rd ed. Ed. Alexander W. Allison, Herbert Barrows, Caesar R. Blake, Arthur J. Carr, Arthur M. Eastman, and Hubert M. English, Jr, 370–71. New York: W.W. Norton and Company, 1983.

Kelley, Joyce E. "Virginia Woolf and Music." In *The Edinburgh Companion to Virginia Woolf and the Arts*, ed. Maggie Humm, 416–34. Edinburgh: Edinburgh University Press, 2010.

Kerman, Joseph. *The Beethoven Quartets*. New York: Alfred A. Knopf, 1967.

Kinderman, William. "Beethoven's Last Quartets: Threshold to a Fourth Creative Period?" In *The String Quartets of Beethoven*, ed. William Kinderman, 279–322. Urbana: University of Illinois Press, 2008.

– Introduction. In *The String Quartets of Beethoven*, ed. William Kinderman, 1–12. Urbana: University of Illinois Press, 2008.

Kosugi, Sei. "Representing Nation and Nature: Woolf, Kelly, White." In *Locating Woolf: The Politics of Space and Place*, ed. Anna Snaith and Michael Whitworth, 81–96. Basingstoke: Palgrave Macmillan, 2007.

Kramer, Lawrence. "Review: Song and Story." *Nineteenth-Century Music* 15.3 (Spring 1992): 235–9.

Latour, Bruno. "On Actor-Network Theory. A Few Clarifications Plus More Than a Few Complications." *Soziale Welt* 47 (1996): 369–81.

– *Reassembling the Social: An Introduction to Actor-Network Theory*. Oxford: Oxford University Press, 2005.

Laurence, Patricia Ondek. "The Facts and Fugue of War: From *Three Guineas* to *Between the Acts*." In *Virginia Woolf and War: Fiction, Reality, and Myth*, ed. Mark Hussey, 225–45. Syracuse: Syracuse University Press, 1991.

– *The Reading of Silence: Virginia Woolf in the English Tradition*. Stanford: Stanford University Press, 1991.

Leaska, Mitchell. "Virginia Woolf, the Pargeter: A Reading of *The Years*." *Bulletin of the New York Public Library* 80 (1977): 172–210.

Lee, Hermoine. *Virginia Woolf*. London: Chatto and Windus, 1996.

Levin, Gerald. "The Musical Style of *The Waves*." *Journal of Narrative Technique* 13.3 (Fall 1983): 164–71.

Levine, Caroline. "Strategic Formalism: Toward a New Method in Cultural Studies." *Victorian Studies* 48.4 (Summer 2006): 625–57.

Levinson, Marjorie. "What Is New Formalism." *PMLA* 122.2 (2007): 558–69.

Lewis, Andrea. "The Visual Politics of Empire and Gender in Virginia Woolf's *The Voyage Out*." *Woolf Studies Annual* 1 (1995): 106–19.

Linett, Maren. "The Jew in the Bath: Imperiled Imagination in Woolf's *The Years*." *Modern Fiction Studies* 48.2 (2002): 341–61.

Lockwood, Lewis. *Beethoven: Studies in the Creative Process*. Cambridge, MA: Harvard University Press, 1982.

López, Francisco. "Profound Listening and Environmental Sound Matter." In *Audio Culture: Readings in Modern Music*, ed. Christoph Cox and Daniel Warner, 82–7. New York: Continuum, 2006.

Lord, Catherine. "The Frames of Septimus Smith: Through Twenty Four Hours in the City of Mrs. Dalloway, 1923, and of Millennial London: Art Is a Shocking Experience." *Parallax* 5.3 (1999): 36–46.

Low, Lisa: "Woolf's Allusion to *Comus* in *The Voyage Out*." In *Milton and Gender*, ed. and intro. Catherine Gimelli Martin, 254–70. Cambridge: Cambridge University Press, 2004.

Manhire, Vanessa. "'The Lady's Gone A-Roving': Woolf and the English Folk Revival." In *Virginia Woolf Out of Bounds: Selected Papers from the Tenth Annual Conference on Virginia Woolf*, ed. Jessica Berman and Jane Goldman, 236–42. New York: Pace University Press, 2001.

– "'The Worst of Music': Listening and Narrative in *Night and Day* and 'The String Quartet.'" In *Virginia Woolf and Music*, ed. Adriana Varga, 134–58. Bloomington and Indianapolis: Indiana University Press, 2014.

Mao, Douglas, and Rebecca L. Walkowitz. Introduction. In *Bad Modernisms*. Durham, NC: Duke University Press, 1999.

– "The New Modernist Studies." *PMLA* 123.3 (2008): 737–48.

Marcus, Jane. "Britannia Rules *The Waves*." *Decolonizing Tradition: New Views of Twentieth-Century "British" Literary Canon*, ed. Karen R. Lawrence, 136–62. Urbana: University of Illinois Press, 1992.

– *Virginia Woolf and the Languages of Patriarchy*. Bloomington: Indiana University Press, 1987.

Martin, Robert. "The Quartets in Performance: A Player's Perspective." In *The Beethoven Quartet Companion*, ed. Robert Winter and Robert Martin, 111–41. Berkeley: University of California Press, 1994.

McClary, Susan. *Feminine Endings: Music, Gender, and Sexuality*. Minneapolis: University of Minnesota Press, 1991.

McGee, Patrick. "The Politics of Modernist Form; Or, Who Rules *The Waves*?" *Modern Fiction Studies* 38.3 (1992): 631–50.

Miller, J. Hillis. *Fiction and Repetition: Seven English Novels*. Cambridge, MA: Harvard University Press, 1982.

Murdoch, Jonathan. *Post-structuralist Geography: A Guide to Relational Space*. London: SAGE Publications, 2006.

Nagel, Rebecca. "Virginia Woolf on Reading Greek." *Classical World* 96.1 (2002): 61–75.

Nattiez, Jean-Jacques. *Music and Discourse: Toward a Semiology of Music*. Trans. Carolyn Abbate. Princeton: Princeton University Press, 1990.

Nattiez, Jean-Jacques, and Katharine Ellis. "Can One Speak of Narrativity in Music?" *Journal of the Royal Musical Association* 115.2 (1990): 240–57.

Pater, Walter. *The Renaissance: Studies in Art and Poetry: The 1893 Text*. Ed. Donald Hill. Berkeley: University of California Press, 1980.

Peitrequin, Raymond. "The Beggar's Song in *Mrs Dalloway*: An Analysis with Some Views on the Poetics of Empathy." *Etudes de Lettres* 3 (1993): 121–37.

Phelan, Peggy. *Unmarked: The Politics of Performance*. New York: Routledge, 1993.

Phillips, Gyllian. "Re(de)composing the Novel: *The Waves*, Wagnerian Opera and Percival/Parsifal." *Genre* 28.1–2 (1995): 119–44.

Phillips, Kathy J. *Virginia Woolf against Empire*. Knoxville: University of Tennessee Press, 1994.

Picker, John. *Victorian Soundscapes*. New York: Oxford University Press, 2003.

Pratt, Mary Louise. *Imperial Eyes: Travel Writing and Transculturation*. New York: Routledge, 1992.

Prettejohn, Elizabeth. "Out of the Nineteenth Century: Roger Fry's Early Art Criticism, 1900–1906." In *Art Made Modern: Roger Fry's Vision of Art*, ed. Christopher Green, 31–44. London: Merrell Holberton Publishers, 1999.

Pridmore-Brown, Michelle. "1939–40: Of Virginia Woolf, Gramophones, and Fascism." *PMLA* 113.3 (1998): 408–21.

Puchner, Martin. "The New Modernist Studies: A Response." *Minnesota Review* 79 (2012): 91–6.

Rajewsky, Irina. "Intermediality, Intertextuality, and Remediation: A Literary Perspective on Intermediality." *History and Theory of the Arts, Literature and Technologies* 6 (2005): 43–64.

Randall, Bryony, and Jane Goldman, eds. *Virginia Woolf in Context*. Cambridge: Cambridge University Press, 2012.

Rosenfeld, Natania. *Outsiders Together: Virginia and Leonard Woolf*. Princeton: Princeton University Press, 2000.

Rumph, Stephen. *Beethoven after Napoleon: Political Romanticism in the Late Works*. Berkeley: University of California Press, 2004.

Ryan, Marie-Laure, Kenneth Foote, and Maoz Azaryahu. *Narrating Space/ Spatializing Narrative: Where Narrative Theory and Geography Meet*. Columbus: Ohio State University Press, 2016.

Sarker, Sonita. "An Unharmonious Trio? Georg Lukács, Music, and Virginia Woolf's *Between the Acts*." In *Virginia Woolf and the Arts*, ed. Diane F. Gillespie and Leslie K. Hankins, 158–65. New York: Pace University Press, 1996.

Sakamoto, Tadanobu. "The Significance of the Old Woman and Her Song in *Mrs. Dalloway*." *Virginia Woolf Bulletin* 20 (2005): 28–32.

Schaeffer, Pierre. "Acousmatics." In *Audio Culture: Readings in Modern Music*, ed. Christoph Cox and Daniel Warner, 76–81. New York: Continuum, 2006.

Schafer, R. Murray. *The Soundscape: Our Sonic Environment and the Tuning of the World*. Rochester, VT: Destiny Books, 1994.

– *When Words Sing*. Scarborough, ON: Berandol Music, 1970.

Schechner, Richard. *Performance Theory*. New York: Routledge, 2003.

Scher, Steven Paul. "Notes toward a Theory of Verbal Music." *Comparative Literature* 22.2 (Spring 1970): 147–56.

Schneider, Rebecca. "New Materialisms and Performance Studies." *TDR: The Drama Review* 59.4 (Winter 2015): 7–17.

– *Performing Remains: Art and War in Times of Theatrical Reenactment*. Abingdon and New York: Routledge, 2011.

– *Theatre and History*. Houndmills, Basingstoke, and New York: Palgrave Macmillan, 2014.

Schröder, Leena Kore. "*Mrs Dalloway* and the Female Vagrant." *Essays in Criticism: A Quarterly Journal of Literary Criticism* 45.4 (1995): 324–46.

Schulze, Robin Gail. "Design in Motion: Words, Music, and the Search for Coherence in the Works of Virginia Woolf and Arnold Schoenberg." *Studies in the Literary Imagination* 25.2 (Fall 1992): 5–22.

Scott, Bonnie Kime. "The Subversive Mechanics of Woolf's Gramophone in *Between the Acts*." In *Virginia Woolf in the Age of Mechanical Reproduction*, ed. Pamela L. Caughie, 97–113. New York: Garland Publishing, 2000.

Scott, Derek. *From the Erotic to the Demonic: On Critical Musicology*. Oxford: Oxford University Press, 2003.

Seeley, Tracy. "Virginia Woolf's Poetics of Space." *Woolf Studies Annual* 2 (1996): 89–116.

Silver, Brenda. "Virginia Woolf and the Concept of Community: The Elizabethan Playhouse." *Women's Studies* 4 (1977): 291–8.

Silver, Brenda, ed., intro., and commentary. "'Anon' and 'The Reader': Virginia Woolf's Last Essays." *Twentieth Century Literature* 25.3–4 (1979): 356–441.

Smith, Mark, ed. *Hearing History: A Reader.* Athens: University of Georgia Press, 2004.

Snaith, Anna. *Virginia Woolf: Public and Private Negotiations.* Basingstoke: Palgrave Macmillan, 2001.

Snaith, Anna, and Michael Whitworth, eds. Introduction. In *Locating Woolf: The Politics of Space and Place*, 1–28. Basingstoke: Palgrave Macmillan, 2007.

Solie, Ruth. *Music in Other Words: Victorian Conversations.* Berkeley: University of California Press, 2004.

Solomon, Maynard. *Beethoven.* New York: Schirmer, 1977.

Spitzer, Michael. *Music as Philosophy: Adorno and Beethoven's Late Style.* Bloomington: Indiana University Press, 2006.

– "Notes on Beethoven's Late Style." In *Late Style and Its Discontents: Essays in Art, Literature, and Music*, ed. Gordon McMullan and Sam Smiles, 192–209. Oxford: Oxford Scholarship Online, 2016. Retrieved 22 October 2017. http://www.oxfordscholarship.com.

Stein, Gertrude. *Lectures in America.* New York: Vintage Books, 1975.

Steinberg, Michael. "Notes on the Quartets." In *The Beethoven Quartet Companion*, ed. Robert Winter and Robert Martin, 143–282. Berkeley: University of California Press, 1994.

Sterne, Jonathan. *The Audible Past: Cultural Origins of Sound Reproduction.* Durham, NC: Duke University Press, 2003.

Sterne, Jonathan, ed. and intro. *The Sound Studies Reader.* New York: Routledge, 2012.

Stewart, Garrett. *Reading Voices: Literature and the Phonotext.* Berkeley: University of California Press, 1990.

Stewart, Jim. "The Birth of Rachel Vinrace from the Spirit of Music." In *Virginia Woolf and Music*, ed. Adriana Varga, 111–33. Bloomington and Indianapolis: Indiana University Press, 2014.

Stone-Davis, Férdia J., ed. *Music and Transcendence.* Farnham: Ashgate, 2015.

Stravinsky, Igor, and Robert Craft. *Dialogues and a Diary.* New York: Doubleday and Company, 1963.

"Style, Form, Formalism." Special issue of *New Literary History* 47.4 (2016).

Subotnik, Rose. *Deconstructive Variations: Music and Reason in Western Society.* Minneapolis: University of Minnesota Press, 1995.

Sultzbach, Kelly. *Ecocriticism in the Modernist Imagination: Forster, Woolf, and Auden.* Cambridge: Cambridge University Press, 2016.

Sutton, Emma. "'Putting Words on the Backs of Rhythm': Woolf, 'Street Music', and *The Voyage Out." Paragraph* 33.2 (2010): 176–96.

– *Virginia Woolf and Classical Music: Politics, Aesthetics, Form.* Edinburgh: Edinburgh University Press, 2013.

Taruskin, Richard. "Chapter 12: The First Romantics." *The Oxford History of Western Music.* Oxford: Oxford University Press, 2010. Retrieved 22 October 2017. www.oxfordwesternmusic.com.

Taylor, Diana. *The Archive and the Repertoire: Performing Cultural Memory in the Americas.* Durham, NC, and London: Duke University Press, 2003.

Theile, Verena, and Linda Tredennick, eds. *New Formalisms and Literary Theory.* Basingstoke: Palgrave Macmillan, 2013.

Thompson, Emily. *The Soundscape of Modernity: Architectural Acoustics and the Culture of Listening in America, 1900–1933.* Cambridge, MA: MIT Press, 2002.

Thompson, Trina. "Sounding the Past: The Music in *Between the Acts."* In *Virginia Woolf and Music,* ed. Adriana Varga, 204–26. Bloomington and Indianapolis: Indiana University Press, 2014.

Transue, Pamela J. *Virginia Woolf and the Politics of Style.* New York: SUNY Press, 1986.

Tratner, Michael. *Modernism and Mass Politics: Joyce, Woolf, Eliot, Yeats.* Stanford: Stanford University Press, 1995.

Tucker, Herbert F. "Tactical Formalism: A Response to Caroline Levine." *Victorian Studies* 49.1 (Autumn 2006): 85–93.

Uhlmann, Anthony. "Virginia Woolf and Bloomsbury Aesthetics." In *The Edinburgh Companion to Virginia Woolf and the Arts,* ed. Maggie Humm, 58–73. Edinburgh University Press, 2010.

Varga, Adriana, ed. and intro. *Virginia Woolf and Music.* Bloomington and Indianapolis: Indiana University Press, 2014.

Vandivere, Julie. "Waves and Fragments: Linguistic Construction as Subject Formation in Virginia Woolf." *Twentieth Century Literature* 42.2 (1996): 221–33.

Virginia Woolf: The Critical Heritage. Ed. Robin Majumdar and Allen McLaurin. London: Routledge and Kegan Paul, 1975.

Wallace, Miriam L. "Theorizing Relational Subjects: Metonymic Narrative in *The Waves." Narrative* 8.3 (October 2000): 294–323.

Weliver, Phyllis. "Music, Crowd Control and the Female Performer in *Trilby."* In *The Idea of Music in Victorian Fiction,* ed. Sophie Fuller and Nicky Losseff, 57–80. Aldershot: Ashgate, 2004.

- *The Musical Crowd in English Fiction, 1840–1910: Class, Culture and Nation.* New York: Palgrave Macmillan, 2006.
- "A Score of Change: Twenty Years of Critical Musicology and Victorian Literature." *Literature Compass* 8.10 (2011): 776–94.
- *Women Musicians in Victorian Fiction, 1860–1900: Representations of Music, Science and Gender in the Leisured Home.* Aldershot: Ashgate, 2000.

Whitworth, Michael. "Woolf's Web: Telecommunications and Community." In *Virginia Woolf and Communities: Selected Papers from the Eighth Annual Conference on Virginia Woolf,* ed. Jeanette McVicker and Laura Davis, 161–7. New York: Pace University Press, 1999.

Wolf, Werner. "Intermediality Revisited: Reflections on Word and Music Relations in the Context of a General Typology of Intermediality." In *Word and Music Studies: Essays in Honor of Steven Paul Scher and on Cultural Identity and the Musical Stage,* ed. Suzanne M. Lodato, Suzanne Aspden, and Walter Bernhart, 13–34. Amsterdam: Rodopi, 2002.
- *The Musicalization of Fiction: A Study in the Theory and History of Intermediality.* Amsterdam: Rodopi, 1999.

Woolf, Leonard. *Downhill All the Way: An Autobiography of the Years 1919 to 1939.* London: Hogarth Press, 1967.
- *Letters of Leonard Woolf.* Ed. Frederic Spotts. New York: Harcourt Brace Jovanovich, 1989.
- "New Gramophone Records [I]." *Nation and Athenaeum,* 13 April 1929, 56.
- "New Gramophone Records [II]." *Nation and Athenaeum,* 18 May 1929, 252.
- "The World of Books: The Man Beethoven." *Nation and Athenaeum,* 26 March 1927, 894.

Woolf, Virginia. "'Anon' and 'The Reader': Virginia Woolf's Last Essays." Ed. with intro. and commentary Brenda R. Silver. *Twentieth Century Literature* 25.3/4 (Fall/Winter 1979): 356–441.
- *The Cambridge Edition of the Works of Virginia Woolf: Between the Acts.* 1941. Ed. Mark Hussey. Cambridge: Cambridge University Press, 2011.
- *The Cambridge Edition of the Works of Virginia Woolf: Mrs. Dalloway.* 1925. Ed. Anne E. Fernald. Cambridge: Cambridge University Press, 2015.
- *The Cambridge Edition of the Works of Virginia Woolf: The Waves.* 1931. Ed. Michael Herbert and Susan Sellers. Cambridge: Cambridge University Press, 2011.
- *The Cambridge Edition of the Works of Virginia Woolf: The Years.* 1937. Ed. Anna Snaith. Cambridge: Cambridge University Press, 2012.
- *The Common Reader.* 2 vols. Ed. and intro. Andrew McNeillie. London: Vintage, 2003.
- *The Complete Shorter Fiction of Virginia Woolf.* Ed. Susan Dick. London: Hogarth Press, 1989.

- *The Diary of Virginia Woolf.* Ed. Anne Olivier Bell. 5 vols. New York: Harcourt Brace Jovanovich, 1979–84.
- *The Essays of Virginia Woolf.* Ed. Andrew McNeillie. Vols. 1–4. New York: Harcourt Brace Jovanovich, 1986–94.
- *The Essays of Virginia Woolf.* Ed. Stuart N. Clarke. Vols. 5–6. London: Hogarth Press, 2009–11.
- *Jacob's Room.* 1922. Oxford: Oxford University Press, 1999.
- *The Letters of Virginia Woolf.* Ed. Nigel Nicolson and Joanne Trautmann. 6 vols. New York: Harcourt Brace Jovanovich, 1975–80.
- "The Moment: Summer's Night." In *The Moment and Other Essays*, 3–8. New York: Harcourt Brace and Company, 1975.
- *Moments of Being.* 2nd ed. Ed. Jeanne Schulkind. San Diego: Harcourt Brace and Company, 1985.
- *Night and Day.* 1919. Oxford: Oxford University Press, 1997.
- *Orlando: A Biography.* 1928. Oxford: Oxford University Press, 1998.
- *The Pargiters: The Novel-Essay Portion of "The Years."* Ed. and intro. Mitchell Leaska. New York: New York Public Library, 1977.
- *A Passionate Apprentice: The Early Journals 1897–1909.* Ed. Mitchell A. Leaska. London: Pimlico, 2004.
- *Pointz Hall: The Earlier and Later Typescripts of "Between the Acts."* Ed. and intro. Mitchell Leaska. New York: University Publications, 1983.
- *Roger Fry.* 1940. London: Vintage, 2003.
- *A Room of One's Own and Three Guineas.* 1929 and 1938. Oxford: Oxford University Press, 1998.
- "Three Pictures." In *Death of the Moth and Other Essays*, 12–16. New York: Harcourt Brace and Company, 1970.
- *To the Lighthouse.* 1927. Oxford: Oxford University Press, 2000.
- *Virginia Woolf "The Hours": The British Museum Manuscript of Mrs. Dalloway.* Transcription and ed. Helen M. Wussow. New York: Pace University Press, 1996.
- *Virginia Woolf's Jacob's Room: The Holograph Draft.* Transcription and ed. Edward L. Bishop. New York: Pace University Press, 1998.
- *The Voyage Out.* 1915. Oxford: Oxford University Press, 2001.
- "Why?" In *The Death of the Moth and Other Essays*, 227–34. New York: Harcourt Brace and Company, 1970.
Zhang, Dora. "Naming the Indescribable: Woolf, Russell, James, and the Limits of Description." *New Literary History* 45.1 (Winter 2014): 51–70.
Zimring, Rishona. "Suggestions of Other Worlds: The Art of Sound in *The Years.*" *Woolf Studies Annual* 8 (2002): 127–56.
Zwerdling, Alex. "*Jacob's Room*: Woolf's Satiric Elegy." *ELH* 48.4 (1981): 894–913.

Index